Commitment to Work and Job Satisfaction

Routledge Studies in Management, Organizations, and Society

This series presents innovative work grounded in new realities, addressing issues crucial to an understanding of the contemporary world. This is the world of organised societies, where boundaries between formal and informal, public and private, local and global organizations have been displaced or have vanished, along with other nineteenth century dichotomies and oppositions. Management, apart from becoming a specialized profession for a growing number of people, is an everyday activity for most members of modern societies.

Similarly, at the level of enquiry, culture and technology, and literature and economics, can no longer be conceived as isolated intellectual fields; conventional canons and established mainstreams are contested. **Management, Organization and Society** addresses these contemporary dynamics of transformation in a manner that transcends disciplinary boundaries, with books that will appeal to researchers, student and practitioners alike.

Commitment to Work and Job Satisfaction

Studies of Work Orientations

Edited by Bengt Furåker, Kristina Håkansson and Jan Ch. Karlsson

LONDON AND NEW YORK

First published 2012
by Routledge

2 Park Square, Milton Park, Abingdon, Oxon OX14 4RN
711 Third Avenue, New York, NY 10017, USA

*Routledge is an imprint of the Taylor & Francis Group,
an informa business*

First issued in paperback 2016

Typeset in Sabon by IBT Global.

Library of Congress Cataloging-in-Publication Data
A catalog record has been requested for this book.

ISBN: 978-0-415-80825-5 (hbk)
ISBN: 978-1-138-20319-8 (pbk)

Contents

Figures

Tables

1 The Relevance of Studying Work Orientations

Bengt Furåker, Kristina Håkansson and Jan Ch. Karlsson

Although the level of living differs enormously across human societies, they are all work societies in the sense that a great amount of labour is needed and carried out to secure the reproduction of the population at some standard of living. The present book does not deal with all kinds of socioeconomic systems but focuses on contemporary developed capitalist societies, in which large numbers of people go to their jobs day after day, week after week, year after year, to take care of various tasks, more or less necessary for sustaining or improving the population's quality of life. Lots of goods and services are continuously being produced and this production cannot take place without a significant quantity of work. Hence it is not surprising that a majority of the working-age population has gainful employment.

A main idea behind this book is that people's subjective relationships to work are important. These relationships are connected with the productive capacities in society; insofar as individuals are positively oriented toward contributing their labour power, we can expect a large amount of work to be done and to be done efficiently, carefully and responsibly. The circumstances under which people participate in various activities colour their subjective relationships to them. If people are being forced to do something the outcome will hardly be the same as if they are willing to do it; their performance is affected by whether their contributions are voluntary or not. Consequently work orientations and work attitudes are significant phenomena in society and this book aims at providing a deeper understanding of different aspects of these phenomena.

It can be debated just how voluntary work in the form of wage labour in a modern capitalist economy really is. Without much other property than their labour power individuals have rather little opportunity to escape the economic necessity to work for a living. This holds even in societies with generous welfare state arrangements. The general rule is that also in these systems individuals have to offer their capacity for work in the labour market; they are exempted only under specific circumstances. Another thing is that rules can be violated, in particular if they are ambiguously formulated.

Changes in the labour market may impinge on work orientations. The development of a 'post-industrial' labour market involves an expansion of highly qualified jobs and such a transformation is significant because these jobs are often associated with certain attitudinal configurations. At the same time, we need to be aware that work in the so-called new economy is often not that different from what we know about the old economy (Baldry et al. 2007). Yet another aspect is what has happened in terms of flexibility, temporary agency work and job insecurity in the last decades. Researchers have paid a great deal of attention to such changes, but it is rather contested which conclusions are to be drawn (e.g., Blossfeld and Hofmeister 2006; Blossfeld, Mills and Bernardi 2006; Fevre 2007; Furåker, Håkansson and Karlsson 2007; Kalleberg 2000; OECD 1997: ch. 5). Anyhow it is important to study work orientations and work attitudes in the light of changing labour markets.

A crucial question for the book is of course what we mean by work. Our simple answer is that the concept stands for gainful employment, in principle as defined in the developed countries' labour force statistics. In spite of the long-standing debate over the definition (Karlsson, 2004) and a possible widening of the concept in ILO statistics (Bollé 2009), we adopt this concept of gainful employment, thereby avoiding the whole discussion about unpaid home work, leisure-time activities, etc. Through this approach we can also benefit from the fact that available datasets and statistics from different countries are based on the same or similar definitions. Work is thus here plainly understood as an activity in exchange for income.

It is unquestionably important that high proportions of both the male and the female population work a lot and perform well, as the totality of these efforts is crucial for the level of living in society. We should, however, qualify this argument a bit by adding two comments. First, it matters not only how much people work and how well they perform but also what they do. There is an ecological or environmental dimension to take into account; some of the work done may lead to global warming, increased pollution and other harmful consequences. As a result, the effects on the standard of living are sometimes dubious or directly negative. Second, we should also be aware of the home- or leisure-based production outside the formal economy, including cooking, gardening, hunting, fishing, work in voluntary associations and the like. It is generally difficult, if not impossible, accurately to estimate the scope of it, but there should be no doubt that activities in the informal sector contribute substantially to the wealth of individuals, particularly in certain regions. We must emphasize that our two comments do not falsify—but just modify—the conclusion that the amount of paid work is crucial in contemporary developed capitalism.

This does not mean that every individual has to participate in work activities. Certain exceptions are obvious, but there are also significant cross-national variations regarding those who are under pressure to participate. At least in advanced welfare capitalism, children, sick, handicapped and old people are commonly exempted. A major task for the architects of contemporary welfare states is to define the circumstances under which people should be allowed public financial support and accordingly be able to refrain from taking on employment. It is a task associated with an incessant debate on the principles and norms with respect to benefit entitlements, the size of benefits relative to wage levels, how much resources are to be spent on various programs and how cheating can be prevented.

The subsequent chapters will deal with work orientations and job satisfaction, both a matter of subjective relationships between human beings and work. It may by and large appear that work orientations refer to something that people bring to their jobs, whereas job satisfaction seems to flow in the opposite direction—as something that people get or at least can get from their work. We should, however, be aware of the interaction that is taking place. There is no question that individuals' work orientations are affected by their job and the experiences it offers, but they usually start out from preconceived notions. At the same time, job satisfaction is partly an effect of expectations, that is, of the work orientations that accompany people to the workplace.

An illustration of the aspects we are interested in can be found in the classical writings of Max Weber (1930: 58–60) on the contrast between 'traditionalism' and the 'spirit of capitalism'. In one of his examples, a farm worker was offered a higher rate per acre for mowing, but instead of working more or doing the same as before (and thus still earning more money) he chose to earn the same by mowing less land. In other words, the worker had not adopted the attitude of striving for as much as possible; he just did what was required to satisfy his customary needs. He may very well have had an instrumental attitude to work—as work was a means to make a living—but within this framework there are at least two different options: to maintain a certain level of living or to increase it. There is a strong tendency in pre-capitalist societies to follow the first route (Sahlins 2004: ch. 1). For the development of capitalism, it is obvious that the attitude entailing willingness to work more in order to earn more was most appropriate.

Actually, the issue outlined above is still present under developed capitalism. In the economics literature on labour supply this is referred to as the substitution and income effects, and there is the idea of a backward-bending supply curve of labour (e.g., Buchanan 1971; Sloman 2010: 229–230). On the one hand, when wages are raised, work becomes more attractive as every hour spent at work is better remunerated, or, to put it another way, leisure time becomes more expensive. This could hence make us expect an increase of the supply of labour. On the other hand, with higher hourly wages employees can afford to refrain from increasing their supply of labour as their income increases anyway. They can also lower their quantity of work and keep the same level of living.

We should of course keep in mind that people cannot simply choose how much they want to work, as flexibility in this respect is far from unlimited. One thing is how much leisure they can afford and another thing is what employers allow. In many cases nobody will be hired unless he or she accepts full-time commitment, but there are also jobs in which part-time is taken for granted. Anyhow, to some extent, people have a choice between working more, with increased earnings as the result, and working less, thus instead having more leisure. In this connection their attitudes are likely to play a significant role.

The standard of living in a given society is not only linked to the amount of work carried out but also to the quality of it. Good performance requires some degree of engagement or dedication, which is another ground for us to stress the importance of work orientations. Wage labour requires a certain amount of consent on the part of the worker. The reason is that the labour contract cannot always specify the tasks the worker is to perform, how to perform them and at which pace, although the scope of freedom or control varies from one job to another. There is thus a fundamental indeterminacy, to use Baldamus's (1961) term, involved in the wage labour process, which makes the attitudes of workers of vital importance. Two types can be distinguished: production and mobility indeterminacy (Smith 2006).

Regarding production indeterminacy, we find two subtypes (Furåker 2005: 80–81). First, formal or informal agreements between employee and employer are subject to changing circumstances in, for example, technologies and markets. Thereby the agreement may become obsolete from the perspective of one or both of the parties. Second, the employer's knowledge of the details of the labour process—what is to be done, how it is to be done and so on—is often incomplete. The employee may be the one having the best understanding of how to perform the work.

Mobility indeterminacy means that the worker can quit his or her present job and go to another employer. This possibility is of course dependent on the state of the economy and of the labour market, but the option is in principle always there. All work contracts are in that sense temporary. From a very different point of departure, Karl Marx (1933: 20) claimed something similar, underlining that workers were subject to 'the whole class of buyers, i.e., the capitalist class' but that they were free to choose between capitalists; they could offer their labour power to anyone of them. Expressed in another way, in this system necessity and indeterminacy coexist.

The indeterminacy of labour makes organizational commitment, that is, employees' loyalty to the employing organization, a crucial theme in the book (e.g., Mowday, Porter and Steers 1982; Meyer and Allen 1997; Meyer et al. 2002; Mowday 1998; Gallie et al. 1998: ch. 9). We are interested in examining the determinants behind this kind of loyalty. There are also other forms of commitment—with the profession, with customers, patients, clients, etc.—that can be very important (e.g., Fukami and Larson 1984; Meyer and Allen 1997; Reichers 1985; Wallace 1993). Moreover, job satisfaction is a key aspect to be dealt with in some of the subsequent chapters. It can be expected that employees who are highly committed to their work have a great deal of satisfaction as well.

Some words of warning are in place. We must not shut our eyes to the risks that people work too much, irrespective of the underlying reasons—whether they are forced to do it because of the income or whether they are extraordinarily engaged in their tasks, clients, etc. There are no doubt great health risks with heavy workloads; many individuals become physically injured because they are too tired to handle their own and others' safety properly, and others get mental health problems because of stress and feelings of inadequacy when facing difficult-to-solve or unsolvable tasks (e.g., Dunham 2001; Karasek and Theorell 1990). Another crucial aspect is the puzzle of combining extensive employment duties with family life, which is evidently also a source of stress (e.g., Bianchi, Casper and Berkowitz King 2005; Frone, Russell and Cooper 1997). We do not want to create the impression that we consider pro-work attitudes something exclusively positive. Such attitudes may be positive for the production of goods and services in society, but they may also hit back by causing problems in other respects.

A main point of departure for the book is that paid work is a key sociological category. We need to emphasize this statement, simply because many authors have tried to detract from it. One of the most well-known attempts of the kind was made by Claus Offe (1985) in an analysis that was first published in German. The author claimed that, for a long time, work had been treated as *the* key sociological concept, but that, at least by the early 1980s, this position had become obsolete. Two main arguments were presented in favour of the thesis. The first is that work had become much more differentiated because of the increased division of labour and the expansion of services. This was supposed to lead to a situation in which people experience their jobs very differently. Work is 'no longer the focus of collective meaning and social and political division' and, therefore, 'with respect to their objective and subjective contents of experience, many wage-earning activities have hardly more in common than the name "work"'(Offe 1985: 136). We find this way of reasoning untenable; it is like saying that 'food' is no longer a relevant concept because there are now so many different dishes.

The second argument refers to an alleged decline in regard to the work ethic (Offe 1985: 140–148). As the argument will be further scrutinized in Chapter 2, this volume, we can leave it out here. It is sufficient to take notice of the principal deduction involved: Offe's whole analysis implies that work must abdicate from its privileged position in sociological analysis. Our position is very different; in contrast, we assume that work is *one* major sociological category and that it will remain that way in the foreseeable future. This conclusion is not undermined by the fact that sociological studies rest on several other crucial concepts. The significance of each concept is dependent on the topic under scrutiny. Whether or not work is generally the most important category is a question which it is a waste of time to pay attention to.

THE CHAPTERS IN THE BOOK

Empirically the analyses in the book are based on different kinds of data. Some of them make use of survey data from various countries to allow international comparisons. These accounts differ from one another as to which countries are involved, but taken together they provide information from Europe, North America and Oceania. To some extent the data entail opportunities of studying changes across time. Furthermore, in two of the chapters personal interviews form the empirical basis for the analyses. The data consist of narratives from workers in low-status occupations and from employees in occupations that have undergone dramatic rationalization measures during the last decades. All these interviews have been carried out in Sweden. Finally, there are some chapters using survey data from a single country, most often Sweden but also Iceland. These chapters deal with different aspects of work and examine how working conditions are related to work orientation and job satisfaction.

All in all, this book contains twelve chapters, written by twelve different authors. In Chapter 2, Bengt Furåker gives an overview of a number of key concepts and theoretical perspectives that will appear here and there in the remainder of the book. To begin with, attention is devoted to the concepts of work orientation, work attitude and job satisfaction. Given the role these notions play in the analyses to come, their respective meaning needs to be spelled out and clarified. Similarly, several related concepts are considered, among others employment commitment—or, rather, non-financial employment commitment—instrumentalism or instrumental work attitudes, organizational commitment, work ethic and work centrality. The task of conceptual clarification is framed by a more general theoretical discussion on the reasons why people work, what factors affect how much effort they put in and how well they perform and what role work plays in their lives.

The subject matter of Chapter 3, written by Frans Hikspoors, Tómas Bjarnason and Kristina Håkansson, is work centrality, defined as individuals' views about the importance of work in their lives. It is asked whether there have been changes in these attitudes during the last two decades in selected Western European countries. The analysis is based on information derived from the surveys of the European Values Study in 1990, 1999/2000 and 2008, which have been conducted in a large number of nations. Data from eleven countries—Belgium, Britain, Denmark, France, (West) Germany, Ireland, Italy, the Netherlands, Norway, Sweden and Spain—are examined. Looking at the whole period from 1990 to 2008, the authors find that the value attributed to work has declined almost everywhere, but this trend is not all that uniform and a few countries show diverging patterns. There is moreover a great deal of continuity in work orientations, as the rank order of different domains in life remains rather stable. Nevertheless work has lost ground to leisure in most countries. Younger individuals tend to put relatively low emphasis on work, and there is evidence of a generational effect in some of the countries, that is, youth keep their outlook as they grow older. With respect to gender, the general pattern is that males value work higher than females do, but by 2008 no significant gender difference could be found among full-time workers. It is suggested that the concept of 'scarcity' can be fruitful when we attempt to explain this increased preference for leisure. The idea is that lack of something increases the demand for it. This would mean that being short of employment and being short of leisure affect people's preferences in different ways.

Departing from Goldthorpe's concepts of instrumental, solidaristic and bureaucratic orientation, Tomas Berglund analyzes a set of significant work orientations in Chapter 4. Using data from the International Social Survey Programme (ISSP), collected in 2005, he distinguishes four categories: the instrumental, the altruistic, the career and the autonomy orientation. A principal question is whether or to what extent there are cross-national differences—in these respects—related to the institutional settings characteristic of the main types of welfare state, production and employment regimes. Patterns regarding work orientations are compared across six countries representing different societal models: France, Germany, Norway, Sweden, the UK and the US. The analyses also include examining the prevalence of the various orientations by gender, age, occupational categories, sector of employment, etc.

In Chapter 5 Bengt Furåker starts out from the observation that so-called non-financial employment commitment is rather strong in several Nordic countries and often stronger than in the Anglo-Saxon world. Non-financial employment commitment simply stands for willingness to have a paid job even if one does not need the money. However, the level of work mobilization—the proportion of the potential work effort that is actually made use of in a society—is largely higher in the Anglo-Saxon than in the Nordic countries. In order to throw more light on these issues Furåker examines the relationship between various work-related attitudes and certain data on employment and work mobilization. The comparison includes six Anglo-Saxon countries—Australia, Britain, Canada, Ireland, New Zealand and the US—and four Nordic countries—Denmark, Finland, Norway and Sweden. Employment and work mobilization data are derived from the OECD presentation of national labour force surveys, covering the period 2003–2007. The attitudinal data derive from ISSP 2005. Among other things, respondents have been asked whether they want to work more than they presently do, how much they want to work in terms of weekly hours and whether they prefer to work more and earn more or vice versa. It turns out that employment rates are positively associated with non-financial employment commitment, but the latter measure is negatively related to work mobilization rates. The attitudinal indicator that corresponds best to work mobilization is willingness to work more and earn more. With some exceptions, employees in the Anglo-Saxon countries are more likely to answer in a pro-work direction on this issue. A possible interpretation is that the more generous welfare-state arrangements in the Nordic countries do not hold back the motivation to have paid employment but that it is nevertheless relatively more important for people in the Anglo-Saxon world to work longer hours and earn more.

Chapter 6, written by Ylva Ulfsdotter Eriksson, deals with attitudes among workers in low-status occupations: blue-collar or lower white-collar occupations. These workers are sometimes assumed to have an instrumental attitude to work, seeing it as nothing else than a means to obtain an income. Ulfsdotter Eriksson shows that this is an untenable simplification. Her empirical findings draw upon a series of interviews conducted in Sweden with workers from six different occupations: waiters/waitresses, garbage men, attendants for mentally handicapped people, stockroom workers, security guards and food industry workers. Besides looking upon their job and current occupation in an instrumental way, the interviewees also express attitudes of commitment to work and to the employing organizations as well as loyalty toward clients, customers and co-workers. They also express engagement in tasks and personal involvement. In other words, the chapter offers a more complex picture of these workers' attitudes.

Anette Karlsson has written Chapter 7 on occupational identity and work orientations in two administrative service occupations in Sweden: medical secretaries and post-office cashiers which have long been female-dominated and which have undergone more or less dramatic rationalization and other changes during the last few decades. Empirically, Karlsson draws on interviews mainly conducted in 2004–2005 but also on various types of text material. Both occupations seem to be characterized by occupational identities that can be described as distinct within certain limits. Even if the occupation is not 'all there is' in life, it typically stands out as either constituting an important and highly valued part of life, or as something that may not be very important in one's life taken as a whole but that one nevertheless engages in quite whole-heartedly during the time spent at work. There is a distinct core of tasks, competences and ethical norms—particularly related to the multifaceted and intertwined themes of 'carefulness' and 'service'—that practitioners of the respective occupations recurrently refer to and that plays a central role for their individual and collective identity. The chapter focuses on the interplay between work orientations, different sources of identification and collective occupational identity. As a part of this, it also discusses some theoretical and practical implications of 'strong but delimited' occupational identities.

Chapter 8 brings up the development of attitudes to work in Sweden. Birgitta Eriksson, Jan Ch. Karlsson and Tuula Bergqvist focus on attitudes to work today and how they have changed during recent years. Their analysis is based on a survey which was first conducted in the middle of the 1990s and repeated in 2010. The authors begin by presenting some theoretical ideas concerning attitudes to work and factors like sex, age, class, work-life balance and work environment. The empirical results are at first presented descriptively and subsequently by means of a multivariate analysis in which the effects of a number of factors—such as the ones just mentioned—are taken into account. The main result is that the general attitude to work in Sweden differs depending on whether it is measured in an absolute or in a relative sense. When work is looked at in itself, the committed attitude dominates strongly, but when it is compared to other spheres of life the non-committed attitude dominates almost as powerfully. Furthermore, the changes found between 1994 and 2010 indicate a clear trend toward growing non-committed orientations.

In Chapter 9, drawing on the *Gemeinschaft-Gesellschaft* distinction and similar notions, Dan Jonsson develops a theoretical analysis of employment relations, regarded as exchange relations. Based on this analysis, three so-called exchange paradigms—represented by 'work-time sellers' (time-for-pay exchange), 'trusted employees' (commitment-for-trust exchange) and 'employed suppliers' (performance-for-pay exchange)—are distinguished. It proves possible to classify most of the respondents in the study as representing one of the three exchange paradigms. The data indicate that the type of exchange paradigm strongly influences employee satisfaction. Related to differences with regard to autonomy, both employed suppliers and trusted employees are much more satisfied with their work, their workplace and their employer than are work-time sellers. In addition, Jonsson shows that the effect of occupation on employee satisfaction is to a large extent mediated by the exchange paradigm. Research on employee satisfaction can thus benefit from being related to a broad theoretical and societal context.

Tómas Bjarnason is the author of Chapter 10. It aims at exploring the impact of a recession on employees' attitudes to their work. Data derive from Iceland, a country that has recently been hit by severe economic crisis. In October 2008 the entire Icelandic bank system collapsed and the Icelandic *krona* lost nearly half of its value in an instant. Downsizing, layoffs and closures became rampant in the weeks and months following the collapse. Unemployment more than tripled from the first quarter of 2008 till the first quarter of 2009. As a consequence, Iceland experienced a period of both political and economic instability and uncertainty. Bjarnason uses data from two large surveys dealing with employees in the Commercial Workers' Union and their work environment, job satisfaction and pay. The surveys have long been conducted in similar ways, thus providing opportunities for estimating how the economic recession affected employee attitudes. Surprisingly, the 2009 survey showed a slight improvement in employee satisfaction and certain other indicators compared to the 2008 survey. In a more detailed analysis, however, it was found that, as expected, employee attitudes were negatively affected by organizational downsizing. An examination of the changes between the two surveys indicates that employees not exposed to downsizing experiences had become more positive to their organization and management than they had previously been. Some explanations for these results are discussed with an emphasis on comparison theories and the effects of 'overpayment'. The long-term effects of the crisis on employees have yet to be explored.

Chapter 11 is written by Kristina Håkansson and Tommy Isidorsson and deals with commitment among temporary agency workers. The specific characteristic of this kind of employment is the dual employment relationship. Agency workers are employed by the agency but managed by the user firm. They thus have two employers to relate to: the legal employer dealing with all issues about the employment and the user firm dealing with all work-related issues. This can be assumed to affect their work orientations and work attitudes. The authors investigate if and how temporary agency workers are organizationally committed and attempt to explain the patterns revealed. It turns out that the majority, 57 percent, of the agency workers are committed to at least one of the organizations, most often to the user firm. Moreover, they are committed to the two organizations for different reasons, although a few similarities appear. Job satisfaction is undoubtedly important in explaining commitment, which has also been emphasized by other researchers. It is linked to the workplace and therefore influences commitment to the user firm but not to the employer. For the latter to have dedicated employees it is crucial to provide organizational support. Finally, factors capturing the specific work situation of temporary agency workers are important for commitment both to the user firm and to the employer.

In the final chapter (12) of the book, Bengt Furåker examines whether people experience job travel as stimulating or stressful, that is, whether it contributes to their job satisfaction or dissatisfaction. For many, travel—outside commuting—is an important aspect of their working conditions, but the conditions differ considerably across occupational categories. The empirical basis for the analysis consists of Swedish survey data from 2005 among a random sample of gainfully employed individuals. A general conclusion is that work travel is clearly more often considered stimulating than stressful. However, people who travel frequently are less likely than others to find it stimulating and there is some weak indication that they are also more likely to find it stressful. Spending many nights away from home mainly appears to be something inspiring and does not seem to generate stress. The experience of work travel as stimulating is enhanced by trips abroad, high degree of control over travel schedules and traveling with workmates. The latter two factors also turn out to have stress-reducing effects. In addition, it can be noted that stress is distinctly related to the sometimes implicated inconveniences of early mornings and/or late homecoming.

2 Theoretical and Conceptual Considerations on Work Orientations

Bengt Furåker

The concepts of *work orientation* and *work attitudes* refer to a subjective dimension of the relationship between a person and his/her job or employment in general. They grasp the person's conceptions, knowledge, beliefs, feelings and evaluations concerning work or various aspects of it. In addition, we find a potential behavioural element to be taken into consideration. According to the conventional notion—agreed with here—attitudes have three different dimensions (e.g., Rosenberg and Hovland 1960; Eagly and Chaiken 1993). The first, the cognitive, aspect has to do with beliefs, that is, conceptions and understandings of the object in question. Second, there is an affective dimension referring to feelings about and evaluations of the object. Individuals' disposition to act makes up the third, the behavioural, aspect of an attitude. It should be stressed that the three dimensions are interrelated. For example, an employer who is convinced that immigrants are just as competent as native workers and who is keen on the principle of equal opportunities can be expected at least not to discriminate against immigrants when recruiting people to vacancies. Nevertheless, it is not unusual to find a mismatch between the dimensions, which in the example given might imply that the employer acts contrary to his/her beliefs and values.

In this book, work orientations and work attitudes are used more or less synonymously, although the former concept is taken to be broader; it can thus include a set of work-related attitudes. Another main concept is *job satisfaction* (e.g., Brooke, Russell and Price 1988; Goldthorpe et al. 1968; Herzberg, Mausner and Snyderman 1959; Herzberg 1966; Kalleberg 1977; Lincoln and Kalleberg 1990). It designates the degree to which people are content with their job. As pointed out in the introductory chapter of this volume, work orientations might appear to be something that people bring to their workplace, whereas job satisfaction might seem to be something that jobs confer on their incumbents. This would however be simplifying the issue. Individuals' work orientations are affected by their job and the experiences emanating from it. Moreover, job satisfaction is partly a function of people's expectations, that is, of the work orientations they bring to the workplace.

Job satisfaction refers to an affective dimension and in that sense it can be counted as belonging to one of the three pillars of the attitude concept.

This does not exclude the fact that the cognitive and behavioural aspects are also present. People may be at ease with their work because they know that they are better off than many others in comparable positions and vice versa. Accordingly, theories of social comparison are highly significant in studying job satisfaction as well as work motivation (e.g., Festinger 1954; Merton 1964: chs. 8–9; Suls and Wheeler 2000). It is then decisive with whom comparisons are being made, that is, whether the reference persons have jobs in the same workplace or not, in the same occupation or not, on higher or lower levels in the occupational hierarchies, etc.

Certain analytical problems arise since satisfaction is dependent on expectations. One individual may be much happier with his/her job than another, in spite of the fact that the two have more or less identical working conditions, and the explanation may be that the former has lower expectations than the latter. Owing to this peculiarity and the fact that people are sometimes satisfied with their work because it makes few demands, it has been suggested that job satisfaction is a less useful concept than *job involvement*, which refers to people's 'active interest in and enjoyment of the work' (Gallie et al. 1998: 209). Nonetheless, I believe that job satisfaction can be a helpful concept, but we must keep its premises in mind.

The subjective relationships at focus have reference not to a single object but to something more complex. One way of dealing with this complexity is to distinguish between work/employment in general and specific jobs, held by the actor himself/herself or by others. Furthermore, the concepts do not necessarily refer to jobs taken as a whole but only to certain aspects of them, for example, working conditions, work tasks, social climate at the workplace and the like. We can expect a great deal of variation across social categories (as defined by sex, age, socioeconomic category, ethnicity, etc.) regarding work orientations, attitudes to work and employment and job satisfaction. One of the main purposes of this book is to spell out some of the variation in these respects.

Work in general is obviously an abstraction, as in working life there are just concrete activities. When people are asked about their work orientations and attitudes, it is rather likely that their own job—or some other specific job (for example, that of their partner)—will cross their minds. In other words, the abstract category tends to be conceived of through existing entities. The abstraction can however also be contrasted with 'non-work'. It is possible, in turn, to specify the latter concept in terms of alternative activities or statuses such as 'staying at home with one's children', 'going to college' or 'being retired.' Still the question remains whether or to what extent people's orientations to work or employment in general are coloured by their experiences from their own job or some other specific job.

Studying work orientations, attitudes to work and employment and job satisfaction, we soon run into several other concepts, such as work centrality, work ethic, instrumentalism, employment commitment and other types of commitment. This chapter aims at presenting and discussing such concepts and at bringing up some of the key issues associated with them. The text is structured around three topics. First, there is the issue of why people work at all. Is it because they must secure their means of survival, because they want to increase their standard of living or because other wishes can be met that way? What is the role of financial and non-financial factors, respectively? Second, how willing are employed individuals to work a lot and to perform well? Again, are they motivated mainly by financial remunerations or by other factors? The third and final question concerns another subjective dimension, namely the role people think that work plays in their lives. Is work conceived of as a central phenomenon in their everyday existence? How does it rank in relation to other spheres of life such as family and leisure? The three sets of questions partly cover the same ground and therefore cut across one another, which in turn means that certain issues are touched upon not only once but twice or even several times.

TO WORK OR NOT TO WORK

We can think of several reasons for people to engage in paid work. One crucial reason may be that it is economically necessary. In the writings by Karl Marx (e.g., 1933, 1996), the capitalist mode of production is based on two main categories: owners of means of production and individuals who own nothing but their labour power—the proletarians—and who therefore have to offer this capacity for hire in the market. The proletarians are free to work for anyone capitalist, but they are forced to do it in order to support themselves. There is hence an economic necessity or coercion to which the property-less are subjected.

Things have unquestionably changed a great deal since the days of Marx. The standard of living has increased dramatically for those at the bottom of the income hierarchy, and we find more or less developed welfare-state arrangements in all advanced capitalist nations. There are some significant implications of these two types of change. First, today most people have more money to spend than they need for securing mere survival. The increased standard of living involves mass consumption in ways which were out of sight in the 19th century. It may be discussed whether the rise of 'consumerism' actually forces people to work; what we can say is that a higher 'normal' standard of living requires either technological progress or more work—or both. Moreover, to increase consumption continually seems to be an attractive goal, or at least it appears to be desirable to 'keep up with the Joneses'. Second, the modern welfare state allows people to escape working under certain circumstances—if they become sick or injured, need to be on maternity leave, etc. Arguably this undermines the necessity for people to work because—as it is expressed in some accounts—it triggers a process of 'decommodification' (Esping-Andersen 1990, 1999). Although we can hardly conclude that people no longer have to work at all, the pressure upon them to do this has no doubt been modified.

The attitude associated with economic motives to work is often referred to as *instrumentalism*. This is a key concept in the 'affluent worker' study by John Goldthorpe, David Lockwood, Frank Bechhofer and Jennifer Platt (1968). Its meaning is that work is an instrument to obtain something else, normally an income that can be used to purchase different kinds of goods and services. Individuals with an instrumental work orientation want to have employment, because they need the money implicated. They conceive of a job as 'a means to an end, or ends, external to the work situation; that is, work is regarded as a means of acquiring the income necessary to support a valued life of which work itself is not an integral part' (Goldthorpe et al. 1968: 38–39). Thus people look upon employment in calculative terms; there is in principle no other reason to keep the job besides the economic return it provides. Although manual workers are assumed to have an instrumental work orientation to a larger extent than others, it is emphasised 'that *all* work activity, in industrial society at least, tends to have a basically instrumental component' (Goldthorpe et al. 1968: 41; italics in original).

In the case of an instrumental work attitude, it is not an issue whether people are forced or not to find employment to make ends meet; no other assumption is made than that they above all work to get paid for it. If they are after the money to survive or just to increase their consumption is another story. The idea of instrumentalism also presupposes that the intrinsic value of the job is weak and that there is a sharp division between work and non-work. However, we may argue that the notion does not have to be, or should not be, interpreted too narrowly. It can as well be considered instrumental to have a job for the purpose of achieving non-financial goals. For example, individuals may take a job mainly because it provides social contacts that they—for one reason or another—consider valuable. An instrumental work orientation is nonetheless commonly regarded as the opposite of non-financial employment commitment, a concept to which I will come back.

Another possibility is that people engage in employment because they feel it is a *moral obligation*. This presupposes the existence of a *work ethic* in society, implying that work is a highly valued activity and that people are subject to normative pressure to take on this kind of activity. The basis for this ethic can be found in religion, as in the classic study *The Protestant Ethic and the Spirit of Capitalism* by Max Weber (1930). Seventeenth-century Christianity provided various views on work which were more or less positive for the development of capitalism. Among other things, Weber emphasised the role of Calvinism for the advance of a suitable work ethic. It might appear strange that the Calvinist doctrine of predestination could have such a role, as it implies that what human beings do does not matter. However, Weber argued that the doctrine took work as a sign of people's fate. Those who toiled by the sweat of their brows could consequently be expected to be predestined to salvation. I will not go deeper into these issues here, but it should be added that a work ethic is an important element also in other religions such as Islam and Buddhism (e.g., Yousef 2001; Niles 1999).

Furthermore, we should observe that more secular societies do not necessarily fall behind regarding work ethics (cf. Anthony 1977). In the contemporary, relatively secular capitalist societies, we find more or less explicit norms regarding employment. Able-bodied individuals of working-age are subject to rather strong pressure to engage in paid work if they do not have sufficient means of subsistence from other sources. This can perhaps most easily be observed in the various policies of workfare and activation oriented toward putting people on welfare (back) into employment (e.g., Alcock et al. 2003; Friedlander and Burtless 1995; Lødemel and Trickey 2001).

The existence of a strong work ethic is linked to the fact that work is a necessity for society as a whole. Human societies would soon fall apart if a lot of vital tasks were not carried out day after day. Even in contemporary developed capitalism, a rather moderate decline in the supply of labour would quickly damage the production of goods and services. This does not have to mean that work is a necessity for every individual. We find socially defined norms regarding who should be available for employment. The general principle is that individuals who are able-bodied and of working-age should be at hand, but they are exempt if they can get their means of subsistence in certain other ways (interest from capital, speculative gains, etc.), that is, without relying on support from the public authorities and without breaking the law.

An important aspect is that the modern welfare state requires large resources to function as intended. There is therefore normally strong pressure upon people to support themselves through paid work rather than through social benefits. The word *duty* may be somewhat obsolete in the contemporary context—but some kind of work ethic is in operation. One way—and perhaps the most adequate—of expressing the present state of things is the following. People who want to be treated as 'ordinary' or 'decent' are expected to work unless they have a due cause (such as being disabled or having small children) not to do it or have other sources through which they can get on. It is simply not easy to live on welfare without a valid reason. There are unquestionably rather strong norms as to the meaning of being a 'normal' citizen in modern society.

It has nevertheless been argued that the work ethic has declined in contemporary societies. Claus Offe (1985: 140–148) is one of those who have put forward such arguments. Already in the first half of the 1980s he claimed that work was in the process of ceasing to be a duty, partly because of the decline of religious and certain other cultural traditions and because of the growth of consumer hedonism. Another of his points is that in order for work to be a duty workers must participate 'as recognized, morally acting persons' and with the 'Taylorization' of working life, 'processes of technical and organizational rationalization', this does not hold any longer (Offe 1985: 141). However, Offe does not provide any empirical evidence in support of his argument but just takes it for granted. It must be questioned to what extent current working life developments are characterized by Taylorization. Although such a process—or processes—may very well be taking place in certain areas, this is hardly the only pattern; there are certainly many jobs which cannot easily be transformed by Tayloristic principles.

In connection with the notion of a demise of the work ethic we must take a number of issues into consideration. To begin with, it is not crystal clear how strong this ethic used to be; it is possible that we often exaggerate its strength in the past. The empirical evidence at hand is indeed limited. For one thing, there was obviously no work ethic covering all social categories to the same extent (cf. Moorhouse 1987; Rose 1985). This observation is valid also today. Actually, concerning both the past and the present—not to mention the future—we lack sufficient empirical knowledge in these respects. We should also not forget the indications that work ethics develop in new directions. In recent decades, there has been a discussion about 'workaholism' or 'heavy work investment', as a possibly growing phenomenon in certain jobs (e.g., Harpaz and Snir 2003; Snir and Harpaz 2009a, 2009b). 'Workaholism' may be an effect of strong job involvement, but it may also have to do with work cultures with powerful norms regarding what can be expected in terms of people's efforts.

Sociologists and other social scientists have repeatedly—and with good reason—brought up the non-financial, 'intrinsic' job rewards and values of work (e.g., Herzberg, Mausner and Snyderman 1959; Herzberg 1966; Kalleberg 1977; Lincoln and Kalleberg 1990; Mottaz 1985; Wang 1996). They emphasise the significance of motivating work tasks such as various kinds of problem-solving and artistic activities. Another thing is the role of social relations—involving colleagues, customers, clients and others—that are associated with most kinds of employment. Being essentially social creatures, human beings are undoubtedly highly dependent on such relations.

We should also pay attention to the concept of *non-financial employment commitment*. It has frequently been used in research on unemployed individuals with the purpose of investigating how their willingness to work compares with that of the already employed (Gallie and Alm 2000; Gallie et al. 1998: ch. 7; Gallie and Vogler 1994; Hammer and Russell 2004; Nordenmark 1999). The concept refers to 'the importance that people attach to employment on intrinsic grounds, that is to say irrespective of the financial implications'; people can be forced to work, simply because they need the money exchanged for it, but '[t]he very notion of commitment implies choice and voluntary consent' (Gallie et al. 1998: 188).

Non-financial employment commitment is in principle the opposite of instrumentalism, as the definition excludes all financial aspects. It is quite common to use the shorter expression employment commitment only, but it seems difficult to exclude the financial dimension completely, even if we reserve the term for 'choice and voluntary consent.' Individuals can very well be engaged in employment because of a need or desire for an income, although they might easily survive without it. Despite having enough money to make a living, they may still want more for 'luxurious' consumption—a larger house, yet another car, travels around the world or whatever.

An important issue with respect to non-financial employment commitment is whether there are gender differences or not (e.g., Bielby and Bielby 1989; Gallie et al. 1998: 188–189; Hakim 1996, 2000, 2003; Halvorsen 1997; Warr 1982). Quite a few studies have demonstrated that men are generally more strongly committed than women, but the difference has not always turned out to be very distinct—some studies show no significant difference and others even uncover the opposite pattern. However, Catherine Hakim (1996, 2000, 2003) has insisted that men and women have different preferences in regard to work and family matters. According to her 'preference theory', women care relatively more about their families and relatively less about their job, which is reflected in their larger proportion of part-time work. These conclusions have certainly been debated (e.g., Crompton and Harris 1998; Crompton 2006; Leahy and Doughney 2006). Among other things, it has been emphasised that people's choices are 'shaped (or constrained) by the context within which choice is being exercised' (Crompton 2006: 12).

Marie Jahoda (1982) has made one of the most well-known contributions to the discussion on why people work. Her argument is that work fulfills a number of latent, social-psychological functions besides the manifest economic function of providing an income. In her view, a job imposes a time structure upon the individual; it provides social contacts outside the family; it means that people can engage in activities for common purposes; it implies regular activities; and it bestows social status and identity. Jahoda has been criticized for underestimating the role of individual agency and for presenting an unacceptable functionalist perspective on work (e.g., Essy 1993; Fryer 1986; Nordenmark 1999). She tends to treat all jobs in the same way; they are all supposed to have positive effects for the individual no matter what characteristics they actually have. It is easy to agree with this criticism, but it still seems that the aspects brought up by Jahoda are worth being considered seriously; they may no doubt be of great interest in research on the role of work.

In a study of Swedish lottery winners, Anna Hedenus and I found that moderately sized or even relatively large winnings seldom made people change their work situation (Furåker and Hedenus 2009). Very few quit working; some took a shorter leave from work; and others shortened their working hours, but the majority—almost two thirds—did not do anything. There are obviously also other than the merely pecuniary mechanisms that tie people to their jobs. To put it briefly, it seems that being 'normal' is an important motive for remaining in employment (Hedenus 2011). The normal thing for working-age individuals in the Swedish context is to have a job, unless they are students, have small children at home or have some other legitimate excuse for not being employed.

DETERMINANTS OF PERFORMANCE

A further aspect of work orientations has to do with people's willing-ness not only to have a job at all but to work a lot and to perform well in their jobs. Performance should be thought of in both quantitative and qualitative terms. The meaning of doing a good job may refer to various dimensions: unrelenting effort but also skilfulness, competence, accuracy, responsibility, reliability, punctuality and the like. It is a common-sense assumption that high job satisfaction goes hand in hand with good per-formance at the workplace.

The concept of *work motivation* is frequently used to grasp the strength in people's willingness to work and to perform as well as possible. In the discussion of motivating factors, it is common to bring up a large number of issues such as the role of financial incentives, conceptions of work as a moral obligation, the character of work tasks, the social climate at the workplace and job security or insecurity (cf. Gallie et al. 1998: 15–21). There is a huge body of research and literature on these topics (e.g., Geller-man 1963, 1998; Kleinbeck et al. 1990; Maslow 1970; McGregor 1985; Vroom 1964). As touched upon earlier, the 'intrinsic' job rewards and the non-financial values of work have caught the attention of many sociologists and other social scientists (besides the references above, see also, e.g., Herzberg, Mausner and Snyderman 1959; Herzberg 1966; Kalleberg 1977; Lincoln and Kalleberg 1990; Mottaz 1985; Wang 1996). The factors stimu-lating people to perform and perform well vary across economic and cul-tural systems; thus we should not look for a single set of driving forces for human beings but for many such sets.

A quick glance at the once 'really existing' socialism may be instructive in this connection. In the country of the October Revolution, the Soviet Union, where the use of market mechanisms was restricted, a great deal of effort was put into finding other mechanisms that would make people work hard and conscientiously. Disciplinary labour norms, rules and legislation were one way of dealing with the problem; such measures were implemented more or less strictly and with varying success over the decades (e.g., Kaplan 1968; Luke 1985). Work was also generally heroized with awards to people who made high-performance contributions. The coal miner Alexey Stakha-nov is perhaps the most well-known (e.g., Siegelbaum 1988; Luke 1985: 201–207). His records in coal mining from 1935 appear to go beyond the humanly possible. He was used as a role model in propaganda, and a whole Stakhanovite movement was organized with him as the front figure. This is an over-explicit example of how the absence of well-functioning material incentives for people to do their best paved the way for other measures to build up work morale and work discipline. Although perhaps sometimes having intended effects, in the long run these other measures could not prevent the presence of poor performance, inefficiency and attitudes of work-avoidance. The concomitant stagnation of the economy played a major role in the fall of the Soviet Union and the whole Soviet bloc.

The reasoning above should not be taken to imply that contemporary developed capitalism provides optimal mechanisms of motivation. People's engagement in their jobs is dependent on employment and working conditions, and these conditions are not infrequently poor in capitalist firms, at least for those at the bottom of the organizational hierarchies. Therefore various forms of protests such as working-pace slow-down, working by the rule, absenteeism, boycotts and strikes are common. Actually, one might even say that resistance is an essential kind of work orientation. The actions taken are sometimes individual and sometimes collective and they can have considerable economic impact on the employer. It is above all by acting collectively that workers are really able to put pressure upon their counterpart. This requires that workers define the problems at hand in basically the same way and imagine similar feasible remedies. It is vital for them to develop common values and norms facilitating joint action. In other words, the key to successful resistance is the formation of a workers' collective (Lysgaard 1967).

There is also the concept of *organizational commitment* (e.g., Porter et al. 1974; Mowday, Porter and Steers 1982; Lincoln and Kalleberg 1990; Meyer and Allen 1997; Mowday 1998; Gallie et al. 1998: ch. 9). It is often taken to refer to a combination of three different attitudinal elements among employees: '(a) a strong belief in and acceptance of the organization's goals and values; (b) a willingness to exert considerable effort on behalf of the organization; and (c) a definite desire to maintain organizational membership' (Porter et al. 1974: 604). A critical issue is then whether or to what extent the values and goals under (a) above are clear, coherent and undisputed. If they are vague or contradictory, it will be difficult to use them for creating support among employees.

In an attempt to find the 'core essence' of the concept of commitment, John Meyer and Natalie Allen (1991) surveyed the literature and made a distinction between affective, continuance and normative commitment. The affective aspect has to do with employees' desires to stay with their organization, continuance refers to their need to remain with it—given the possibilities and costs of exiting—and the normative component is based on a moral belief or obligation to stay on. Meyer and Allen (1991: 67) argue that the three approaches have a common point of departure; they all treat commitment as 'a psychological state that (a) characterizes the employee's relationship with the organization, and (b) has implications for the decision to continue or discontinue membership in the organization' (see also, e.g., Meyer and Allen 1997; Meyer and Herscovitch 2001; Meyer et al. 2002).

Actually, commitment does not have to be tied to the employing organization as such but to actors/phenomena connected with it (e.g., Fukami and Larson 1984; Meyer and Allen 1997; Reichers 1985; Wallace 1993). For example, employees can be committed to their profession or occupation rather than to their employer. It may be more important for lawyers to stick to the moral code of the profession than to be loyal to a certain lawyer's office, and doctors may be more willing to help their patients than to follow the hospital's bureaucratic rules. Workers may also have strong ties with unions, professional associations, the local community or other actors. There can thus be competing loyalties at a workplace, which in turn are likely to affect the overall backing of the organization's values and goals. It has been argued that we need a multiple commitments approach to handle this complexity (Reichers 1985). By way of example, in a British study of 'new economy' workplaces—carried out by Chris Baldry and his colleagues (2007: 99–103)—it turned out that employees' commitment to colleagues and to customers was generally much stronger than it was to the employer.

A few words should also be said about another concept, namely the *'psychological contract'* (e.g., Grant 1999; Herriot, Manning and Kidd 1997; Rousseau 1995, 2001). It is generally aimed at grasping the more informal beliefs among employers and their employees about what the two parties are supposed to give and receive, respectively. Why this kind of contract should be labeled 'psychological' rather than 'social' remains an unanswered question; contracts always involve at least two actors and therefore have a 'social' character. A sociological perspective would entail some other elements. It would start out from the simple assumption that employers and employees normally agree on some kind of contract that can be formal (written) or informal (oral or tacit). No matter what form it takes, the agreement is crucial for the relationship between the two parties, although its contents can vary a great deal. According to Talcott Parsons and Neil Smelser (1956: 105) contracts can be analyzed either in terms of the *quid pro quo* (the workers' performance for the organization and the organization's remuneration for that effort) or of their conditioning rules that are 'socially prescribed and sanctioned'; in the latter respect there is a focus on such aspects as 'the interest of third parties' and the need for 'restrictions on fraud and coercion.' Thus, Parsons and Smelser echo what Émile Durkheim (1964: 200–229) called the 'non-contractual' elements of contract.

There is, however, also a power aspect to take into account. In juridical terms the contract appears as an agreement between two equal parties, but as Marx (1996: 177–186) underlined this is not the whole truth. Behind the idea that capitalists and workers voluntarily and on equal terms exchange money for the use of labour power, he saw an asymmetric relationship in which the one party dominates the other. This is a main theme in his analysis of the capitalist rule in the factory and it was in fact also recognized by Weber (1978: 729–730): 'The formal right of a worker to enter into any contract whatsoever with any employer whatsoever does not in practice represent for the employment seeker even the slightest freedom in the determination of his own conditions of work, and it does not guarantee him any influence on this process. It rather means, at least primarily, that the more powerful party in the market, i.e., normally the employer, has the possibility to set the terms, to offer the job "take it or leave it", and, given the normally more pressing economic need of the worker, to impose his terms upon him.' In these accounts, there is not much room for agreements between employers and employees, although some understanding—explicit or tacit—will always be present. One might say, however, that the less asymmetric the power relationship between the two parties is or becomes, the more space is left for employer-employee agreements.

It may be less important whether we call the informal contract between employers and their employees 'psychological' or something else. A significant observation is that both parties may have more or less articulated expectations of each other, regardless of what the formal agreement states. Not least because of the indeterminacy incessantly associated with how work tasks are to be carried out (cf. Furåker 2005: 80–81), formal regulations and agreements must be complemented by some mutual understanding and trust. This insight might help us explain why people are sometimes doing their best at the workplace but sometimes are pretending to be working, are working to the rule or are going slow. It may also contribute to our understanding of open labour disputes and conflicts.

WORK CENTRALITY

Many sociologists and other social scientists have paid attention to the role of work in people's lives. Is it a main activity in terms of time or significance or both? A concept frequently appearing in the literature is *work centrality*. In an often-quoted sentence in the report on the *Meaning of Work* project it has been defined as 'the degree of general importance that working has in the life of an individual at any given point in time' (MOW 1987: 81; italics deleted). When measuring work centrality, it is rather common to make a distinction between an absolute and a relative dimension, depending on whether work is assessed without being related to anything specific or by a comparison with other spheres in society such as family, leisure and religion. However, it seems likely that some comparison is embedded even in the absolute case. Human beings hardly evaluate phenomena in the world without having some point of reference in mind. In my opinion, apart from the different ways of phrasing survey and interview questions, work centrality is essentially a matter of the *relative* significance that individuals attach to working in their life situation. It can be added that this is also the point of departure of the MOW (1987: 80) project.

Claus Offe (1985: 141; italics in original) maintains that there are two ways in which work can play a crucial role in people's lives: (a) if it is 'normatively sanctioned as a *duty*'; and (b) if it is 'a *necessity*' for physical survival. In his view, the prerequisites for this vital role have ceased to exist or at least are on their way out. I have already touched upon some of Offe's reasoning with respect to the decline of the work ethic, but he also mentions certain other processes. In contemporary societies, life is no longer organized around gainful employment the way it used to be and job biographies show more discontinuity. The time structure and the location of work within people's biographies have become increasingly variable. For example, people are often trained for one kind of job but actually hold another. Moreover, working time has been shortened and people have more time for other activities. These descriptions are overall in line with what we know about developments in the last century, but it nevertheless remains unclear to what extent work ethics have been affected.

The quotation from Offe above appears to say that the second point is limited to physical survival only. However, in his discussion, the author focuses on the general motivating effects of a wage income. He obviously believes that there is a saturation effect so that an increase of income is not accompanied by a corresponding increase in utility. With rising standards of living people become less interested in supplying the same amount of labour as before and instead look for other ways of improving the quality of their lives, including improvements of working conditions. This is Offe's own version of the substitution and income effects that were mentioned in Chapter 1, this volume. It seems to me, however, that Offe is too quick to dismiss people's desires for higher income and tends to overestimate the saturation effect; the evidence available is at least inconclusive.

Some authors have put forward the idea that work society has been replaced by a consumer society or—in a more cautious version—perhaps will be so in some more or less distant future. This implies that people reorient themselves in several different ways. One example is given by Zygmunt Bauman (1998: 24–25, 2007: 28–29) in his discussion of the transition from 'producer' to 'consumer' society. The argument is that although both production and consumption exist everywhere, we can speak of a transition from one type of society to another because there has been a change in the norms to which citizens are socialized. Individuals were previously supposed to become producers, but now they are above all expected to be consumers.

For the transition from producer to consumer society, two circumstances are claimed to be particularly important: the decline in industrial mass production—as a consequence of the rapid progress of technology which allows both an increase in production and a decrease in the labour required—and in the scope of the military service. These changes mean that fewer individuals are now subject to the kind of organization that the two sectors are associated with. Large-scale industry and military services are very much institutions that train people to monotonous, routine behaviour. This kind of drill has little or no room for freedom of choice and basically represents the opposite of what is anticipated in the consumption markets. As consumers people must continuously be prepared to choose between diverse goods and services for sale.

It is hence assumed that people's orientations in society have changed; individuals are now less work-oriented and more consumption-oriented. Obviously, the role as consumer has become more important over time, simply because the standard of living has increased compared to some decades ago. There is much more to consume and if people buy more—and do it in a premeditated way—they must devote more attention and energy to what is offered in the markets (Bauman 1998: 25, 2007: 17–19). One aspect is simply that consumption tends to take more time. The process of purchasing things has changed people's everyday life, for example, through the expansion of shopping centres and not least Internet commerce.

There should be no doubt that consumption has got a more central place in present-day advanced capitalism. Yet it does not automatically follow that the producer role has been put into the shade by the consumer role. One omitted aspect in Bauman's reasoning is that people who are not employed in large-scale industries are nonetheless supposed to work unless—as pointed out above—they have valid reasons for not doing it. Workers in other types of jobs are also socialized into work roles; this socialization process may be somewhat different, but it certainly takes place. The empirical evidence in support of Bauman's argument is generally weak and can hardly justify the far-reaching generalization that producer society has been replaced by consumer society.

A more developed analysis on the same theme is presented by Paul Ransome (2005). He classifies societies on the basis of subjective criteria, that is, on people's experiences and feelings. In work-based society, people regard paid work as their essential life interest in the sense that they ascribe the exchange from this activity greater importance than the exchange from any other field (Ransome 2005: 15). The corresponding criteria are used with respect to consumption-based society. To put it in another way, the idea is to use people's orientations for the purpose of categorizing societies. Ransome is nevertheless careful to point out that production and consumption hang closely together. All production aims at some consumption—and this holds even if not everything produced is consumed—and all consumption requires some kind of production. It is thus stated that the goal of both activities is to satisfy needs.

In his analysis of work-based society Ransome (2005: ch. 2) focuses on what he calls its 'work-centeredness' and 'productivist' ethic. With reference to empirical research he concludes that people by and large expect work to generate material and psychological security, opportunities for creative activity and possibilities of establishing and maintaining social contacts. No alternative way of obtaining these goals seems to be within reach. Apparently, it does not matter that people are more or less forced to work. All the same, they tend to ascribe work a central role; it simply has a hegemonic position in their worldview.

The concept of consumption-based society requires that individuals receive greater satisfaction from consumption than from production (Ransome 2005: 61). An important observation is then that people today have greater opportunities to borrow money. This means that their liquidity can be increased rapidly, allowing them to buy goods and services that otherwise would be beyond reach; they can consume now and pay later. Ransome (2005: 55–57) suggests that a post-modern mind-set here challenges the dominant productivist ethic, as loans for consumption open the door for people to spend and squander. Whether this is the most adequate description of the situation can be disputed. Loans must usually be paid back and people are then required to have the necessary money, which in turn makes income-generating employment important. It is even possible that this mechanism ties people more closely to paid work. Increased consumption may very well lead to an increasing amount of work, that is, a situation in which people need to earn more in order to be able to consume more. As Ransome himself points out, it has already been proposed that developments in recent decades could be characterized as a 'work-and-spend-culture' (Cross 1993: 5).

Ransome's criteria for defining different types of society are highly questionable and the lack of data makes them impossible to use. In concluding, however, he is careful to emphasise that the fully developed consumption-based society has not yet—in the beginning of the 21st century—arrived (Ransome 2005: 188–189). On the other hand, the author claims, we cannot be satisfied with the conclusion that work-based society has not been affected by the changes during the last decades. He therefore suggests a compromise implying a change in the balance between the two phenomena. Consumption has become more important and—with the increased standard of living—we must admit that pleasure and enjoyment have become permanent features of people's lives. If things continue to develop in this direction we can expect a transformation of society to take place. Ransome's entire approach seems to imply that this scenario is likely to be realized, but as he knows that the empirical basis for it is too weak—not to say non-existent—he is wise enough not to go the whole way with it.

CLOSING WORDS

Theories and concepts should be seen as scientific tools that can help us explain phenomena in the world. It is only in their empirical application that they can prove their value for social analysis. This chapter has aimed at bringing up some theoretical and conceptual issues connected to work orientations, attitudes to work and employment and job satisfaction, and the remainder of the book consists of empirical chapters, which formulate and attempt to answer various research questions. For that purpose, they make use of theoretical approaches such as those discussed here.

3 Declining Work Centrality in Western Europe

Myth or Reality?

Frans Hikspoors, Tómas Bjarnason
and Kristina Håkansson

For the bulk of the adult population, work provides a major frame of reference. As Freud (1930) remarked, work is a person's strongest tie with reality. The impact of employment on the use of our time, for example, is profound: 'Working defines the time structure for days, weeks and years. It marks the division between the productive and reproductive, and often between auto- and hetero-determined activities. It lends itself to legitimize socially biographic phases: training, work life, retirement' (Ruiz-Quintanilla and Wilpert 1988: 9).

Several concepts have been developed concerning the meaning of work. A key concept in this discussion is *work centrality*, which is defined as individuals' beliefs concerning the importance of work in their lives (MOW 1987: 81; Paullay, Alliger and Stone-Romero 1994: 224–228; see also Chapter 2, this volume). Dubin's (1956) early formulation of the concept has been influential, and it is in turn based on Weber's (1930) analysis of the Protestant work ethic (Hirschfeld and Field 2000). Work centrality is a matter of how we think about work, its importance and how crucial it is in our lives. Such beliefs are linked to how we prioritize our time and effort. They are likely to affect whether or not we work, how much we work and the types and levels of reward we seek, or assume we can obtain, from work.

Work centrality has been measured in both absolute and relative terms (e.g., Harpaz and Snir 2003). In absolute terms, work is thought of as varying in importance in one's life without any comparison with other spheres. The relative concept refers to the importance attributed to work while also considering other domains in life such as family, religion or politics.

Work values are rooted in larger value systems (Figure 3.1), which are in turn associated with national cultures (Parboteeah and Cullen 2003). They are transferred to individuals via primary and secondary socialization (e.g., family, education, vocational training). Through socialization, individuals learn and internalize behaviour in accordance with what is required and expected of them in their work roles (Kraimer 1997; Harding and Hikspoors 1995). What is expected of people, however, is dependent on specific circumstances and individual characteristics, for example, gender, age and social status. The concept of 'age culture' is sometimes used to refer to perceptions 'that structure people's ideas of the age-work relationship' (De Vroom 2004: 8). Various societal policies and workplace practices affect the social conditions under which we are brought up and live (Parboteeah and Cullen 2003). There are different welfare and labour market policies that either encourage or restrain labour market involvement (Bleijenbergh and Roggeband 2007; Crompton and Lyonette 2006; Esping-Andersen 1990). Furthermore, the economic conditions under which people are raised put their mark on people's values and practices (Inglehart 1990, 2008; Welzel and Inglehart 2010). Finally, work experiences are likely to either validate our work values or create conditions according to which these must be re-evaluated. For example, Smola and Sutton (2002) report that individuals' values change upon leaving college and becoming part of the workforce.

Previous studies have found work to be perceived as relatively important compared with other areas of life (Ruiz-Quintanilla and Wilpert 1991). Only family appears to have greater importance (Harding and Hikspoors 1995; Sharabi and Harpaz 2007). There is, however, some debate about the significance of work. Politicians, managers, teachers and parents continually express their concerns regarding a declining work ethic. Similarly,

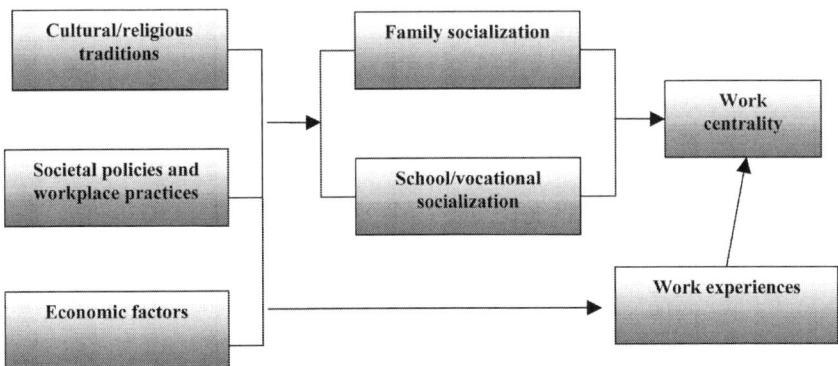

Figure 3.1   The work socialization process, adapted from Harding and Hikspoors 1995.

the symbolic and economic centrality of work in post-industrial society has been called into question by a number of scholars (Offe 1985; Gorz, 1999; Beck 2000; Vecernik 2003). Some authors argue that we are facing a 'new capitalism' that fosters short-term thinking and erodes mutual commitments (Sennett 1998), or even that we are approaching the end of work (Rifkin 1995). Others, such as Bauman (1998), have emphasised the expansion of consumerism and the 'aesthetic' value of work (see also Furåker's discussion in Chapter 2, this volume).

This chapter aims to explore whether or not there have been any changes in perceptions of work centrality over an eighteen-year period in selected Western European countries. The question is whether work has declined in importance and, if so, why this has happened. To our knowledge, recent developments in Western Europe, in this respect, have not been fully explored. Nor have such changes, if they exist, been accounted for; that is, we need to look for the causal factors. We start with an overview of previous research and present our hypotheses. Then there follows an analysis of changes in work centrality in eleven countries during the period 1990 to 2008. In this analysis, differences between men and women, age categories and various employment statuses are taken into account. Finally, we discuss the findings and the limitations of the study.

IS WORK DECLINING IN IMPORTANCE?

Recent studies suggest that there is a declining trend in the importance being ascribed to work in Western Europe. Ruiz-Quintanilla and Wilpert (1991: 97ff) examined the perceived value of work in Germany and found that it had decreased over a six-year period during the 1980s. This ran parallel with an increase in the importance of leisure, with leisure even surpassing work in 1989. Smola and Sutton (2002) claimed that there was a weakening in work centrality and the work ethic between 1974 and 1999 in the US, consistent with a rise in the value of leisure; however, these results were questioned on methodological grounds (Twenge et al. 2010; Sharabi and Harpaz 2010). In a longitudinal study of work centrality in Israel, Sharabi and Harpaz (2007) actually found an increase in the importance of work and leisure, while the value put on religion declined.

All in all, there are few recent internationally comparative studies exploring changes in people's perceptions of the significance of work. We will examine whether the assumptions of a declining importance of work and an increasing importance of leisure will hold true in a large number of European countries. The following hypotheses are thus suggested:

Hypothesis 1: There is a trend toward less value being placed on work (declining work centrality) in a number of Western European countries between 1990 and 2008.

Hypothesis 2: Concurrent with the decreasing value of work, leisure is becoming more important.

AGE, GENERATION AND WORK CENTRALITY

Studying West European countries, Inglehart (1990) showed that, in past decades, there has been a shift from materialist to post-materialist values with each generation. He argues that this cultural shift is due to two factors: 'scarcity' and 'socialization.' The scarcity hypothesis states that 'priorities reflect one's socioeconomic environment: one places the greatest subjective value on those things that are in relatively short supply' (Inglehart 1990: 68). Therefore, people who are economically deprived will put a greater emphasis on material acquisition than those who are more affluent. This helps to explain short-term fluctuations in material values; an example could be that people's concerns about money increase during economic downturns and higher levels of unemployment (Inglehart 2008; Welzel and Inglehart 2010). Such a situation could possibly shift values temporarily from post-materialistic to materialistic. Accordingly, Sharabi and Harpaz (2007) argue that the rise in the relative importance of work between 1981 and 1993 in Israel mainly resulted from the 'scarcity' of work brought about by increasing unemployment during the 1980s and early 1990s. However, Inglehart emphasises socialization much more as an explanation for such a shift, maintaining that 'one's basic values reflect the conditions that prevailed during one's pre-adult years' (Inglehart 1990: 68).

In a similar way, recent contributions by Inglehart (2008) and by Welzel and Inglehart (2010) strongly support a trend toward a generational shift in values. It has been demonstrated that each generation mostly keeps its outlook regarding materialism or post-materialism throughout its life cycle. A shift in values occurs because of the economic, social and political circumstances during formative years, putting a permanent mark on each generation. Through this process, a gap in values is created between generations, which is maintained throughout the life cycle of each generation (see also Abramson and Inglehart 1999; Peterson and Ruiz-Quintanilla 2003; Smola and Sutton 2002).

As the first decade of the 21st century has been characterized by relative economic prosperity, we may now predict a decreasing emphasis on work and an increasing emphasis on leisure.[1] A recent study provides support for such a trend. Twenge et al. (2010) found an increase in the importance of 'leisure rewards' and a slight decrease in the importance of 'intrinsic [work] rewards' among young people in the US. Compared with 'Boomers' (born between 1946 and 1964), 'GenX' (born between 1965 and 1981) and 'GenMe' in particular (born between 1982 and 1999) place a greater emphasis on leisure and extrinsic work rewards. The authors argue that this mirrors GenX and GenMe members' 'desire for [a] work-life balance' (Twenge et al. 2010: 1133)—which reflects the exceptionally long working hours in the US. Several earlier studies also indicate a generational shift toward work becoming less important and leisure becoming more important (Smola and Sutton 2002).

Overall, then, it is argued that a number of factors could have contributed to lower work centrality among the youngest generations. In cross-sectional research, such shifts are, however, only observed as differences in attitudes, values or preferences between age categories. Looking solely at differences like these, one is unable to determine whether or not they are due to generational changes (cohort effects), to life-cycle changes or to temporary economic shocks. Thus, for the purpose of determining whether or not there are generational effects in the data, shifts in values need to be studied in each age category separately.

Consequently, we will compare different age categories in order to distinguish between generational and life-cycle effects. Since a large body of evidence suggests that the basic values of individuals are largely fixed by the time they reach adulthood (see Inglehart and Baker 2000: 42), changes among the youngest cohort may provide an indication about future changes in the population. In the analysis, we will use age categorizations that correspond to transitional phases in life in general and to working life in particular. The following hypotheses are proposed:

Hypothesis 3: There is a life-cycle effect regarding work centrality in such a way that younger people ascribe less importance to work and greater importance to leisure than do older people.

Hypothesis 4: There is also a generational effect such that the perceived importance of work among the youngest cohort is reflected in older cohorts at later times.

GENDER AND WORK CENTRALITY

There has been extensive discussion regarding whether or not differences in work values are related to gender. For example, Rowe and Snizek (1995) found no evidence of gender differences in work orientations, while Hult (2008) discovered diverging gender patterns in various countries. Warr (2008) reported small but significant work centrality differences between men and women. These differences also remained significant after taking employment status into consideration.

Gender differences can be due to at least two factors: structural constraints and differences in preferences. Constraints affect opportunities and, in doing so, people's choices, thus pushing men's and women's attitudes in different directions (Crompton and Lyonette 2006; Kan 2007). Vlasblom and Schippers (2006) found that the presence of children decreases female labour participation; however, in Europe, there are considerable national differences in female labour market participation, which are dependent on, for example, policies governing education, care and the labour market (Crompton and Lyonette 2006; Björnberg, Eydal and Ólafsson 2006; Bleijenbergh and Roggeband 2007). Care policies, particularly those aimed at the care of preschool children, alleviate some of the constraints on women's labour market participation.

Hakim (2002), in contrast, argues that values (or preferences) determine women's emphasis on family formation and interest in employment. She makes a distinction between 'home-centred,' 'adaptive', and 'work-centred' women. For example, home-centred women give priority to their homes and families and 'avoid paid work after marriage except in times of financial stress' (Hakim 2002: 437). In contrast, work-centred women focus on making a career, prioritizing work over family life. Kan (2007: 459) found evidence in favour of as well as against Hakim's theory. Women's preferences and constraints in relation to the labour market interact with each other, with both being important as regards shaping women's careers.

However, research indicates that the importance given to work may differ with labour market attachment, for example whether people have full- or part-time jobs. It is possible that the same employment status makes men's and women's work attitudes and values similar (Rose 1994; Nordenmark 1999; Kan 2007). We should also note that women tend to be in part-time employment more than men. If part-time workers hold work to be less important than full-time workers, then a trend toward increasing part-time work will lead to an overall decline in the emphasis on work. Changes as regards work centrality thus need to be examined separately for men and women, with employment status taken into account. In the light of this, we hypothesize:

Hypothesis 5: Women will attach lower importance to work than men, but such a relationship will be mediated by employment status.

DATA AND VARIABLES

The data used in this study are derived from the European Values Study (EVS), conducted by the European Values Systems Study Group in 1990, 1999/2000, and 2008. Norway was not included in 1999, but in this case we have instead used the World Values Survey (WVS) 1996. The European surveys have been conducted using national samples in a large number of countries; here, we will focus on the following European countries: Norway, Sweden, France, Britain, Ireland, (West) Germany, Spain, Italy, Denmark, Belgium and the Netherlands. The 1990 results were based on about 900 to 2,500 responses for each country; in 1999, there were approximately 900 to 1,800 responses, and in 2008, about 1,000 to 1,500 responses.

The EVS's questions regarding work values were part of a large questionnaire. The opening question was: 'For each of the following aspects, please indicate how important it is in your life'—with 'very important', 'rather important', 'not very important', 'not at all important' as response options (scored from 4 to 1, respectively). The score is used as the indicator of absolute work centrality. Moreover, work as a potential value target was presented among other value domains: family, friends, leisure time, politics and religion. Ratings regarding the importance of work were taken as an indicator of relative work centrality. Leisure and family orientations were operationalized using similar means. Labour market status was measured using a question about whether people had a paid job or not, with the response alternatives also covering different working hours. In our analysis, we have a variable that focuses on full-time workers, part-time workers and the unemployed, which is labeled employment status. Age categories were classified on the basis of transition phases during working life: 15–29, 30–49 and 50 years and above.

RESULTS

Hypotheses 1 and 2 propose that a decrease in the importance attached to work will be found in the selected European countries between 1990 and 2008 and that this decrease will go hand-in-hand with a greater emphasis on leisure. In Table 3.1, we report on the perceived importance of work in comparison with other domains of life (friends, leisure, religion and politics). There are similarities as well as differences between the countries. First, family is regarded as the most important of all the domains of life. This is true for all the nations. Second, politics and religion are regarded as least important in almost all the countries over the eighteen-year period. Work, friends and leisure lie between these two extremes. Similar patterns have been reported in other studies (Harding and Hikspoors 1995; Harpaz, Honig and Coetzier 2002).

The table shows that a relatively great value is placed on work in the Mediterranean countries of France, Italy and Spain, but also in Belgium, where work is ranked as the second most important domain in life and where this ranking has not changed over the two decades. Work is, hence, perceived as more important than friends, leisure, politics and religion in these four countries. The other extreme is constituted by countries where work has generally less significance in life: Britain, West Germany and the Netherlands. In these cases, work ranks fourth in importance after family, friends and leisure across all three measurement points. Accordingly, in the above-mentioned countries, there is some stability in the perception of work in relation to other domains in life. However, there is also a group of countries showing a decline in the ranking of work centrality (Norway, Sweden, Denmark and Ireland) in favour of friends or leisure. Ireland distinguishes itself through having the greatest change; its ranking of work has declined from the second most important in 1990 to the fourth most important in 2008. To sum up, when compared to other domains of life, work has retained the same relative position in seven countries, but has lost ground to other areas of life in four countries.

Turning to the perceived value of work in absolute terms (i.e., with the mean values given to the question about the importance of work), we discover slightly lower means on the aggregate level in 2008 (3.36) and in 1999 (3.38) than in 1990 (3.45). A decreased emphasis on work appears in five countries between 1990 and 2008, but there is a reverse trend in two countries. Between 1990 and 1999, a significant decrease in the perceived importance of work is found in Ireland, Denmark, Norway, Sweden and the Netherlands. Belgium and France show the opposite trend during the same period. Between 1999 and 2008, the value of work declined in Britain, Belgium, Spain and Sweden, while there was an increase in West Germany and Denmark. In other words, while there is a small overall decline in the means for work centrality in the eleven countries between 1990 and 2008, the patterns are still somewhat inconclusive.

Examining work centrality with control for labour market status, we can identify some interesting differences. The self-employed put the highest value on work, followed by full-time employees. The retired and those labeled housewives in the EVS have the lowest scores. The unemployed, students and part-time workers lie in between, sharing almost the same score. When looking at the change for each category over time, we see that full- and part-time employees have increased their work centrality scores over the two decades, while the retired and the 'housewives' show a decrease.

A closer look at the samples reveals that the proportions of these categories vary considerably between countries. However, there is also variation in the sample composition in some of the countries between the three surveys. Accordingly, we have to examine whether the changes in work centrality reflect changes in the attitudes of the same categories over time or whether they are due to an altered composition of the samples.

In total, the proportion of retirees has increased over time while the proportion of 'housewives' has decreased. Both of these categories have lower scores regarding work centrality, and their respective relative increase and decrease might level out. The most noteworthy change in composition applies to Sweden. The decline in the importance of work in Sweden from 1990 to 1999 is probably due to a considerably larger proportion of

Table 3.1   Ranking of Work Centrality in Comparison with Other Domains. Eleven Countries, 1990, 1999 and 2008

	Ireland			Britain			Sweden		
	1990	1999	2008	1990	1999	2008	1990	1999	2008
Work	3.53 (2)	3.29 (3)	3.29 (4)	3.12 (4)	3.09 (4)	2.90 (4)	3.62 (3)	3.42 (4)	3.28 (4)
Family	3.89 (1)	3.90 (1)	3.89 (1)	3.84 (1)	3.89 (1)	3.87 (1)	3.83 (1)	3.87 (1)	3.90 (1)
Friends	3.48 (3)	3.58 (2)	3.73 (2)	3.40 (2)	3.54 (2)	3.59 (2)	3.66 (2)	3.69 (2)	3.50 (2)
Leisure	3.11 (5)	3.26 (4)	3.46 (3)	3.29 (3)	3.40 (3)	3.38 (3)	3.50 (4)	3.48 (3)	3.49 (3)
Religion	3.28 (4)	3.07 (5)	2.87 (5)	2.44 (5)	2.19 (5)	2.33 (5)	2.03 (6)	2.24 (6)	1.91 (6)
Politics	2.03 (6)	2.18 (6)	2.25 (6)	2.30 (6)	2.10 (6)	2.29 (6)	2.41 (5)	2.60 (5)	2.44 (5)

	Norway			Denmark		
	1990	1996	2008	1990	1999	2008
Work	3.68 (2)	3.50 (3)	3.54 (3)	3.39 (3)	3.19 (4)	3.33 (4)
Family	3.86 (1)	3.86 (1)	3.90 (1)	3.86 (1)	3.85 (1)	3.86 (1)
Friends	3.65 (3)	3.56 (2)	3.63 (2)	3.46 (2)	3.48 (2)	3.56 (2)
Leisure	3.34 (4)	3.29 (4)	3.47 (4)	3.36 (4)	3.32 (3)	3.47 (3)
Religion	2.34 (6)	2.30 (6)	2.28 (6)	2.10 (6)	2.05 (6)	2.18 (6)
Politics	2.51 (5)	2.41 (5)	2.62 (5)	2.36 (5)	2.36 (5)	2.62 (5)

Table 3.1 (continued)

	W. Germany			Belgium			Netherlands		
	1990	1999	2008	1990	1999	2008	1990	1999	2008
Work	3.09 (4)	3.12 (4)	3.24 (4)	3.46 (2)	3.55 (2)	3.42 (2)	3.38 (4)	3.29 (4)	3.26 (4)
Family	3.64 (1)	3.75 (1)	3.72 (1)	3.80 (1)	3.86 (1)	3.85 (1)	3.73 (1)	3.72 (1)	3.80 (1)
Friends	3.25 (2)	3.42 (2)	3.38 (2)	3.37 (3)	3.35 (3)	3.38 (3)	3.54 (2)	3.55 (2)	3.58 (2)
Leisure	3.23 (3)	3.16 (3)	3.25 (3)	3.25 (4)	3.23 (4)	3.26 (4)	3.40 (3)	3.45 (3)	3.47 (3)
Religion	2.24 (6)	2.24 (6)	2.22 (6)	2.39 (5)	2.43 (5)	2.24 (5)	2.36 (6)	2.27 (6)	2.41 (6)
Politics	2.38 (5)	2.27 (5)	2.33 (5)	1.92 (6)	2.10 (6)	2.10 (6)	2.52 (5)	2.60 (5)	2.63 (5)

	Italy			Spain			France		
	1990	1999	2008	1990	1999	2008	1990	1999	2008
Work	3.57 (2)	3.55 (2)	3.59 (2)	3.57 (2)	3.56 (2)	3.49 (2)	3.52 (2)	3.62 (2)	3.59 (2)
Family	3.85 (1)	3.88 (1)	3.91 (1)	3.81 (1)	3.85 (1)	3.83 (1)	3.79 (1)	3.87 (1)	3.86 (1)
Friends	3.30 (3)	3.24 (3)	3.30 (3)	3.36 (3)	3.24 (3)	3.33 (3)	3.26 (3)	3.43 (3)	3.42 (3)
Leisure	3.16 (4)	3.09 (4)	3.10 (4)	3.22 (4)	3.09 (4)	3.30 (4)	3.10 (4)	3.23 (4)	3.17 (4)
Religion	2.87 (5)	2.97 (5)	2.98 (5)	2.52 (5)	2.29 (5)	2.24 (5)	2.27 (5)	2.17 (5)	2.21 (6)
Politics	2.05 (6)	2.18 (6)	2.35 (6)	1.82 (6)	1.82 (6)	1.93 (6)	2.07 (6)	2.13 (6)	2.41 (5)

Source: EVS 1990, 1999 and 2008 (as Norway was not included in the EVS 1999, we have used data from the WVS 1996).
(1) Most important
(2) Second most important
(3) Third most important
(4) Fourth most important
(5) Fifth most important
(6) Least important

full-time workers in 1990 than in 1999 and 2008 (71, 54 and 55 percent, respectively). There are no big differences like these in the other countries that show a decline; consequently, in these cases, the changes have not been caused by differences in the composition of the samples. Nor do countries with an increased work centrality indicator show any major changes in the sample composition.

The conclusion thus far is that there is an overall trend toward a fall in the importance of work during the first period, 1990–1999, followed by stabilization during the 2000s. There is a weakening of work centrality in most of the countries, but this is not always continuous and some countries show a trend in the opposite direction. When looking at the ranking of work in relation to other domains of life, we find that the decline in this ranking is limited to a third of the countries examined. It would seem, rather, that work has a fairly stable position over time. Notably, both full- and part-time employees have put a greater emphasis on work during the last two decades. Thus, Hypothesis 1 has only partly been confirmed since our detailed analysis reveals a more complex picture containing slightly divergent developments.

The second hypothesis was that a decline in the perceived significance of work would go hand-in-hand with a greater preference for leisure. Looking at the latter dimension, we found almost the reverse pattern as regarding work. Less importance is placed on leisure in countries where work is highly valued, and vice versa. With respect to the ranking of leisure, there is stability over time. In Italy, Spain, France and Belgium, where work comes across as the second most important domain in life, leisure only shows up as number four. In Germany, Britain and the Netherlands, where work turns out to be ranked number four, leisure is valued more highly and takes third place.

For the purpose of testing the hypothesis regarding the relationship between work and leisure, the score for work is subtracted from the score for leisure. Figure 3.2 shows the results for 1990 and 2008. In 2008, Italy, France, Spain, Belgium and Norway had positive work-minus-leisure scores, while Britain, the Netherlands, Ireland, Denmark, Sweden and West Germany had negative scores.

More important, the analysis reveals that work has generally lost ground to leisure during the period as seen by the positive scores in 1990 (indicating higher importance of work compared to leisure) and the negative scores in 2008 (indicating higher importance of leisure compared to work). This development is due to the increasing value placed on leisure as well as to the decreasing value placed on work, although this trend is not continuous across our three occasions of measurement (not shown in the figure). There is also a reverse trend in a few countries. West Germany and Spain show an increase in the significance of work in relation to leisure during 1990 to 1999, and the same trend applies to Belgium during 1999 to 2008.

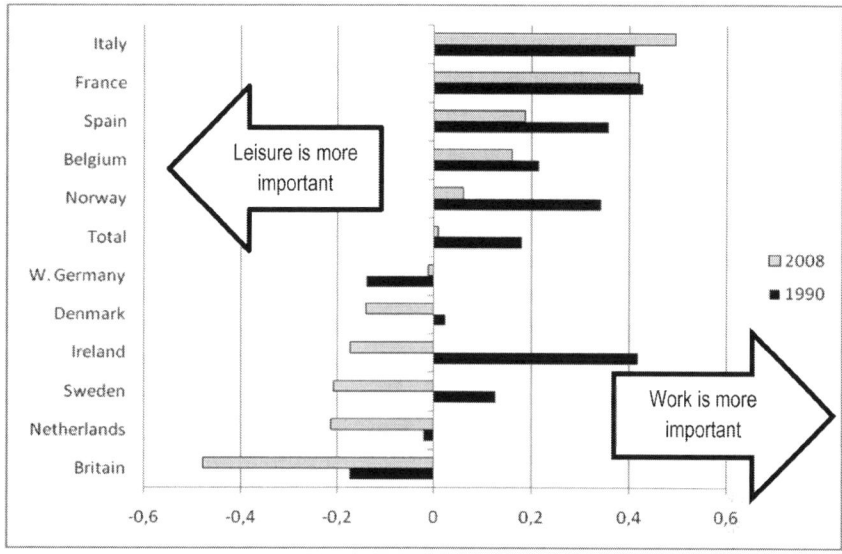

Figure 3.2 Importance of work minus leisure. Eleven countries, 1990 and 2008.

The most remarkable results apply to Sweden, Ireland and Denmark. In these countries, there is not only a general trend of work losing in importance to leisure, but of leisure actually becoming more important than work. In West Germany, Belgium, Italy and France, we find either an increase, or stability, in the relative importance of work in comparison to leisure across the three surveys. In conclusion, in the countries where there is a decline in the significance of work, this is accompanied by an increase in the significance of leisure. Hypothesis 2 is thus confirmed.

Age and Generation

Hypotheses 3 and 4 suggest that younger people would ascribe less importance to work and greater importance to leisure compared to older individuals. In order to separate generational effects from life-cycle effects and economic and labour market factors, work centrality was analyzed in three age categories. Each cohort corresponds to a particular phase in people's lives and careers. Work centrality was calculated for each cohort, for each year, and for all eleven countries.

The analysis shows that, in 1990, work centrality was increasing with age in all the countries except Ireland and Britain. In 1999, this effect only applied to Italy, Spain and France, while in 2008, it only applied to Italy and France. In fact, in several cases, we find the reverse trend in 2008—the relative value of work compared to leisure is decreasing with age; this result

applies to Denmark, Britain and West Germany. The evidence of a generational effect is visible in Norway, Sweden and Spain. In these countries, the
low value put on work in relation to leisure found in 1990 and 1999 in the
youngest cohort is reflected in older cohorts at later times.

In some of the countries, work is relatively more important than leisure among prime-age individuals (30 to 49 years) than among the others.
In these cases, work particularly loses ground in the oldest age category
(50 years and above). Hypothesis 3 is supported for most of the countries
examined in 1990, but the relationship between age and work centrality
becomes weaker in 1999 and shows diverging trends in 2008.

When examining the trend of the indicator work minus leisure over the
eighteen-year period, a general pattern of a relatively lower importance for
work is noted in all cohorts, but most clearly among the oldest. However,
this decrease is not continuous, and a great deal of variation appears in
individual countries. In Denmark and West Germany, the youngest cohort
switched its preferences and perceived work as even more important than
leisure in 2008.

Table 3.2 shows examples of diverging trends in work centrality in different cohorts and different countries. These countries could be divided
into four clusters. First, a trend toward 'disengagement' in the oldest cohort
can be observed in, for example, Denmark, Spain, Belgium and Britain.
In these cases, there is a trend toward a weakening of the importance of
work in the oldest cohort, while less change is found in the other cohorts.
A second pattern is a negative trend in all three cohorts and this applies
to Ireland, Norway and Sweden. As a third model, we have countries like
Italy and France, which show very small changes or almost none regarding
work centrality in all cohorts. Yet another pattern is found in West Germany, where there is a clear and positive trend for work among the youngest cohort but a small negative trend among the oldest cohort. Table 3.2
shows the figures for Denmark as an example of the first pattern, Ireland
as an example of the second, Italy as an example of the third and Western
Germany as an example of the fourth.

Gender

We assumed in Hypothesis 5 that women would have a lower level of work
centrality than men, but that such a relationship would be mediated by
employment status. In 2008, men in general still place a slightly higher
importance on work (3.40) than women do (3.33), as they also did in 1999
and 1990 (not shown). This difference was significant in 1990 irrespective
of employment status, but the independent effect of gender concerning full-
time workers disappeared in 2008.

Figure 3.3 shows that full-time working men and women attach a greater
importance to work than do those who are less attached to the labour

Table 3.2 Work minus Leisure by Age Category. Selected Countries, 1990, 1999, and 2008

	Denmark								
	1990			*1999*			*2008*		
Age group	*Mean*	*N*	*SD*	*Mean*	*N*	*SD*	*Mean*	*N*	*SD*
15–29	-0.12	269	0.89	-0.11	207	0.98	0.04	204	0.96
30–49	-0.03	403	0.90	-0.13	412	0.95	-0.06	554	0.87
≥ 50	0.20	349	1.10	-0.09	379	1.20	-0.24	734	1.10
P-value	0.00			0.85			0.00		
Eta	0.13			0.02			0.10		

	Ireland								
	1990			*1999*			*2008*		
Age group	*Mean*	*N*	*SD*	*Mean*	*N*	*SD*	*Mean*	*N*	*SD*
15–29	0.32	245	0.89	0.15	181	0.94	-0.21	204	0.92
30–49	0.41	369	0.99	0.14	383	0.95	-0.05	356	0.90
≥ 50	0.47	374	1.00	-0.14	404	1.20	-0.31	358	1.08
P-value	0.20			0.00			0.00		
Eta	0.05			0.14			0.12		

	Italy								
	1990			*1999*			*2008*		
Age group	*Mean*	*N*	*SD*	*Mean*	*N*	*SD*	*Mean*	*N*	*SD*
15–29	0.24	626	0.89	0.20	445	0.90	0.27	319	0.82
30–49	0.38	736	0.97	0.39	731	0.87	0.42	523	0.92
≥ 50	0.62	638	1.00	0.69	796	0.98	0.65	635	0.92
P-value	0.00			0.00			0.00		
Eta	0.15			0.20			0.17		

	W. Germany								
	1990			*1999*			*2008*		
Age group	*Mean*	*N*	*SD*	*Mean*	*N*	*SD*	*Mean*	*N*	*SD*
15–29	-0.44	503	0.95	-0.08	503	0.78	0.08	140	0.90
30–49	-0.11	692	0.93	-0.14	692	0.86	0.07	422	0.86
≥ 50	-0.02	804	1.30	-0.16	804	1.20	-0.11	498	1.21
P-value	0.00			0.00			0.02		
Eta	0.16			0.13			0.08		

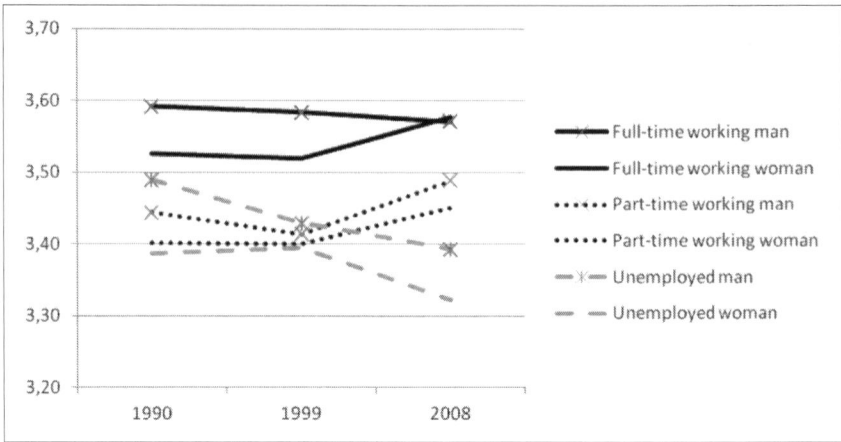

Figure 3.3   Unweighted aggregate means of work centrality by sex and employment status.

market, that is, part-time workers and the unemployed of both genders. Those outside the labour force place an even lower emphasis on work (not shown in the figure). Although full-time working men and women put the same importance on work in 2008, there are clear gender differences with respect to the other years and the other categories. Hypothesis 5 thus has to be modified slightly.

SEARCHING FOR EXPLANATIONS

The main conclusion of this study is that the perceived work centrality in eleven European countries shows both continuity and change over time. In relative terms—when compared with other domains of life—it was found to be stable in the majority of the countries, while it had declined in four of the countries. At the same time, the absolute value put on work has decreased in most of the countries. However, this decrease is not continuous throughout the decades and there are diverging trends in some of the countries. Accordingly, there is only partial support for Hypothesis 1.

When analysing work centrality in relation to leisure at an aggregate level, we find that work has lost ground in terms of importance over the two decades. This development applies to most of the countries examined. But again, this change is not continuous and a few of the countries show a different pattern. All in all, we conclude that there has been an increase in the perceived importance of leisure in relation to work. Hypothesis 2 is thus supported.

Most of the countries showing a high preference for leisure over work—Sweden, Norway, Denmark, Britain, Ireland and the Netherlands—have had quite high overall employment levels, around 70 to 75 percent during the 2000s. Where work is perceived to be more important than leisure—in Italy, France, Spain and Belgium—we find rather low employment levels, especially among females, in spite of some increases over the last two decades. In order to explain this pattern, it would seem fruitful to look at the role of different cultural and societal contexts (cf. Figure 3.1).

One possible explanation for this is that there is a 'scarcity' of leisure in countries with higher employment levels and a scarcity of employment in countries with lower levels. This is in line with the conclusions by Inglehart (2008) and Welzel and Inglehart (2010). Accordingly, the increased preference for leisure may reflect a desire among people in Northern European and Anglo-Saxon countries to reduce their working hours. In contrast, the low employment levels in the Mediterranean countries suggest that the people there have more leisure and thus a

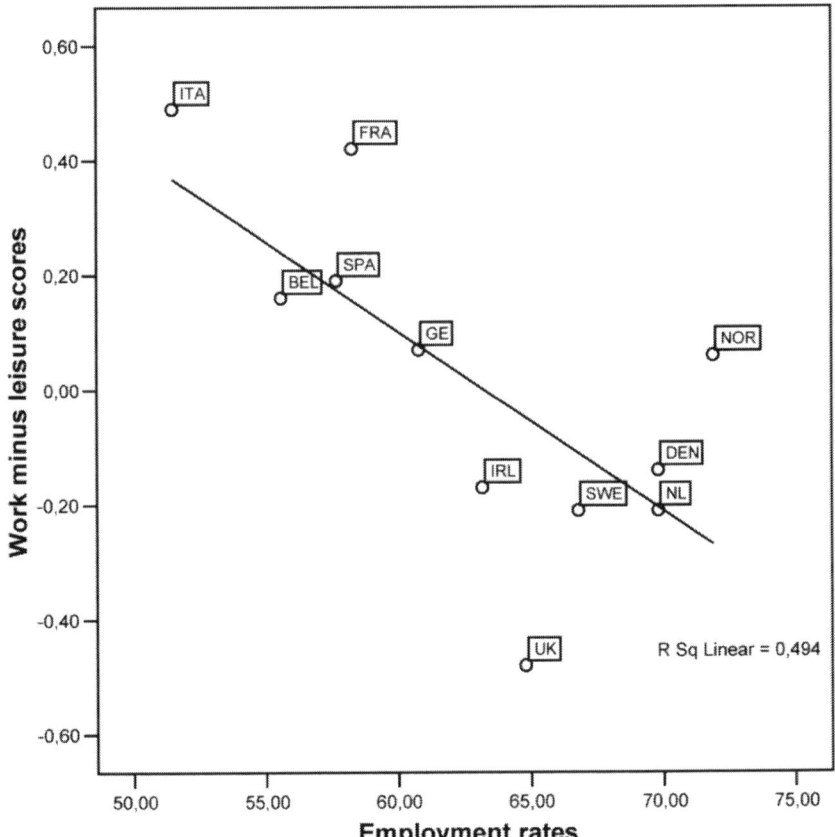

Figure 3.4 Work-minus-leisure scores by employment rate among people aged 15–74. Eleven countries, 2008.

relatively greater preference for work. This relationship is illuminated in Figure 3.4, which shows work-minus-leisure scores and employment levels. There is obviously a clear negative relationship between the two. Lower employment levels go hand-in-hand with higher work-minus-leisure scores. Although not shown in the figure, this holds true for both men and women.

Could changes in employment levels explain changes in work centrality? Ireland distinguishes itself from the rest through a large decrease in the relative importance ascribed to work, which was the second most important domain in life in 1990 and the fourth in 2008. In this country, there is a simultaneous increase in employment levels. In fact, Ireland has the highest growth in employment levels of all the countries studied, from 52 percent in 1990 to 68 percent in 2008. This is primarily due to a remarkable expansion in the proportion of women in the labour market. Along with this increase in the Irish employment level, it turns out that work is given less emphasis. This pattern is not, however, visible in the other countries that show a decline in work centrality; employment levels can thus only constitute one possible explanation.

The impact of scarcity may also appear in the relationship between unemployment and work centrality. The scarcity hypothesis suggests that, during periods of economic insecurity, a greater emphasis is put on earning money and thus also on the importance of work. We find a positive correlation between unemployment levels and work-minus-leisure scores in the countries examined (not shown). This supports the assumption that economic deprivation causes people to place a higher value on material factors, increasing the relative importance of work in comparison with leisure. In most of the countries showing a decrease that pertains to work centrality, there was also a fall in unemployment. This applies to Ireland, Britain, the Netherlands, Denmark and Norway. Ireland distinguished itself by having the largest fall in unemployment rates, from 13.4 percent in 1990 to 6.3 percent in 2008. Falling unemployment may thus be one factor that explains the decreasing significance of work.

The third hypothesis concerned the correlation between work centrality and age; here we expected less emphasis on work in the youngest age category. Our analysis provides support for this hypothesis in most of the countries examined in 1990, while this relationship becomes weaker in 1999 and shows diverging trends in 2008. At the aggregate level, a decrease in the work-minus-leisure score was found among the youngest across the eighteen-year period, but several countries diverge from this pattern. Moreover, there is a tendency in some of the countries for the low emphasis on work in this cohort to be reflected in the middle cohort one or two decades later, indicating a generational effect. Hypothesis 4 thus obtains some support. Such a pattern is probably due to a changing economic, cultural and social environment in the formative years of the youngest cohort. For some of the nations, our results thus support the socialization theory and the assumption that there is a generational effect. This is in line with the conclusions drawn by Inglehart (1990, 2008) and by Welzel and Inglehart 2010). However, our analysis also reveals a life-cycle effect in some of the countries, for example, France and Italy.

Surprisingly, the strongest trend observed in our data was the weakening of work centrality among the oldest cohort during the period examined. This picture appears among those approaching retirement in most of the countries but particularly in Ireland and Sweden in 2008. The result is consistent with what England and Misumi (1986) found among people aged 60 or older in Japan and the US, although they used an absolute measure of work centrality.

The trend toward disengagement is stronger in countries with higher employment levels among older people of working-age, which is shown in Figure 3.5. In other words, there seems to be a discrepancy between what

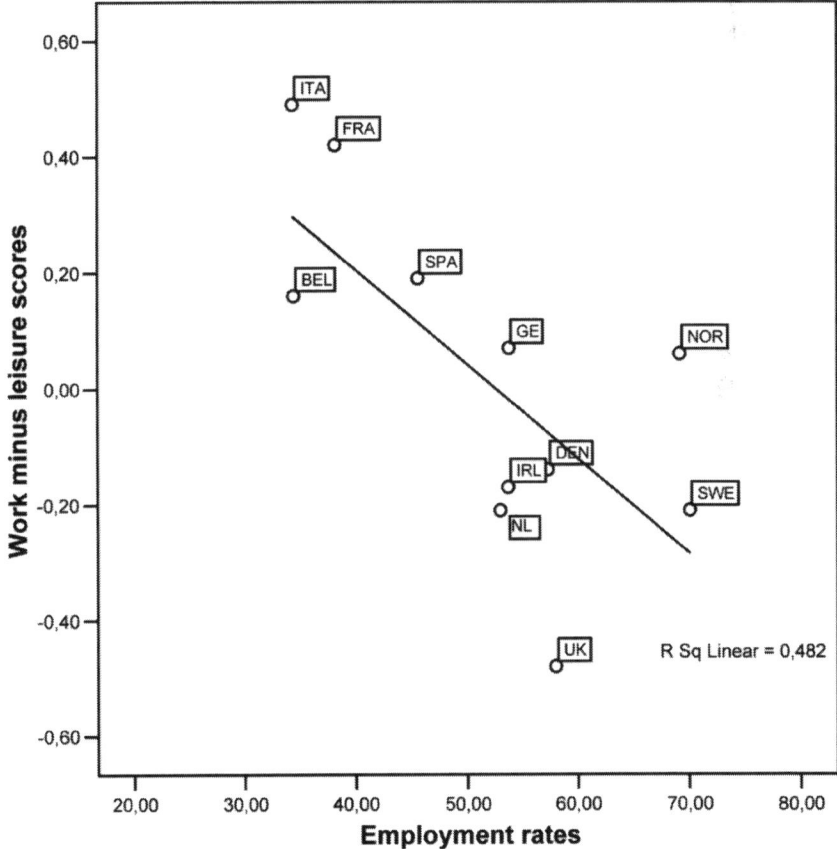

Figure 3.5 Work-minus-leisure scores by employment rate among people aged 55–64. Eleven countries, 2008.

people do and what they appreciate. The scarcity of leisure also seems to apply to the oldest age category, where higher activity rates go hand-in-hand with relatively strong preferences for leisure over work.

In contrast to Warr (2008), we found that differences between men and women as regards the importance of work were no longer significant in 2008 when we checked the hours worked (full-time/part-time). As shown in Figure 3.3, the gender differences among full-time workers regarding work centrality declined during the examined period and disappeared in 2008, while the differences remained in the case of part-time workers and the unemployed. Hypothesis 5 thus has to be modified slightly. When examining the relative importance of work in comparison with family (work minus family), we discover that full-time working women put a greater value on family, in comparison with work, than full-time working men do (see Figure 3.6).

Figure 3.6 shows work-minus-family scores for men and women in three employment statuses. All the categories prefer family over work, but there are clear gender differences throughout. Irrespective of their employment status, women value family over work to a greater degree than men do. These results apparently echo socialization into rather traditional gender roles.

An analysis of the impact of having children on the importance of work further indicates that family formation differently affects men's and women's view of work centrality. In 2008, the importance attached to work was basically the same among men (3.40) and women without children (3.44), whereas fathers (3.40) placed a greater importance on work than did mothers (3.29). The presence of children thus simply had no overall effect on men's attitudes in the eleven countries, while it turned out to have a significant effect on women's priorities.

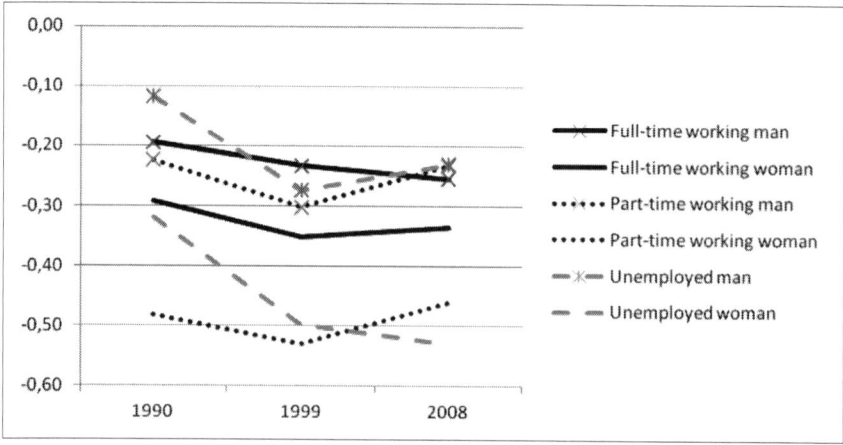

Figure 3.6 Work-minus-family scores by sex and employment status. Eleven countries, 1990, 1999 and 2008.

There is also a correlation between work centrality among women and female employment levels. Countries with high female employment levels score lower on work centrality. One possible explanation for this is that there are more conflicts between work and family in these countries. The welfare and care policies of dual earning models encourage female employment, but the traditional division of domestic labour means that women generally have more responsibility for housework and child care than men. Women also have a greater preference for family matters than do men (as shown above). They can thus be expected to experience conflicts between work and family more often, and to adjust their working hours to the needs of their families. In other words, their labour market participation can be stressful, which in turn is likely to decrease their preference to work. In contrast, insofar as women withdraw from the labour market during their child-bearing years, another pattern may arise. When faced with no conflicts regarding family obligations, women's preference for work may actually be enhanced.

In Figure 3.3, we were able to see that the importance of work among the unemployed declined between 1990 and 2008. Yet, we find a greater emphasis on work in countries with higher levels of unemployment. Thus, we have the strange situation of a positive relationship between levels of unemployment and work centrality on the national level, while the importance of work has decreased among the unemployed since 1990. One possible reason for this surprising result might be tension between values and reality. If the unemployed regard re-employment as unlikely in the near future, but still hold employment to be very important, tension will be created. This can only be solved either by getting a job or by attaching less significance to work. Adapting one's values to reality in such a situation could resolve the conflict, as suggested by the cognitive dissonance theory (Wiendieck 1980).

Limitations

Like all other studies, this study has its limitations. If one wants to include institutional differences as explanatory factors and cover many countries, one has little choice but to carry out secondary analyses on existing international data. Although operationalizations are frequently not optimal, one can at least investigate a limited number of highly relevant variables in a large number of countries.

The question about work centrality ('how important is work in your life') offered four alternative responses: very important, rather important, not very important, and not at all important. The mean response was close to the maximum of this continuum, substantially reducing potential variance. Response options that provide greater measurement sensitivity, a wider range of alternatives, and a less skewed distribution would be preferable (Warr 2008). Besides that, it was not mentioned explicitly that the question referred to paid employment. Even though there are some methodological limitations, the contribution made by this chapter is a broad empirical examination of work centrality.

CONCLUSION

In this chapter, some assumptions regarding declining work centrality have been examined empirically and we find that they obtain only partial support. Looking at the entire period, 1990 to 2008, we find a decline in the significance attributed to work in most of the countries; however, there is no clear uniformity in the trend and a few countries show rather different patterns.

We should also note that there is a great deal of stability in work orientations. The ranking of work seems to be the same over time in most of the countries. At the same time, even though the order of ranking of life's different domains is not changing, work has lost ground to leisure in most of the countries. We suggest that the concept of 'scarcity' is fruitful when it comes to explaining this increased preference for leisure. This concept might explain why work is rated lower in countries where employment levels are higher. 'Scarcity' affects values in such a way that the lack of something increases the demand for it. Thus, unemployment increases the value of work, while high employment levels can increase the preference for leisure. This is particularly evident in Ireland, with its large decrease in the importance of work—from the second most important domain in life in 1990 to the fourth in 2008. During this period, there was a simultaneous increase in employment and a fall in unemployment.

Our analysis provides some support for assumptions concerning both life-cycle and generational effects, but the evidence is inconclusive. While, generally speaking, leisure has become more important vis-à-vis work among the youngest across the two decades, several countries diverge from this pattern. Moreover, there is a tendency in a few of the countries for the low importance given to work in this cohort to be reflected in the middle cohort one or two decades later, which indicates a generational effect. Evidently, however, work has also lost ground in terms of importance in the oldest age category. The effects of different institutional conditions under which people 'disengage' from work when approaching retirement age need to be the subject of further research.

NOTES

1. The effects of the financial crisis in the last years of the first decade of 2000s is unlikely to be visible in our data.

4 Work Orientations in Western Europe and the United States

Tomas Berglund

The question of work orientation has long been of interest in sociology. Work orientation is often defined as an individual's attitudes toward work in general and is closely related to work values, that is, the qualities that people regard as important in a job (Parker et al. 1972). In the 1960s, John Goldthorpe, David Lockwood, Frank Bechhofer and Jennifer Platt (1968) found what they called three 'ideal-typical' orientations toward a job: an instrumental, a solidaristic and a bureaucratic orientation. The instrumental orientation is one in which a job is regarded as just a way to get the financial means for life outside work. For a worker with a solidaristic orientation, a job is viewed as an end in itself, that is, as a meaningful group activity and as important for one's identity. The bureaucratic orientation also characterizes a job as something more than just a way to get the financial means for life outside work. The bureaucrat often has a commitment to the organization, and is hence more involved in his/her job. This commitment, however, is not independent of expectations of advancement.

In a previous study I investigated work orientations in six countries using data from the International Social Survey Programme (ISSP), 'Work Orientations II 1997' (Berglund 2001). The countries were Sweden, Norway, West Germany, France, Britain and the US. Theoretically, the study used Goldthorpe et al.'s typology of three orientations toward work as its point of departure. If these orientations are viewed in relation to Weber's action typology (Weber 1978: 24–25), we can also include what I called an individualistic orientation. This resembles the bureaucratic orientation in the sense that opportunities for advancement are of importance in a job, but it may instead be seen from a post-materialistic perspective of self-fulfillment and self-realization (Inglehart 1990, 1997; Inglehart and Welzel 2005). Furthermore, commitment to a particular organization is not that relevant for the individualist; instead job mobility is important in finding a suitable match between the individual's preferences and the offers in the labour market.

In a factor analysis of items from the work-orientation questionnaire, four patterns appeared that resemble the theoretical pre-understanding, but the empirical dimensions did not completely correspond to the model. First, an instrumental orientation was found, constituted by the responses to the following two items: 'A job is a way of earning money—nothing more'; and 'I would enjoy having a paid job even if I did not need the money' (reversed). This dimension is more common among manual workers, men and those with only primary education. Second, a career orientation was detected in which good opportunities for advancement and high income are regarded as important in a job. This dimension resembles the bureaucratic orientation to work and characterizes managers in particular, but also the youngest age group (18–29 years). Third, an altruistic orientation was distinguished: a job that is useful to society and a job that allows one to help other people are regarded as important work values. It is more prevalent among women and public employees. And last, an orientation was found in which work autonomy (working independently; deciding on one's own working hours) is of importance. This especially characterizes the self-employed and professionals (only in Sweden, Norway and Germany) and resembles the expected individualistic orientation. However, a more precise term in this context is 'autonomy orientation' toward work.

In this chapter, I will return to the question of work orientation and examine whether the findings from 1997 can be detected in a newer set of empirical materials, that is, ISSP's Work Orientations III 2005. As in the earlier study, the same six countries will be in focus. The chapter tries to answer the following questions: Do we find the same patterns regarding work orientations in 2005 as in 1997? How have the orientations evolved over time? In which social categories, for example gender, age and occupational categories, are the different work orientations most common? And, last, do the six countries differ concerning work orientations, and if so, why?

THE SIGNIFICANCE OF WORK VALUES

Why study work values and work orientations? The legacy of Max Weber has shown the potential importance of changes in the cultural sphere for economic and cultural development. Goldthorpe and Lockwood's interest in the work orientation of employees was a consequence of a more general concern with possible cultural shifts in modern industrial and affluent societies. The question was whether the working class had begun to replace its traditional lifestyle with a more bourgeois way of life emphasizing the private sphere (Goldthorpe et al. 1968). Such a perspective implies that working life no longer has any profound influence on workers' self-identity. Instead, family and leisure time are the significant domains affecting work orientation. An indication of these tendencies would be a more widespread instrumental orientation toward work among the working class—which Goldthorpe et al. also found. This view has subsequently been put forward several times, with claims being made that consumption, rather than the production sphere, is what influences attitudes and identities (du Gay 1996; Offe 1985; Pakulski and Waters 1996).

In other research, an instrumental orientation is not regarded as primarily an effect of cultural values. Instead, it is the individual's experience of the quality of the work situation that matters (Blauner 1964; Korpi 1978). An alienating job—stripped of intrinsic values—will foster an instrumental orientation toward work. Looked at from this point of view, a widespread instrumental attitude in society could be an indication of impoverished working conditions rather than the rise of a bourgeois middle-class culture.

There is, however, no general agreement on how work values and work orientations are created and shaped (see Dose 1997 for an overview). It seems that neither primary socialization processes, personal experiences, secondary socialization processes in working life nor value changes during the course of life can be neglected in the shaping of work values. Consequently, the work values observed in the working population at a certain point in time can be the result of either matching processes between individual preferences and jobs, or of individuals' adaptation to working conditions and organizational cultures.

In the present study, we will not be able to resolve the question of whether work orientations are an effect of matching or adaptation processes. The main reason for this is that the data at hand are cross-sectional. To study the directions of causality, longitudinal information is needed. In any case, the data used here are international and comparative, which makes it possible to investigate how work orientations and work values vary not only among groups and work situations but also among nations.

INTERNATIONAL COMPARISONS

Many studies on international differences in work orientations have had a middle-range focus and have studied the significance of institutional differences between countries, instead of the national cultures per se (Esser 2005; Hult 2004). Generally, an institution can be defined as 'a set of rules, formal or informal, that actors generally follow, whether for normative, cognitive, or material reasons' (Hall and Soskice 2001a: 9). Individuals who are addressed by institutions are therefore believed to be influenced in terms of their cognitions, evaluations and actions (March and Olsen 1989).

Two ways of clustering countries and states have emerged from the institutional perspective on welfare states and labour markets. The first of these recognizes different welfare or employment regimes (Esping-Andersen 1990; Korpi and Palme 1998; Gallie 2007a). It studies the emergence of different national welfare or labour market institutions from a power-resource perspective. As an effect of the relative power of labour and capital and the relative success of channeling these interests into the political system and into welfare and labour market policies, welfare states are said to have greater or lesser decommodifying effects on labour; that is, they make employees more or less dependent on paid work for their material survival. From this perspective, Esping-Andersen (1990) distinguishes the following three main welfare state regimes: the social democratic, the conservative and the liberal. Gallie (2007a) broadens the perspectives by using the concept 'employment regimes' to underline the connection between the welfare state and labour market institutions. He distinguishes between three models in Europe: inclusive, dualist and market regimes. However, this typology corresponds to a large extent with the typology of Esping-Andersen.

In the inclusive regime, organized labour has strong power resources, which generally affects the design of labour market policies in a way beneficial for workers (Gallie 2007a: 18ff). There is a focus on general policies that minimize differences between labour-market categories, for example between employed and unemployed. Furthermore, full employment tends to be a central policy goal, which further strengthens the relative position of employees. On the workplace level, the presence of unions makes concerns about quality of work and participation into important issues. In the dualist regime, organized labour has a weaker position than in the inclusive regime. Regulations and policies tend to make a sharp distinction between employed and unemployed, and between core and peripheral employees. And in general, the unions have an easier time mobilizing core employees. This may lead to very different working conditions between employees with standard and non-standard contracts, with the former category tending to have much better terms with regard to job protection, training and working conditions. Finally, in market employment regimes, organized labour is a much weaker social partner in the regulation of labour markets. This leaves the floor open for employers to shape working conditions. One consequence of this is that working conditions and salaries will vary strongly as an effect of employers' relative dependence on employees' skills. This, in turn, will stratify employees and accentuate class differences.

The second perspective focuses on different production regimes, with liberal market economies (LMEs) and coordinated market economies (CMEs) as the two main types (Hall and Soskice 2001b; Hall and Gingerich 2009). This perspective emphasises the strategic actions and interactions of firms in relation to other actors (unions, governments, other firms, their employees, etc.) and the most important institutions conditioning these relationships and interactions. In the LMEs, hierarchies and markets are the main mechanisms of coordination. In the CMEs, the actors' interaction and coordination are more influenced by non-market relationships, for example, by the relations between unions and employers (Gallie 2007a).

One important difference between LMEs and CMEs has to do with the character and quality of employees' work and work situations (Gallie 2007a: 13ff; Soskice 1999). The CMEs are characterized by a focus on competing with quality products that demand the use of advanced technology and a skilled workforce. A major problem for the employer is to get access to highly skilled workers and to train them for specific work tasks. Furthermore, the large knowledge component in the work process usually implies relatively high levels of discretion in work. Both these factors—the investments in training, and the employees' relative work autonomy—make the employer more dependent on the employees and therefore more prepared to cooperate with unions and work councils.

The LMEs are to a higher degree characterized by mass production, which demands a less skilled labour force and therefore less investment in training. On the other hand, highly skilled professional and managerial segments are also needed, both to secure innovations, thereby keeping up in the market competition, and for administrative purposes in more hierarchical organizations. This creates a polarization of working conditions between low- and high-skilled employees. Furthermore, a production system intended for quantity production is generally characterized by greater volatility to market changes, which in turn demands greater numerical flexibility, that is, the potential to change the size of the workforce. The working conditions in LMEs are therefore less favourable for low-skilled employees, the relations between management and employees are more hierarchical and management is more antagonistic to unions.

The countries selected for comparison here are usually regarded as some of the prime examples of different production and employment or welfare regimes (Esser 2005; Gallie 2007a). Britain and the US are examples of LMEs or market employment regimes. The two Nordic countries—Norway and Sweden—are unmistakable examples the inclusive employment regimes. However, in the production regime literature, they are placed together with France and Germany as examples of CMEs.

VARIATIONS IN WORK ORIENTATIONS

Besides investigating whether the types of work orientations found in 1997—the instrumental, the career, the altruistic and the autonomy orientation—are also salient in the 2005 data and how they vary between social categories, the purpose is to analyse whether these orientations vary between countries. Cross-national variation could either be an effect of differences in the types of jobs and working conditions that are offered in the countries' respective labour markets, or an effect of general cultural differences. An institutional perspective, as described above, could be regarded as a sort of middle way. Working conditions are the result of social interactions in the labour market in tripartite relations between the state, employers and employees (unions). These interactions have resulted in an institutional framework, that is, rules, norms and practices which may affect individuals' cognitions, values and actions. Accordingly, it is reasonable to believe that these institutions also affect individuals' work orientations.

The autonomy orientation refers to an attitude where self-direction in work is regarded as an important work value. This orientation can be seen as an aspect of post-materialism and as an example of what have been called individualistic self-expression values (Inglehart 1990, 1997; Inglehart and Welzel 2005). It should be a typical orientation in post-industrial labour markets and in jobs with high levels of discretion and autonomy, for example, in professional occupations. Furthermore, in welfare states with a relatively high degree of social security, post-materialistic motives for working are believed to be more important than in welfare states with lower social security. In accordance with the theories of production regimes we should expect this orientation to be more prevalent in CMEs than in LMEs. If we also consider the employment regime perspective, it is possible to qualify the hypothesis and expect the autonomy orientation to characterize the inclusive Nordic labour markets, where the decommodifying effects of the welfare state and the influence of the unions on working conditions are the greatest.

The career orientation first and foremost values high salary and career opportunities in a job. This orientation should be more common in LMEs than in CMEs, because of the former's more hierarchical work relations, greater income dispersion, less regulated labour markets and less generous welfare benefits. This makes employees very dependent on their salaries, creating greater incentives for job mobility to find better opportunities in terms of salary and job protection. Using Inglehart's terminology, the career orientation expresses a higher degree of materialistic values (Inglehart 1990, 1997; Inglehart and Welzel 2005). In many respects the Nordic inclusive employment regimes exhibit the opposite characteristics. It is therefore reasonable to believe that the career orientation is least prevalent in these countries.

The instrumental orientation resembles the career orientation insofar as it emphasises wages as a decisive facet of a job. When viewed in a positive light, the instrumental orientation is regarded as a sign of an affluent working class placing value on private life instead of on work (Goldthorpe et al. 1968). However, it is hard to differentiate between these countries when it comes to wealth and affluence, which makes it difficult to use this perspective to formulate any expectations concerning the spread of an instrumental orientation. Another, less optimistic perspective views the instrumental orientation as an attitude of withdrawal that characterizes employees in a labour market offering impoverished employment and working conditions—that is, as a sort of defeatist attitude (Blauner 1964). Following the literature, the CMEs should in general offer better working conditions than the LMEs, and, if we add the employment regime perspective, the inclusive Nordic labour market should offer the best conditions. Consequently, the instrumental attitude should be more widespread in the liberal market regimes than in the Nordic inclusive employment regimes.

The last work orientation is called the altruistic orientation. Here, helping other people and being useful to society are important values. From the institutional perspectives, there are no obvious hypotheses to expect. On the one hand, the Nordic welfare model may foster attitudes that are in accordance with the values that imbue the institutional system. We would therefore expect to find the altruistic orientation to be more prevalent there than in the liberal market economies. However, we know from earlier research (Berglund 2001), that the altruistic orientation is least strong in the five European countries and most strong in the US. This may indicate more general cultural differences between the US and Europe. Such differences have also been found in other studies (Inglehart and Welzel 2005: 65). Americans are characterized by stronger community feelings, patriotism and religious beliefs than are the citizens of most European countries. The altruistic orientation to work may therefore have other connotations in the American context than in the European. However, another interpretation of these values is that they serve as a functional alternative in the absence of a strong welfare state, that is, as a driving force for charity and social work in the civil society. If this is the case, we should also expect the altruistic orientation to be more widespread in Britain, alongside the US.

DATA AND METHODS

To study work orientation in France, West Germany, Britain, Norway, Sweden and the US, data from ISSP are used. ISSP is an international collaboration that was launched in the 1980s to collect comparable international attitudinal data (Hult and Svallfors 2002). In general, such data are hard to collect because of problems in formulating survey questions that retain the same meaning and connotations in different national contexts. This can create serious validity problems in measurement. ISSP tries to solve such problems through genuine international collaboration in the development of the questionnaires.

Data for the ISSP Work Orientation module have been collected on three occasions: 1989, 1997 and 2005. In 1989, eleven countries participated; in 1997, there were twenty-five; and in 2005, thirty-two countries. The choice to focus on only six countries has to do with the goal of replicating the findings from my previous analysis, hereafter called the 1997 study (Berglund 2001). In the German case separate samples are collected in the former East and West Germany. The 1997 study concentrated on West Germany, and for the sake of comparability, West Germany is still in focus in the present study.

The sample sizes in each of the countries are quite ambitious (Scholz et al. 2008). The smallest samples are in Britain (1,954) and Sweden (1,979). The West German sample size is 2,844, the Norwegian 2,665, and the American 2,224. In France the sample is as large as 9,710 individuals.

However, the French have another view on how to use reminders compared to the other countries—they are used very sparsely—which explains their large sample size. It is obvious, however, that response rates are becoming a large problem for the Work Orientation Survey. In France, the response rate is only 17 percent; in Germany 39 percent; and in Britain 47 percent. The response rate was highest in Sweden with 69 percent, followed by the US with 55 percent and Norway with 50 percent. These low response rates (except for Sweden) create risks of biased data. In many of the countries attempts were made to compensate for this through weighting (F, GB, US). The weights are used in the analyses to come.

Principal component analysis (PCA) and ordinary least square multiple regressions are the statistical techniques mainly used in the analyses. The variables are to a large extent the same as in the 1997 study (Berglund 2001). As described above, four work orientations make up the dependent variables: an instrumental orientation, a career orientation, an altruistic orientation and an autonomy orientation. The construction of these dimensions will be presented below. Although the independent variables are largely the same as in the models run in 1997, some changes have been made. First, variables that did not have any substantial impact on the dependent variables have been removed. These are marital status and religion. Second, education is operationalized by grouping years of education into three categories: ten years or less, eleven to thirteen years, and fourteen years or more. In addition, the following variables are included in the regression models: gender, age, private and public sector of employment and occupational category. The last variable has been constructed by, first, differentiating between employees and employers/self-employed, and then, for the employees, merging ISCO-88 occupational categories.[1]

RESULTS

In the work orientation questionnaire, there are ten items that can be used to extract different dimensions of work orientation. In the analyses below, two are dropped and only eight of the items are used. The two dropped items are questions on the importance of job security and having an interesting job. These questions are very skewed—with more than 90 percent thinking these factors to be important or very important in a job—and can be regarded as valence items, that is, questions that express self-evident values with which very few disagree (Stokes 1963). In the 1997 study, these two items were dropped from the analysis for the same reason (Berglund 2001).

The remaining items are analysed using factor analysis (PCA). In Table 4.1 the rotated factor loadings are shown. The first two items are statements with which the individual could agree or disagree on a five-point scale. The remaining six measure the importance of various aspects of a job on five-point scales (from very important to very unimportant). When the samples from the six countries are pooled together in the analysis, four dimensions

Table 4.1 Dimensions of Work Orientation. PCA. Rotated Solution (Varimax)

	1	2	3	4
A job is just a way of earning money—no more	-0.059	0.174	**-0.783**	0.033
I would enjoy having a paid job even if I did not need the money	-0.001	0.073	**0.824**	0.032
[How important is] high income	-0.048	**0.819**	-0.167	0.180
[. . .] opportunities for advancement	0.208	**0.832**	0.059	-0.034
[. . .] a job that allows someone to help other people	**0.889**	0.047	0.030	0.151
[. . .] a job that is useful to society	**0.892**	0.104	0.032	0.061
[. . .] a job that allows someone to work independently	0.232	0.121	0.097	**0.708**
[. . .] a job that allows someone to decide their times or days of work	-0.008	0.013	-0.087	**0.850**
Eigenvalues (initial)	2.080	1.508	1.092	1.066
Variance explained (rotated solution)	21.3	17.8	16.8	16.1
n		6,711		

Source: ISSP 2005.

emerge. These dimensions correspond to what was found in the 1997 study. First, there is the dimension consisting of the two items 'a job that allows someone to help other people' and 'a job that is useful to society.' This dimension is called an altruistic orientation toward work. Second, the two items 'high income' and 'opportunities for advancement' load together to one dimension that can be called a career orientation. Third, the instrumental orientation is found to consist of the two items 'A job is just a way of earning money—no more' and 'I would enjoy having a paid job even if I did not need the money.' And last, the two items 'a job that allows someone to work independently' and 'a job that allows someone to decide their times or days of work' constitute an autonomy orientation toward work.

This analysis confirms the factor structure found in the 1997 study (Berglund 2001). If one studies the separate samples of the countries, the factor structures reveal some differences in the overall picture. In all the countries, the instrumental orientations emerge as a separate dimension. The items concerning the autonomy orientation load together with the altruistic orientation in France, West Germany, Britain and the US. In Norway and Sweden, the items instead load on the career orientation. In general, the loadings of the autonomy items are quite weak on these other dimensions compared to the central items in the altruistic and career dimensions.

The next step of the analysis is to create indexes, which has been done by summating the items that are connected in Table 4.1 (the first item in the table has been reversed). The scales range from 0 to 8 indicating stronger orientation in the named direction.[2] These four scales have been constructed in the same way as in the 1989 and 1997 studies. This makes it possible to study changes of means and rankings of the countries over time (not shown). In general, however, the general rank order of the countries is quite stable.

For the instrumental orientation, the highest means are found in Britain and France and the lowest in Norway and Sweden. This rank order of the countries is also found in 1997. In 1989, not all the countries are included, but Norway is still at the bottom of the list. Concerning the altruistic orientation, the rank order of the countries is quite stable throughout the three survey years. The US is at the top together with Britain. In 2005 West Germany joins Britain at the same rank. France, Norway and Sweden have stable levels and are clearly below the two top countries and especially the US. For all the years, the career orientation is most widespread in the US and least widespread in the two Nordic countries. For the autonomy orientation, Sweden is at the top both in 1997 and 2005. Norway and West Germany share second place in 2005.

Further on in this chapter, these rankings will be analysed when some important factors are controlled for. We will now study which factors are related to the different orientations to work in each of the countries. Table 4.2 presents the figures concerning the instrumental orientation toward work and reveals some general patterns for the countries. Occupational group is especially relevant; the instrumental orientation is more common among manual workers and service workers than among professionals, managers and the self-employed. This pattern was also found in the 1997 study (Berglund 2001), indicating that the working class has a greater tendency to evaluate a job as a means to provide for material necessities than as a value in itself. It lends support to the view that, relatively speaking, working-class jobs offer less rewards apart from the wages.

As for the other factors, education also has a quite general impact on the instrumental orientation. Individuals with ten or fewer years of education are more instrumentally oriented than individuals with fourteen or more years. In Britain, however, there is no effect of education. Gender is also a variable with a quite general relation to the instrumental orientation; men tend to a higher degree than women to have an instrumental view of work. In Germany and the US this difference is not significant.

In Table 4.3, the altruistic orientation is analysed. Here, two general patterns are found. First, women tend to have a more altruistic orientation toward work than do men. Only in two of the countries are there no statistically significant differences. Second, public employees also tend to have a more altruistic orientation than do private employees, with the exception of the US, where no statistically significant difference is found (in West Germany the variable is not available). These results are wholly in line with the findings from 1997

Table 4.2 Factors Affecting Instrumental Orientation. Multiple OLS-regression

	SE	NO	GE(W)	FR	GB	US
Gender (ref: Woman)						
Man	0.37**	0.28*	0.33	0.49**	0.40*	0.12
Age (ref: 18–29 years)						
30–39	0.28	0.10	0.26	0.61**	0.33	0.31
40–49	0.17	-0.08	0.36	0.80***	-0.08	0.40*
50–59	0.24	0.10	0.11	0.29	0.00	0.15
60–	0.42	-0.01	0.34	0.16	-0.40	0.18
Occupational category (ref: Manual worker)						
Employer, Self-employed	-1.09***	-0.79***	-0.86**	-1.09***	-0.72*	-0.58**
Manager	-1.80***	-0.84***	-1.49*	-1.30***	-1.36***	-0.91***
Professional	-1.12***	-0.67***	-0.95***	-1.23***	-1.23***	-0.43*
Service worker	-0.49*	-0.22	0.03	-0.56*	-0.55	-0.03
Years of education (ref: 14 years or more)						
–10 years	0.51**	0.52*	0.68*	0.77**	0.10	0.60**
11–13 years	0.33*	0.36**	0.35	0.05	0.01	0.51***
Sector (ref: Private)						
Public	0.26	0.06	-	0.12	0.04	-0.07
Intercept	2.69	2.25	2.70	3.38	3.90	2.67
R^2_{adj}	0.10	0.07	0.10	0.11	0.05	0.07
n	785	799	467	787	471	991

Levels of significance: * p< 0.05; ** p< 0.01; *** p< 0.001.
Source: ISSP 2005.

except that there were significant differences for both variables in Germany (sector available in 1997), and for gender in the US (sector not available that same year) (Berglund 2001). The conclusion is that concerning the altruistic orientation, there are quite large differences between the sexes and between employees in different sectors in the countries analysed. When it comes to the other variables, there are no effects except for France, where age, occupational category (also found in GB) and education have some influence.

Some general patterns are also found for the career orientation (Table 4.4). The most important of these has to do with age, implying that individuals tend to be less career-oriented the older they get. It is most distinct in Britain followed by the two Nordic countries, but less so in France and Germany and not at all in the US. In the 1997 study, the same patterns were

Table 4.3   Factors Affecting Altruistic Orientation. Multiple OLS-regression

	SE	NO	GE(W)	FR	GB	US
Gender (ref: Woman)						
Man	-0.47***	-0.38**	-0.02	-0.42**	0.03	-0.28**
Age (ref: 18–29 years)						
30–39	0.07	0.14	0.06	-0.35*	-0.11	0.17
40–49	0.16	0.15	0.10	-0.43*	-0.03	-0.10
50–59	0.16	0.08	0.28	-0.32	0.18	0.06
60–	0.41	0.21	-0.02	-0.73	-0.11	-0.08
Occupational category (ref: Manual worker)						
Employer, Self-employed	0.29	0.09	0.32	0.54*	0.20	-0.09
Manager	-0.47	-0.19	0.91	0.10	-0.36	-0.21
Professional	0.08	-0.04	0.19	0.65***	0.52	-0.06
Service worker	0.35	0.18	0.15	0.46**	0.64*	-0.05
Years of education (ref: 14 years or more)						
–10 years	-0.17	0.04	-0.21	0.43*	0.02	0.25
11–13 years	-0.09	-0.23	-0.11	0.48**	0.09	-0.07
Sector (ref: Private)						
Public	0.75***	0.85***	–	0.40**	0.58**	0.20
Intercept	5.14	5.18	5.51	5.16	5.10	6.86
R^2_{adj}	0.10	0.12	0.00	0.07	0.07	0.02
n	820	821	473	842	494	991

Levels of significance: * $p < 0.05$; ** $p < 0.01$; *** $p < 0.001$.
Source: ISSP 2005.

revealed, including the non-significant results in the US (except for the oldest who were significantly less career-oriented than the youngest) (Berglund 2001). However, it seems possible to state that in most of the countries analysed here, the career orientation toward work diminishes with age. We can suggest two reasonable hypotheses. On the one hand, individuals tend to make a career throughout the course of their working lives. These values, therefore, become less and less important the older one becomes. On the other hand, advancing to a job with a high salary may not be that easy, which people tend to realize the older they become. The decreasing proportion of individuals with a career orientation may therefore be looked upon as an expression of balancing values and attitudes with reality (Festinger 1957). In the US, we do not find this pattern.

Table 4.4 Factors Affecting Career Orientation. Multiple OLS-regression

	SE	NO	GE(W)	FR	GB	US
Gender (ref: Woman)						
Man	-0.06	0.06	0.38**	0.31**	0.31*	-0.07
Age (ref: 18–29 years)						
30–39	-0.10	-0.10	-0.03	-0.00	-0.41*	0.25
40–49	-0.41*	-0.22	-0.23	-0.15	-0.79***	0.10
50–59	-0.51**	-0.35*	-0.42*	-0.37*	-0.93***	-0.10
60–	-0.50*	-0.51*	-0.32	-0.27	-1.53***	-0.10
Occupational category (ref: Manual worker)						
Employer, Self-employed	0.17	0.33	-0.06	-0.60**	0.02	-0.12
Manager	0.55	0.64**	0.37	0.21	0.19	-0.34*
Professional	0.35*	-0.01	0.05	-0.18	-0.07	-0.47**
Service worker	0.36*	0.04	0.30	0.15	-0.15	-0.18
Years of education (ref: 14 years or more)						
–10 years	-0.08	-0.07	0.42*	0.19	0.20	0.91***
11–13 years	0.03	-0.05	0.31	0.18	-0.06	0.39***
Sector (ref: Private)						
Public	-0.04	0.12	–	-0.09	-0.10	0.20
Intercept	5.35	5.21	5.29	5.94	6.34	6.16
R^2_{adj}	0.02	0.02	0.04	0.04	0.09	0.07
n	831	822	485	848	496	990

Levels of significance: * p< 0.05; ** p< 0.01; *** p< 0.001.
Source: ISSP 2005.

There are also some other results of interest. First, there is a gender difference in three of the countries—France, West Germany and Britain—but not in the Nordic countries and the US. Second, occupational category has some role to play. In Norway, managers are more career-oriented than are manual workers. This was also found in the 1997 study, in which managers in Sweden tended in that direction as well. Here, the coefficient for managers in Sweden is quite high but not significant. Instead, both professionals and service workers are more career-oriented than manual workers. It is interesting to compare this Nordic pattern to the one found in the US. Both managers and professionals in the US are less career-oriented than manual workers. In 1997 a similar tendency was found. It seems that it is not entirely accepted to express career ambitions in some managerial and

professional contexts in the US, even though (or because) a career orientation is a very common and general value. Perhaps the strong effect of education can be understood by means of a similar interpretation.

In Table 4.5 the figures for the autonomy orientation are presented. The
most general patterns here follow the occupational categories. In all the
countries except for the US, employers and the self-employed have a stronger autonomy orientation than do manual workers. The same patterns were
also present in the 1997 study (Berglund 2001). However, in that study professionals were also characterized by an autonomy orientation in three of the
countries: West Germany, Norway and Sweden. In 2005, we find a significant difference for manual employees only in Norway and Sweden, but not
in Germany. Furthermore, in Norway and Sweden in 1997, professionals

Table 4.5   Factors Affecting Autonomy Orientation. Multiple OLS-regression

	SE	NO	GE(W)	FR	GB	US
Gender (ref: Woman)						
Man	-0.13	-0.11	0.25	-0.42***	0.17	0.01
Age (ref: 18–29 years)						
30–39	0.26	0.55**	0.36	0.41**	0.29	0.35*
40–49	0.42**	0.61***	0.24	0.42**	0.26	0.66***
50–59	0.31*	0.13	0.34	0.21	0.33	0.46**
60–	0.19	0.20	0.22	0.12	0.29	0.48*
Occupational category (ref: Manual worker)						
Employer, Self-employed	0.53**	0.82***	0.89***	0.91***	0.90***	0.31
Manager	0.35	0.72***	0.11	-0.30	0.38	-0.09
Professional	0.35*	0.52**	0.36	0.13	0.23	0.16
Service worker	0.15	0.26	0.29	0.16	0.55*	0.31*
Years of education (ref: 14 years or more)						
–10 years	-0.11	-0.19	-0.24	-0.25	-0.05	0.21
11–13 years	-0.14	-0.12	-0.04	0.24	-0.22	-0.15
Sector (ref: Private)						
Public	-0.01	0.06	-	-0.13	0.22	-0.09
Intercept	5.72	5.02	5.18	5.14	4.83	5.08
R^2_{adj}	0.03	0.07	0.04	0.06	0.03	0.03
n	827	828	477	839	497	986

Levels of significance: * $p < 0.05$; ** $p < 0.01$; *** $p < 0.001$.
Source: ISSP 2005.

contrasted very much to managers in their preference for autonomy values. This is not confirmed in this study; managers in Norway even seem to have a somewhat stronger autonomy orientation than professionals.

There is one more general result that needs to be commented upon. In Sweden, Norway, France and the US, there is a quite distinct age pattern. The most autonomy-oriented age categories are in the middle of the age span. In particular, the category 40–49 years has the strongest autonomy orientation. Generally, when age patterns are found in cross-sectional data, as in this dataset, there are two main explanations, sometimes competing, sometimes complementary. The first is to understand the pattern as an effect of individuals' life cycles, that is, phases in life that most people must go through, for example entering and establishing oneself in the labour market, building a family, exiting the labour market for retirement, etc. These phases may influence the individual's preferences. In this case, the autonomy orientation consists of two valuable facets of the work situation: being able to work independently and having the possibility to decide when to work. These characteristics of the work situation may be most appreciated during the years when people start a family and have small children. In many of the countries (Sweden, West Germany and France) the 1997 study showed the highest coefficient for those aged 30–39 years, which appears to fit well with the life-cycle hypothesis about family building (Berglund 2001). However, in 2005, especially in Sweden and the US, it is people between 40 and 49 years who have the strongest autonomy orientation and not the 30–39 year olds. This is not wholly consistent with the hypothesis.

A competing hypothesis for interpreting age differences is that they mirror generational differences. Ronald Inglehart put forward this explanation in his theory of cultural shifts in affluent societies from materialistic to post-materialistic values (Inglehart 1990, 1997; Inglehart and Welzel 2005). The younger generations went through adolescence—the period when individuals tend to develop many important basic values—under different material circumstances than older generations. This makes them develop different values. During times of scarcity, materialistic values concerning economic and personal security tend to be of great importance. In good times, when basic material needs are met, people stress the importance of self-expression and personal freedom.

However, this theory places very much weight on changing material circumstances and on need. Another theoretical strand is to focus on the general cultural climate—the *Zeitgeist*—of different generations. For example, the generations who entered the labour market during the 1980s are said to emphasise individualism as a result of changing cultural and political landscapes (Phelps Brown 1990).

Above all, the relevance of these theories in this context concerns whether value changes can be traced in the value differences between different birth cohorts. From 1997 to 2005, eight years elapsed. Most of the individuals aged 30–39 years in 1997 were 40–49 years old in 2005. If the autonomy orientation that underlines freedom and autonomy in a job is a generational phenomenon—characteristic of the generation born in the 1960s who had their adolescence during the 1980s—one would expect these values to follow this birth cohort into the age category 40–49 in the 2005 survey. There is some support for this hypothesis in Sweden, but none in the US, where no statistically significant age differences at all were found in 1997.

The last table to present is an analysis of the pooled data using regressions with country dummies and controlling for the variables from the analyses above (Table 4.6). The first column shows the instrumental orientation toward work. It is most common in Britain and France, and least common in Norway and Sweden. As for the altruistic orientation, it is very prevalent in the US but less common in the two Nordic countries and France. The career orientation is also less widespread in the two Nordic countries than in the other four. Sweden is the most autonomy-oriented country in the analysis. It stands in particular contrast to France, Britain and the US.

If we go back to the hypothesis of national differences concerning the instrumental orientation, it was expected that it would be more typical of the LMEs than the CMEs, and that it would be least common in the Nordic countries. This last qualification of the hypothesis finds support. However, between the other two CME countries, West Germany and France, and the LMEs the results are less straightforward.

As for the altruistic orientation, from earlier research it was expected to be more widespread in the US than in the five European countries. The results support this expectation, but we find no backing for the hypothesis that the altruistic orientation is a consequence of the institutional set-up of

Table 4.6 Work Orientations. Country Comparisons. Control for Variables in Tables 4.3 to 4.5, except Sector. Multiple OLS-regression

	Instrumental orientation	Altruistic orientation	Career orientation	Autonomy orientation
Countries (ref: Sweden)				
Norway	-0.39***	-0.03	-0.11	-0.38***
West Germany	0.25*	0.29**	0.37***	-0.28**
France	0.84***	0.01	0.67***	-0.67***
Britain	0.77***	0.32***	0.49***	-0.58***
US	0.32***	1.38***	0.95***	-0.49***
R²	0.14	0.14	0.11	0.05
n	4,301	4,441	4,472	4,454

Levels of significance: * p< 0.05; ** p< 0.01; *** p< 0.001.
Source: ISSP 2005.

the Nordic inclusive welfare states. Another idea was that altruism could serve as a functional alternative to a generous welfare state. This hypothesis also finds only limited support; Britain does not join the US in having a very widespread altruistic orientation among the working population.

The career orientation was believed to be more common in the LMEs than in the CMEs and especially in comparison to the inclusive Nordic welfare states. There is some endorsement for the hypothesis; the US has the most career-oriented working population and the two Nordic countries the least career-oriented. However, France is second in this respect, not Britain as expected.

Finally, it was expected that the autonomy orientation would be more prevalent in the CMEs than in the LMEs, and especially prevalent in the Nordic welfare states. The patterns found in Table 4.6 provide some support for this expectation. Sweden is at the top, and Norway is in third place just behind West Germany. It was anticipated that the two liberal economies would be at the bottom of the ranking, but France is the country with the lowest level.

DISCUSSION

The present study largely replicates a 1997 study using newer data from 2005. In general, the results are consistent with the findings from 1997. The same factor structure is extracted in the 2005 data, strengthening the conclusion that these four dimensions represent important orientations toward work. However, the reliability of some of the scales is questionable, indicating that more reliable constructs would need more items in the questionnaire to capture the four orientations.

The factors that explain variations in these orientations in 2005 are quite similar to those in 1997. Concerning the instrumental orientation, the main factors are occupational category and education. This result is very consistent across countries and over time (with some exceptions). Two different hypotheses are, on the one hand, that it is a cultural trait of the working class that has become more bourgeois and only values private life; and, on the other hand, that it is an effect of poor working conditions fostering an alienated attitude toward work. Perhaps the explanation lies in a combination of the two perspectives. If poor working conditions create an instrumental orientation toward work, it is reasonable to believe that these experiences are communicated and discussed in the working class and that this affects new generations' expectations and attitudes toward paid work.

In the literature, the same construct that has been interpreted here as an instrumental orientation has also been interpreted as an indicator of employment commitment (Gallie et al. 1998; Hult 2004; Esser 2005). Hult (2004: 6) defines the latter concept in the following way: 'By "employment commitment" is meant the perceived values in a job other than financial ones'. There are quite obvious similarities between the two concepts, representing the poles of each side of a dimension. The instrumental orientation is when the individual looks at work mainly as a means to get the financial resources for private life. In contrast, an individual who has a strong employment commitment sees paid work as a goal in itself.

The problem with this conceptualization is the concept of 'commitment.' When we speak of commitment, a willingness or readiness to perform some kind of action seems essential. As regards employment commitment it is reasonable to believe that it concerns a readiness to take part in paid work. However, we cannot exclude that people who have a low score on the scale may still be very willing to perform paid work, for example, in cases with less generous welfare systems compensating for income loss, or with low salaries, forcing individuals to many working hours (see Chapter 5 by Furåker, this volume). It therefore seems quite misleading to call the construct employment commitment.

Furthermore, the construct of instrumental-orientation/employment-commitment that is used here is considered by some authors to involve a quite strong normative element, that is, a duty to work. Esser (2005) posits the normative pressure to participate in paid work in generous welfare states (the Nordic ones) as one explanation of the high employment commitment in these countries. If the scale used here represents normative beliefs, it would seem to imply that the strong differences between occupational categories indicate a relatively weak work ethic in the working class. However, another hypothesis that finds even stronger support in Esser's analysis is the influence of the industrial relations systems on employment commitment, that is, the significance of organized labour on the quality of working conditions in the labour market (Esser 2005: 84–85). This finding strengthens the argument that the construct mainly represents an instrumental orientation as being an effect of the working conditions to which individuals are exposed.

The international differences in instrumental orientation found in the present study support the hypothesis that the instrumental orientation is least widespread in the Nordic inclusive labour markets. The explanation is probably that the Nordic labour markets offer a greater proportion of 'good' and stimulating jobs compared to the other countries because of the characteristics of the industrial relations system—in particular the impact of strong unions. However, the pattern is not that clear-cut if we look at it from the perspective of CMEs and LMEs. We expected the instrumental orientation to be more widespread in the US and Britain than in France and Germany, but this was not the case.

The findings concerning the altruistic orientation are also in line with the 1997 study. These work values prevail most strongly among public employees and women. For public sector employees, the essential character of the work they do is for the common good, and their organizational cultures may therefore be permeated by these values. This, in turn, may affect employees' work orientation in such workplaces. When it comes to women's altruistic orientation, it is tempting to try to explain it by traditional gender roles. However, in two countries, Germany and Britain, no differences were found, which makes the results more ambiguous. The rankings of the countries are quite the same as in the 1997 study. The US is the country with the most altruistic population, and the two Nordic countries, together with France, are the least altruistic. It therefore seems possible to conclude that the inclusive Nordic welfare states are not accompanied by an altruistic orientation toward work to a higher degree than other countries. Instead, it is among the liberal market economies that these work values are strongest. There is no straightforward explanation of these results; but one quite functionalistic explanation could be that altruistic values serve as a motivational force to work for the common good as a sort of a compensation for the lack of more extensive welfare programs. However, in the case of the US, we cannot discard the possibility of a distinctive national culture that puts great emphasis on communal values.

Concerning the career orientation, there are also distinct national differences. The US, together with Britain and France, is the top scorer in career orientation. Norway and Sweden, on the other hand, are at the bottom. This is the pattern to expect when the welfare states vary in their decommodifying effects. Pecuniary reasons to work and the opportunities for advancement should be more important in societies where paid employment is almost the only source of income and where income differentials are large. The internal patterns in each country are essentially the same as in the 1997 study. Younger people are more career-oriented than older ones. The most reasonable explanation of this is the life-cycle hypothesis. However, we cannot rigorously test this explanation with the cross-sectional data at hand.

The last kind of work orientation studied in this chapter is the autonomy orientation. The analysis has shown some general patterns in the six countries. The first has to do with occupational category; employers and the self-employed tend to express such an orientation to a higher degree than do manual workers. This was also found in 1997. The second is an age pattern; individuals in the middle of the age span seem more autonomy-oriented than both the youngest and the eldest. The best explanation for this pattern has to do with the life cycle. Members of the age categories 30–39 and 40–49 years presumably value independence in work for the sake of the flexibility to combine work and family. However, in Sweden there is a sign of a possible generational effect; the generation born in the 1960s is the bearer of a post-materialistic culture of independence and self-fulfillment. When it comes to national differences, there is some support for the view that the generous Nordic welfare states tend to foster these individualistic and post-materialistic work values.

NOTES

1. Managers are ISCO codes 1000–1319; professionals 2000–3480; service workers 4000–5230 or 9100–9162; manual workers 6000–8340 or 9200–9333.
2. Cronbach's alpha has been calculated. Best internal consistency is found for the scale measuring altruistic orientation (alpha ranging between 0.81 and 0.74) and the second best for the career orientation (0.63–0.52). Least reliable are the scales measuring the instrumental (0.61–0.26) and the autonomy orientation (0.51–0.38). The reliability of the scales, except for the altruistic orientation, is quite low in many of the countries.

5 Work Attitudes, Employment and Work Mobilization

A Comparison between Anglo-Saxon and Nordic Countries

Bengt Furåker

Previous research on attitudes to work has triggered the analysis in this chapter. As we will see below, several studies have shown that willingness to engage in employment is at least as strong as—or even stronger—in Scandinavia than in Anglo-Saxon countries. These results are highly interesting, in particular in relation to the debate on the welfare state. In this debate, which incessantly revolves around the effects of social benefits on people's incentives to be available for the labour market, the Anglo-Saxon and the Scandinavian (or Nordic) families of nations represent very different models. There is no doubt that the Nordic welfare state arrangements are much more comprehensive and generous. Research indicating that generous systems do not harm individuals' interest in taking on employment may thus have important political implications.

The picture is however more complicated. As will soon be demonstrated, the Nordic countries do not keep up with the Anglo-Saxon in terms of the amount of work carried out. Generally a larger proportion of the population's potential work effort is made use of in the latter than in the former countries. In the light of these facts, I believe there is a need to further explore the relationship between work attitudes and levels of employment and work mobilization. This is also the overriding purpose of this chapter, in which six Anglo-Saxon countries—Australia, New Zealand, Britain, Ireland, Canada and the US—and four Nordic—Denmark, Finland, Norway and Sweden—are the subject of comparison.

Another aim of this chapter has reference to theoretical and methodological issues. I want to discuss and elaborate our analytical tools in the field. For one thing, it seems that the concept of non-financial employment commitment is insufficient when we want to grasp attitudes to a great work effort. Social researchers sometimes have a tendency to ignore people's financial motives or to treat them as secondary, but we need an inclusive approach in examining the relationship between subjective, attitudinal information and actual employment and work mobilization rates. In fact there is here a whole complex of issues, to which I will come back in the next section.

The chapter is organized in the following way. To begin with, I consider some theoretical perspectives relevant for my research questions and this part includes a discussion of the crucial concepts. Second, I present data for the ten countries under scrutiny on employment, hours worked and work mobilization. With this end in view, information from national labour force surveys 2003–2007, put together by the OECD, is being used. Thereby we get a background for the analysis of attitudes. In a third step I examine data from the International Social Survey Programme (ISSP) 2005 on non-financial employment commitment and the data's association with employment rates and work mobilization rates. The program furnishes survey information from a large number of countries, including those considered here. A fourth task is to look for other measures of work preferences in the ISSP dataset to see what they can contribute. The chapter ends with a discussion of the results and how they can be interpreted.

PREVIOUS RESEARCH AND THEORETICAL PERSPECTIVES

Basing themselves on data from ISSP 1997, Carl Hult and Stefan Svallfors (2002) have demonstrated that employment commitment—referring to people's non-financial motivation to have paid work—was stronger in particularly Norway but also in Sweden than in New Zealand, the US and Britain. These results spring from an analysis with controls for sex, age, social class, education and working time. Parenthetically it can be mentioned that West Germany was also included and it came right after Sweden in the ranking on employment commitment. The most interesting for us is the comparison between the two Scandinavian and the three Anglo-Saxon countries. A main conclusion in the study is 'that fears of a comparatively generous welfare state, such as in the Scandinavian countries, undermining the work ethic are exaggerated' (Hult and Svallfors 2002: 326).

Similar results have been presented by Ingrid Esser (2005) in another cross-national comparison on employment commitment, defined in the same way as in the study by Hult and Svallfors and also based on data from ISSP 1997. Esser deals with twelve countries, including four Anglo-Saxon—Britain, Canada, New Zealand and the US—and three Scandinavian—Denmark, Norway and Sweden. Separate analyses are run for working men and working women with controls for a large number of individual-level characteristics (Esser 2005: 75–77). Among men all the Scandinavian countries got significantly higher scores on employment commitment than did Britain and Canada, whereas the advantage over New Zealand and the US could not be verified statistically. With the same measure applied to women, Denmark, Norway and Sweden clearly outdistanced Britain, Canada and the US, but their lead over New Zealand remained uncertain.

In a later publication Esser (2009) has come back to these issues by analyzing data from ISSP 2005, in other words the same data as used here. Her comparison entails non-financial employment commitment, measured in the same way as in the previous study. Amid the thirteen nations included we find the six Anglo-Saxon countries to be treated in this chapter—Australia, Britain, Canada, Ireland, New Zealand and the US—and the same three Scandinavian countries as before—Denmark, Norway and Sweden. The results are very much in line with what we have already seen. Among both men and women, employment commitment tends to be strongest in Scandinavia. Esser also uses a measure of welfare regime generosity, according to which Norway, Sweden and Denmark all score higher than each of the Anglo-Saxon countries. Among both men and women, this measure turns out to be positively correlated with employment commitment. In a separate analysis with only four nations (including Norway, Britain and the US), data from 1989, 1997 and 2005 are compared to see whether there have been changes across time. There are no signs that employment commitment has been weakened in the country with the most generous welfare state, that is, Norway. It is rather the other way around, while the data for Britain and the US do not reveal much change. On the basis of this whole study it is therefore concluded that 'work morale cannot be described as being undermined by generous welfare states today' (Esser 2009: 98).

The results briefly presented above seem to be robust. At the same time, however, we know that people in Anglo-Saxon countries perform a great deal of labour. Employment rates are generally rather high and the same can be said about annual hours worked per employed person. In a comparison some years ago of Western labour markets, I examined cross-national differences with respect to work mobilization (for the definition see below) (Furåker 2003: 249–250). The patterns are not entirely consistent, but in 2000 all five Anglo-Saxon countries in the comparison—the US, New Zealand, Australia, Canada and the UK—scored higher than each of the four Nordic countries included—Denmark, Finland, Norway and Sweden.

Non-financial employment commitment is a crucial concept in this chapter. As pointed out in Chapter 2, this volume, it refers to how people look at having a job irrespective of the pecuniary remunerations involved (Gallie et al. 1998: 188). To be committed in this sense means to be willing to work, although one does not have to for the sake of money. The opposite is instrumentalism, that is, the attitude implying that the motive for working lies exclusively in the income generated by a job. Notably, measures of non-financial employment commitment have often been made use of in assessing whether unemployed individuals are willing to work or not (Gallie and Alm 2000; Gallie et al. 1998: ch. 7; Gallie and Vogler 1994; Hammer and Russell 2004; Nordenmark 1999). In the present analysis, however, this is not an issue to be dealt with.

As 'non-financial employment commitment' is a somewhat clumsy concept, it is frequently replaced by the shorter expression 'employment commitment.' One problem with doing this is obvious; then we have no concept left for grasping the totality of relevant motives, including also financial motives. There is a need for a broad category to cover all kinds of drives that make people engage in paid work. It appears as self-evident that the concept of employment commitment should be reserved for that purpose. This notion would include both financial and non-financial aspects.

Another point is that we can benefit from making a distinction between willingness to work at all and preferences with respect to how much work to perform. It seems reasonable to say that this distinction has its 'objective' equivalents in employment rates and hours worked, respectively. Non-financial employment commitment may be a good indicator of whether people are interested in having a paid job, but perhaps not the best indicator of the amount of work they are prepared to carry out. The empirical analysis below will tell whether this is a realistic assumption or not.

One important issue is whether financial motives for working are to be considered voluntary or involuntary. It has been emphasised that non-financial employment commitment entails voluntariness and consent (Gallie et al. 1998: 188). Whether this is the case is certainly not always easy to determine. Without question, millions of people throughout the world are forced to work, because, literally, they cannot survive without doing it. However, in the economically advanced societies treated here it is seldom physical survival that is at stake, but rather survival at a certain standard of living—usually far above the mere subsistence level. It is simply difficult to be a citizen in these societies without adjusting to a 'normal' life. Paying for common necessities such as food, clothes and housing requires a considerable income, which is in turn often hard to get unless one has a job. This is brought to life, for example in Barbara Ehrenreich's well-known book *Nickel and Dimed* (2002), which is a close description of low-income earners' difficulties in getting by in the US. We might say that necessity rules over voluntariness, and the coercive mechanism consists of the pressure upon people to lead a socially passable life, which requires a certain standard of living.

Nevertheless financial motives for working may not be due as much to necessity as to a desire to increase income for consumption. For individuals who have sufficient money to live on, it can still be very appealing to have a little more to spend. Nor are people who are unmistakably rich automatically free from such enticements. Sayings such as 'the more you have the more you want' and 'appetite grows with eating' might be taken to illustrate this point; individuals with plenty of money may all the same want more to expand their consumption, sometimes perhaps merely to show that they can do what they want. More than a century ago Thorstein Veblen (1953) launched the concept of conspicuous consumption that is definitely still a relevant notion. He also called attention to leisure as another way of demonstrating wealth; whether this holds today is less obvious.

A main purpose of this chapter is to throw some further light on the possible differences between Anglo-Saxon and Nordic countries. Although these societies all have capitalist market economies, their societal models are far from the same. In recent decades, social scientists have increasingly paid attention to the fact that capitalist nations are not cast in the same mould and that it is indispensable to take the existing diversity into account when dealing with work attitudes and phenomena such as employment rates and work efforts. I am concerned about whether, in these regards, there are significant differences related to the Anglo-Saxon and Nordic societal models and, if so, how they should be interpreted. The literature contains several attempts to classify welfare state regimes (Esping-Andersen 1990; Castles 1993, 2004; Gallie and Paugam 2000; Korpi and Palme 1998; Korpi 2000). In spite of some divergence regarding which and how many categories should be distinguished, most of these attempts seem to have one thing in common: the Anglo-Saxon and the Nordic countries end up in separate categories because they so clearly differ in terms of welfare institutions and welfare generosity.

At bottom there is the issue of whether welfare state arrangements affect people's incentives for working and, if so, how. Critics of the welfare state commonly claim that the provision of various kinds of benefits undermines recipients' readiness to take a paid job and to contribute a substantial work effort (e.g., Lindbeck 1995, 2003). The opposite argument is that welfare state arrangements do not have such effects or, at least, that this is not the general rule. Sometimes it is even suggested that it can be the other way around, because certain mechanisms in the welfare arrangements encourage people to put up a good work record (the so-called entitlement effect; see, e.g., Hamermesh 1979, 1980). Such a record is advantageous when individuals want to get as much as possible out of the systems of unemployment insurance, sickness insurance, pensions, etc. The rules are simply to a large extent designed to make benefits dependent on previous employment and work carried out.

The two 'families of nations' also seem to differ in another respect, namely, regarding the quality of jobs. When jobs are relatively attractive or decent, we can expect people to be more motivated to be employed and perhaps also to work a great deal. According to some studies, in comparison with their Anglo-Saxon colleagues, job incumbents in the Nordic countries generally have stronger employment protection, more task discretion or autonomy and better opportunities for training and development (e.g., Dobbin and Boychuk 1999; Gallie 2007a). These differences are often tied to a classification of 'production regimes' or of 'employment regimes' and, again, the Anglo-Saxon and Nordic countries fall into separate categories. In the production regime approach the Anglo-Saxon cluster belongs to the 'liberal market economies' (LMEs) and the Nordic to the 'coordinated market economies' (CMEs); in LMEs firm activities primarily depend on market relationships and in CMEs they are much more dependent on non-market actors (Hall and Soskice 2001a). Another distinction is that between 'market employment regime' and 'inclusive employment regime' (Gallie 2007b: 16–19). The Anglo-Saxon countries come under the first category and the Nordic under the second. In this case the decisive factor is the role ascribed to markets and organized labour, respectively. If, as suggested in the literature, CMEs or the inclusive employment regimes generally provide better jobs, it is likely that, all other things being equal, people in these countries are more inclined for having paid work.

Summing up this rhapsodic account of differences in terms of societal models, we should keep in mind that it remains highly contested how generous welfare state arrangements should be evaluated. As emphasised, we also need to take the quality of jobs into consideration. The available evidence suggests that countries with generous systems frequently offer relatively attractive jobs. There are hence several aspects to reflect on when examining whether different sets of welfare institutions have detrimental effects on employment. This chapter does not have the ambition to answer all these much debated questions, but it can, I hope, contribute some pieces of relevant knowledge.

DATA AND MEASURES

As mentioned, six Anglo-Saxon and four Nordic countries are included in the empirical analysis. The Anglo-Saxon family of nations is represented by Australia, Britain, Canada, Ireland, New Zealand and the US. In the Nordic case, Denmark, Finland, Norway and Sweden are included. Several types of empirical data are being employed. A first section presents 'objective' information, derived from labour force statistics and compiled by the OECD. It includes employment rates, average annual hours worked and work mobilization rates, given as averages for the period 2003–2007. The period is chosen because the attitudinal data to be examined later were collected in 2005; with this solution two years before and two years after 2005 are also covered, thus evening out some of the fluctuations caused by business cycles.

Employment rates are simply the percentage of a given population in employment. They are here supplied for persons aged 15–64 and for men and women separately. Thereafter I bring up figures (in hours) on annual averages of employed persons' time spent in a paid job. We are then ready to calculate work mobilization rates, offering an overall measure of how much of a population's work potential is actually being utilized. Assuming that each individual could contribute 40 hours per week during 50 weeks, a full annual effort equals 2,000 hours. These two assumptions are of course somewhat arbitrary; instead we might presuppose that people are able to work 45 hours per week (implying overtime) and 52 weeks (no vacation). It is, however, not so important exactly which number we choose to represent a full annual work effort, as this number is simply used as a dividend for all the countries in the calculation of work mobilization rates. The idea is to take into account both the degree to which the population is gainfully employed and how much work (in hours) each employed individual does. Accordingly the measure is calculated in the following way. For each country, the employment rate, expressed as a number between 1 and 0, is multiplied by the average number of annual hours worked and the result is divided by 2000.

The second type of information is survey data, collected through the ISSP in 2005, on people's attitudes and preferences regarding paid work. I have chosen to limit the analysis to employed respondents, aged 15–64 years. There are several reasons for this limitation. The number of unemployed is rather small in most of the country samples and it would be difficult to draw any firm conclusions about them. Furthermore, some of the questions are not that relevant for individuals who are older and/or outside the labour force. At any rate, responses would be difficult to interpret. The selected respondents amount to a total of 8,306 and the numbers vary from just over 500 in Britain to 1,185 in Australia.

As for the subjective information, there is first an indicator of what is usually referred to as non-financial employment commitment. It is measured by a statement that respondents have been requested to agree or disagree with: 'I would enjoy having a paid job even if I did not need the money.' People were asked whether they (a) strongly agree, (b) agree, (c) neither agree nor disagree, (d) disagree, or (e) strongly disagree with this statement. It is common to build an index with the help of this item and another statement that is also available in the ISSP data set: 'A job is a just way of earning money—no more' (see Berglund's Chapter 4, this volume; Hult and Svallfors 2002; Esser 2005, 2009). However, like Gallie et al. (1998: 188–190) I just use a single item.

The ISSP dataset also contains information on a number of other issues of interest. One item deals with people's preferences regarding weekly working hours. Respondents could choose between four options: (a) full-time (defined as at least 30 hours); (b) 10–29 hours; (c) fewer than 10 hours; and (d) no paid job at all. Yet another question is about whether people would like to spend more or less time in paid work than they did at the time of the survey. Actually, this was part of a battery of questions, also asking about time for household work, family, friends and leisure activities. Five response alternatives were given: (a) much more; (b) a bit more; (c) the same as now; (d) a bit less; and (e) much less. Finally, there is a question asking whether people—compared to their present situation—would want to work (a) longer hours and earn more money; (b) work the same number of hours and earn the same; or (c) work fewer hours and earn less. It thus explicitly focuses on the financial consequences of a change in the amount of work to be carried out.

EMPLOYMENT RATES, HOURS WORKED
AND WORK MOBILIZATION RATES

This first empirical section provides an account of employment, hours worked and work mobilization in the ten selected countries (Table 5.1). The purpose is to present information to which the subjective data can be related. In the first three columns of figures I present employment rates, referring to all persons, and males and females, aged 15–64 years. We discover that employment rates are generally somewhat higher in the Nordic countries, in spite of Finland being far below the other three which make up the top trio in the total ranking. However, the Anglo-Saxon cluster also has an outlier, Ireland, scoring even lower than Finland.

The figures for men vary between 76 and 81 percent in nine of the ten countries; Finland is the obvious deviant with 71 percent. There is some gap between the Anglo-Saxon and the Nordic countries, but it disappears if Finland be excluded. On the female side we find more variation. Three Nordic countries–Norway, Sweden and Denmark—have the top scores with more than 72 percent. Most of the other countries hover around 64–69

Table 5.1 Employment Rates, Annual Hours Worked per Person in Employment and Work Mobilization Rates. Anglo-Saxon and Nordic Countries, Averages 2003–2007

	Employment rates	*Male employment rates*	*Female employment rates*	*Annual hours worked per employed*	*Work mobilization rates*
Countries					
Australia	71.4	78.3	64.4	1725	61.5
Canada	72.7	76.7	68.7	1740	63.3
Ireland	67.1	76.3	57.8	1653	55.5
New Zealand	74.1	81.1	67.3	1800	66.7
UK	72.5	78.7	66.6	1674	60.7
US	71.5	77.5	65.7	1801	64.4
Denmark	76.3	80.3	72.2	1578	60.2
Finland	68.9	71.0	66.7	1715	59.0
Norway	75.8	78.7	72.7	1414	53.6
Sweden	74.4	76.3	72.3	1601	59.6
Families of nations					
Anglo-Saxon[a]	71.6	78.1	65.1	1732	62.0
Nordic[a]	73.9	76.6	71.0	1577	58.1

[a] Means unweighted with respect to size of countries.
Sources: OECD (various years).

percent and in this case Ireland is the straggler with less than 58 percent. The average for the Nordic countries is higher than for the Anglo-Saxon countries and it does not help much to exclude Ireland.

As for the figures on annual hours worked, it should be emphasised that countries with high female employment rates usually have a large proportion of part-time work. The figures are also a function of other factors such as how full-time jobs are defined, the quantity of absence from work and the existence of overtime. As we can see, the Anglo-Saxon countries score much higher than the Nordic, and two of the former nations—the US and New Zealand—even reach the 1,800-hour limit. With high female employment rates and a large proportion of women in part-time jobs, Norway shows by far the lowest number of hours worked per person in employment. Denmark and Sweden also have low figures on this criterion.

Finally we arrive at the work mobilization rates that represent the most comprehensive measure in the table. With the exception of Ireland, all the Anglo-Saxon countries score higher than each of the countries in the Nordic cluster, but Denmark is quite close to the UK. New Zealand has the highest score, followed by the US, Canada and Australia. Norway has the lowest mean of all, even below that of Ireland. The outcome in the Irish case is very much an effect of the low female employment rate.

To summarize, the general pattern is that employment rates are slightly higher in the Nordic than in the Anglo-Saxon area. In terms of the average number of hours worked per person and work mobilization it is the other way around. The main explanation as to why the Nordic countries score higher on total employment rates is that women have jobs to a larger extent. At the same time, the average number of annual hours worked is negatively affected because women more often than men work part-time. If we count the number of hours worked, several other factors need to be taken into account as well: the definition of full-time and, accordingly, of part-time, the prevalence of overtime, etc. All in all, with respect to work mobilization rates the Anglo-Saxon countries outdo the Nordic. In the next step we will turn to data on attitudes and the patterns uncovered here will then serve as a background.

NON-FINANCIAL EMPLOYMENT COMMITMENT

Let us start by looking at some of the ISSP figures regarding non-financial employment commitment measured as the proportion agreeing that they would enjoy having a paid job even if they did not need the money. Finland is not included in this analysis, simply because its figures are so much lower than any of the other countries that one must suspect some problem with the translation of the questionnaire. A Finnish-speaking colleague has pointed out that the word 'enjoy' has been given a translation that makes it difficult for Finns to agree with the statement. Therefore, on this item, I just deal with the nine remaining countries.

Respondents commonly agree that they would like to have a paid job even if they did not need the money. A total of more than 70 percent of all respondents in the sample used (Finland excluded) have responded in that way. The difference between the two families of nations is negligible, but for each cluster there is some significant internal variation. Thus the Anglo-Saxon and Nordic countries mingle with one another in the integrated ranking. Norway shows the highest percentage, Denmark is second and New Zealand and Ireland third and fourth, respectively. At the other end, Britain has the lowest figure. Men throughout score lower than females.

To look more closely at the country differences logistic regressions have been run with controls for sex, age, composition of household, socioeconomic category (based on a simple version of the so-called EGP-scheme; see, e.g., Erikson and Goldthorpe 1993: ch. 2) and working time (self-reported). After this operation the country differences mentioned above remain, although with some modifications. I do not intend to go into the details of all the results regarding the control variables, but just mention that non-financial employment commitment is particularly salient among female and among younger respondents. Compared to working class members this also holds for those who belong to the 'service' and 'intermediate' classes.

In Figure 5.1 the data on non-financial employment commitment are run against one of our objective measures: employment rates. The scatter plot shows a positive correlation between the two variables (Pearson's R

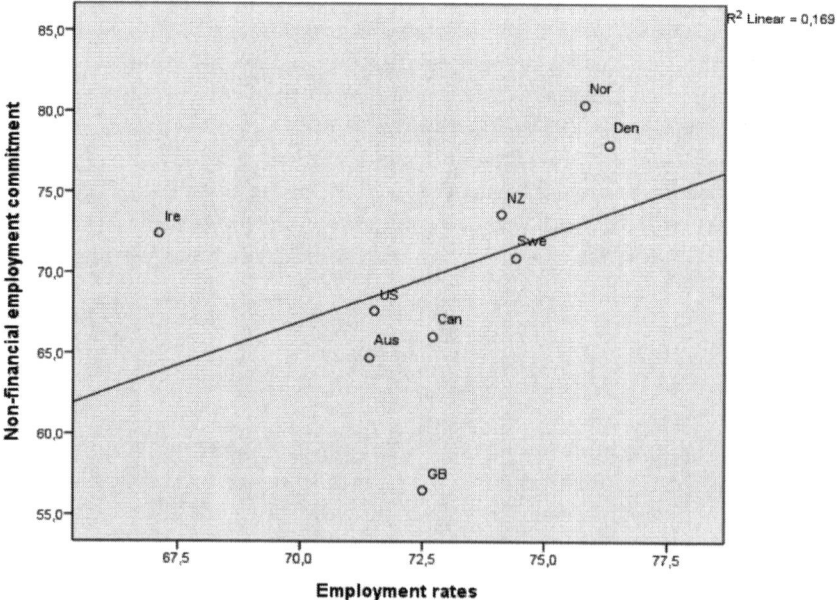

Figure 5.1   Non-financial employment commitment and employment rates. Nine countries, around 2005.

= 0.41). Denmark, Norway and Sweden are all—together with New Zealand—located in the upper, right-hand corner of the diagram. Two countries appear as outliers: Ireland with a very low score on employment rate and Britain (GB) with a very high score on non-financial employment commitment. As there are huge differences between men and women, above all with respect to employment rates, I have run separate scatter plots for the two sexes (not shown). It turns out that the correlation between the two variables is clearly stronger among women than among men.

Although non-financial employment commitment cannot be taken to be the cause behind employment rates, there is a positive association between the two, in spite of some considerable cross-national variation. If non-financial employment commitment is a common attitude in a society, we should not have to worry about the supply of labour. The three Nordic countries Denmark, Norway and Sweden score relatively high on both non-financial employment commitment and employment rates. This is partly due to the fact that Nordic women have high figures on both indicators. I can therefore just concur with what other researchers have already said: A generous welfare state and high levels of employment can obviously coexist.

A quite different picture emerges when we focus on work mobilization rates. Figure 5.2 shows a scatter plot with non-financial employment commitment on the Y-axis and work mobilization rates on the X-axis. As can be observed, there is some correlation between the two. It is roughly as strong as in the previous

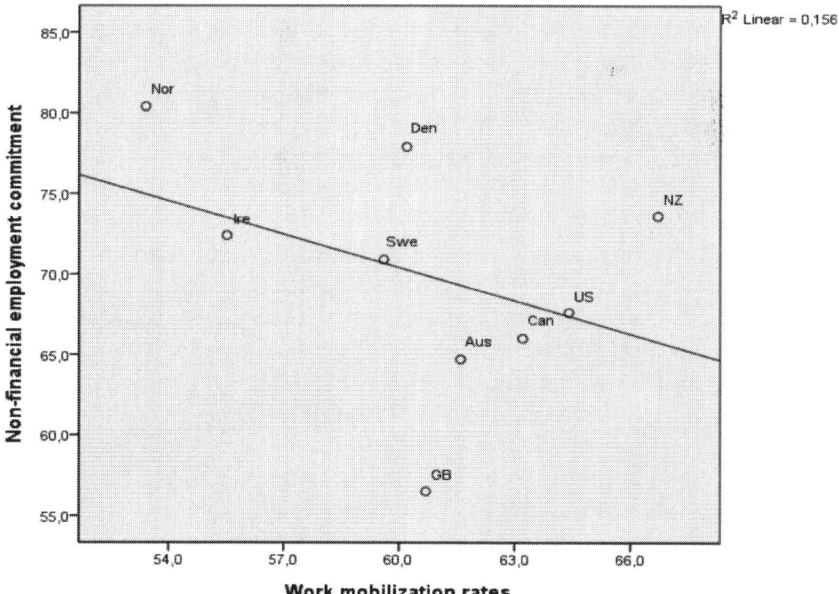

Figure 5.2 Non-financial employment commitment and work mobilization rates. Nine countries, around 2005.

scatter plot, but by contrast it is now negative (Pearson's R =—0.40). The Nordic countries have rather high scores on non-financial employment commitment, but their work mobilization rates do not correspond to this outcome. Unfortunately we cannot make a division between males and females in this regard, because the OECD does not report average annual working hours by sex.

Non-financial employment commitment is thus positively related to employment rates and negatively related to work mobilization rates. Moreover, the Nordic countries mostly fall behind concerning work mobilization. We must ask how these outcomes are to be interpreted. Evidently a generous welfare state does not have to lead to, or be an obstacle to, either non-financial employment commitment or high employment rates, but substituting the latter aspect for amount of work carried out we cannot draw the corresponding conclusion.

OTHER MEASURES

The question is now whether the ISSP dataset includes other attitudinal information that can be of interest in relation to work mobilization rates. Table 5.2 gives us a simple overview of three different measures that might be worth looking at. Data are shown for each of the countries involved in the comparison and for the two families of nations. All three variables focus on how much people want to work and the table therefore also includes separate rows for full-time and part-time workers.

The first item shows the proportion who has expressed a preference for working full-time. In the questionnaire full-time is defined as 30 hours or more. Because there is a great deal of cross-national variation as regards this definition, instructions have been adjusted to the characteristics of each country. This may create certain problems for the interpretation of the data. In other words, it is a rather rough measure, but it may nevertheless tell us something about work preferences.

In all ten countries, except Sweden, a majority of the respondents have chosen to answer 'full-time.' The Swedish figure is surprisingly low and makes us again be doubtful about the quality of the data. However, also other countries such as Britain and Finland score rather low. The top figure is found for the US with Ireland as second and, notably, Norway as third in the ranking. There is thus considerable variation within each of the families of nations. If we rely on unweighted means, we see that about 62 percent in the Anglo-Saxon countries have indicated a preference for full-time work compared to 56 percent in the Nordic cluster.

Unsurprisingly, figures are much higher among full-time workers than among part-timers. For the former category the difference between the two families of nations is relatively large. Still the general pattern is rather similar to what we have seen for all respondents. With respect to part-time workers, there is some difference between the two families of nations, but it is not that big.

Table 5.2   Responses on Three Work-related Attitude Measures. Anglo-Saxon and
Nordic Countries, 2005

	% who prefer to work full-time	% who would like to spend more time in a paid job	% who prefer to work longer and earn more
Countries			
Australia	56.5	13.6	23.0
Britain	53.0	8.6	21.7
Canada	60.0	11.6	22.7
Ireland	67.8	14.0	22.2
New Zealand	59.5	12.7	23.9
US	75.8	20.0	32.3
Denmark	59.5	6.7	8.4
Finland	54.1	8.0	14.4
Norway	66.3	10.3	12.7
Sweden	43.4	5.5	17.2
Families of nations			
Anglo-Saxon[a]	62.1	13.4	24.3
Nordic[a]	55.8	7.6	13.2
Full-time			
Anglo-Saxon[a]	72.0	10.0	24.0
Nordic[a]	60.1	5.0	11.2
Part-time			
Anglo-Saxon[a]	29.4	29.1	25.7
Nordic[a]	25.0	26.7	27.3

[a] Means unweighted with respect to size of countries and samples.
Source: ISSP 2005.

Table 5.2 also shows the proportions who have answered that they want
to spend much or a bit more time in a paid job. These proportions are
commonly rather or very low, roughly varying between 5–7 percent (Sweden and Denmark) and 20 percent (the US). On average the Anglo-Saxon
countries score almost twice as high as the Nordic: 13.4 percent compared
to 7.6. We come across one significant exception from this general pattern;
the figure for Norway is higher than that for Britain.

Moreover, there are some noteworthy differences between full-time and
part-time workers. Part-time workers much more often want to increase
their time in a paid job. This holds for both families of nations. In the
Anglo-Saxon countries, about 29 percent among part-time workers have
answered that they want to work more than presently, compared to 10

percent among full-time workers. The corresponding figures for the Nordic cluster are just below 27 percent compared to 5 percent. These results also imply that there is one clear family-of-nation difference. Among full-time workers, the Anglo-Saxon countries score twice as high as the Nordic countries. In regard to those who are in part-time employment, the average figure for the Anglo-Saxon cluster is also higher but not that much.

We cannot know whether people take an increased income for granted when answering that they want to spend more time in a paid job, although it seems reasonable to make such an assumption. The third item in Table 5.2, however, explicitly includes the pecuniary consequences of changes in working time. It asks whether people want to work longer hours and earn more money, work the same number of hours and earn the same or work fewer hours and earn less. The outcomes on this variable and the previous cannot be compared directly because the response options are very different. Nevertheless it is worth observing the generally higher proportions reporting that they would prefer to work and earn more.

Most interesting, the proportion answering that they prefer to work longer hours and earn more money is considerably higher in the Anglo-Saxon than in the Nordic countries: 24.3 percent against 13.2, that is, once again the Nordic figure is about half of the Anglo-Saxon. The US shows the clearly highest proportion, whereas Denmark has by far the lowest. With the exception of the US, the Anglo-Saxon countries stay close to 22–24 percent on this measure. Exempting Denmark, the Nordic figures vary between about 13 and 17 percent.

Continuing to the differences related to working time we can make some simple observations. The proportions saying that they want to work longer hours and earn more money are roughly the same among three categories: full-time and part-time workers in the Anglo-Saxon countries and part-time workers in the Nordic countries. These three categories have figures revolving around one fourth. In contrast, not much more than one tenth of the Nordic full-time workers have given the same answer.

In spite of some significant inconsistencies it might seem that the response patterns on all three variables in Table 5.2 are in line with the higher work mobilization rates in the Anglo-Saxon countries. A closer look at the data reveals that this assumption does not hold all the way. As regards the first of the three variables, the proportion preferring full-time work, there is hardly any correlation at all with work mobilization rates (and it is in fact slightly negative). The next variable, indicating the proportion of respondents who have expressed a wish to spend much or a bit more time in a paid job, seems to be more interesting for our analysis. It is positively associated with the work mobilization measure (Pearson's R = 0.33). However, the third variable, on whether respondents wish to work and earn more, is more strongly correlated (Pearson's R = 0.57). The scatter plot in Figure 5.3 presents further details of this interrelationship.

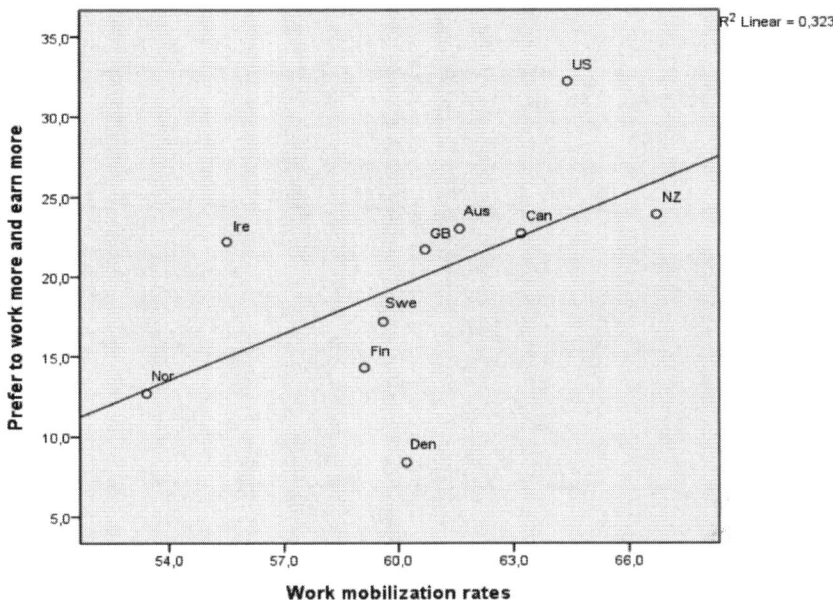

Figure 5.3   Relationship between preferences for working more and earning more and work mobilization rates. Anglo-Saxon and Nordic countries, around 2005.

The four Nordic countries are found in the lower middle or left-hand part of the figure, still without being very close to one another. With the exception of Ireland, the Anglo-Saxon nations are located in the upper right-hand quarter of the diagram, but the US is rather remote from the fit line. In other words, in countries with high work mobilization rates people are more likely to answer that they want to work more in order to earn more. The correlation is rather strong and it is obvious that this third variable is a better indicator of work mobilization than the others dealt with here. The reason is probably that it explicitly includes financial motives.

Because of the outcome on the work-more-earn-more variable, I want to control for the impact of various other factors by using multinomial logistic regression. Again, sex, age, composition of household, socioeconomic status and self-reported working time are controlled for. The dependent variable includes three response options with a natural centre value, which makes multinomial logistic regression suitable. We can thus distinguish between those who want to work more and earn more, those who want to work the same and earn the same as today, and those who want to work less and earn less.

Table 5.3 summarizes the results of the multinomial regression. In order to avoid too many figures the outcomes on the control variables are not shown, but some of the most important can be mentioned. Males tend to be more willing than females to increase their work effort and to earn more

Table 5.3   Factors Affecting Wish to Work More and Earn More and to Work
Less and Earn Less. Controlled for Sex, Age, Type of Household,
Socioeconomic Category and Working Time. Multinomial Logistic
Regression. Odds Ratios

	Would prefer to work longer hours and earn more money		Would prefer to work fewer hours and earn less money	
	Model 1	Model 2	Model 1	Model 2
Countries				
Australia	1.70***		0.82	
Britain	1.41*		0.57**	
Canada	1.79***		0.88	
Ireland	1.31		0.72	
New Zealand	1.76***		0.61**	
US	2.58***		0.45***	
Denmark	0.59**		0.97	
Finland (ref.)	1		1	
Norway	0.93		0.66*	
Sweden	1.24		0.97	
Families of nations				
Anglo-Saxon		2.02***		0.74***
Nordic (ref.)		1		1
Nagelkerke R²	0.12	0.10	0.12	0.10
Intercept	-1.77 ***	-1.79***	-1.74***	-1.86***
n		7,139		

Levels of significance: * = p<0.05; ** = p< 0.01; *** = p< 0.001.
Source: ISSP 2005.

and, likewise, less willing to decrease it and hence earn less. As for age, we find that, compared to the reference category (45–54 years of age), the two younger categories are more prone to increase their income by working more and less prone to do the opposite. The effect is particularly strong among the youngest. In addition, the oldest are less apt to express a desire for working and earning more. We might also expect them to be more willing to reduce their work effort and income, but this cannot be confirmed statistically. Household type shows rather few clear results and they are somewhat difficult to interpret; for that reason I refrain from commenting on them here and instead jump to socioeconomic status. Relative to working class respondents, members of the service class tend to turn down more work and higher income and to express a preference for the reverse.

The intermediate class is probably somewhere in between, but the outcome is not that clear. Finally, compared to full-time workers, part-timers to a higher degree choose more work and money and to a lower degree less work and money.

The figures shown in Table 5.3 demonstrate some clear-cut results with respect to the country variable. Except for Ireland all the Anglo-Saxon countries have significantly higher odds than Finland (the reference category) regarding willingness to work more and earn more (Model 1) and the Irish coefficient is both high and close to being statistically confirmed. Actually Sweden also scores rather high, but in this case the coefficient is more remote from statistical verification. In contrast, compared to the reference category Denmark turns out to have a significantly lower score. When the Anglo-Saxon countries are lumped together and the same is done with the Nordic countries (Model 2), we find a distinct difference between the two clusters. It is definitely more common in the Anglo-Saxon world to express a preference for working and earning more.

The results in the right-hand part of Table 5.3, showing the outcome on willingness to work less and earn less, are on the whole rather much in line with the above. Respondents in the US, Britain and New Zealand are less apt to express such a preference, but the same also goes for respondents in Norway, whereas none of the other countries can be confirmed to deviate from the reference category. Taken together the Anglo-Saxon nations score clearly lower than the Nordic. It is less common among respondents in the former to prefer shorter working hours when this means less income.

CONCLUDING DISCUSSION

What conclusions can be drawn from the analysis above? Except for Finland, the Nordic family of nations shows high levels of non-financial employment commitment. The degree of such commitment is higher in Denmark, Norway and Sweden, with their generous welfare state arrangements, than in most of the six Anglo-Saxon countries, with their less open-handed welfare systems. This outcome is in line with previous studies (Esser 2005, 2009; Hult and Svallfors 2002). Moreover, the three Nordic countries have the highest female employment rates in the comparison and their male employment rates are also rather high. Thus, although generous welfare state systems may create various kinds of problems, we have no evidence that they are associated with low employment rates or a low degree of non-financial employment commitment. We can add that previous research has shown the quality of jobs to be generally higher in the Nordic than in the Anglo-Saxon countries. It is possible that this factor contributes to the relatively widespread non-financial employment commitment in the Nordic cluster.

The association between non-financial employment commitment and employment rates is positive and rather strong. There is, however, a clear difference between men and women and the association is stronger among the latter. In a society with high employment rates we can expect that most individuals of working-age prefer to have a job and this may be the case even if the income is not that decisive. High levels of employment are no doubt mainly due to the demand for labour, and when this demand is great people's wishes for a job have good prospects of being fulfilled—which is an important factor for the maintenance of such wishes. Actual circumstances thus contribute to shaping their attitudes. At the same time, attitudes may have an impact of their own. For example, it should be easier to fill vacancies in the labour market if people have a positive attitude toward getting a job.

The above reasoning may hold for both men and women, but interestingly non-financial employment rates tend to be higher among women. How can we account for that? It seems that we need to consider the role of the long-standing increase in female labour market participation. This development means that an older role, in which paid work has low priority, is more or less substituted for a new role, in which paid work is a clear preference. The process is uneven and has not kept the same pace in all the countries examined here, but its long-term direction is the same everywhere. Once women realize that change is taking place they may become particularly eager to have paid work—perhaps even before it has become a self-evident option. Jobs with large proportions of women are above all found in the service sector and the size of the public sector is therefore essential. Consequently it is not surprising that female non-financial employment commitment is high in Denmark, Norway and Sweden.

However, we should not confuse employment rates with the amount of work that people carry out. People may have a job but still work relatively little; they can have part-time contracts or high levels of absence because of sickness, parental leave or other circumstances. In terms of work mobilization rates, the Anglo-Saxon countries as a rule surpass the Nordic. For some forms of non-attendance at the workplace, welfare state provisions may be highly important as much as they allow people to stay away from their job. Attractive jobs—which tend to be relatively frequent in the inclusive employment regimes of the Nordic cluster—may on the other hand increase people's interest in spending many hours in paid employment.

As non-financial employment commitment is only weakly related to work mobilization rates, I directed my attention to other subjective items in the ISSP dataset. The most interesting item is then a question aimed at capturing people's willingness to increase or decrease their work effort and accordingly their income. This turned out to have the strongest correlation with work mobilization rates. The proportion reacting to the item in the affirmative is not that big and, as is almost always the case, the data analysis delivers somewhat inconsistent results. Largely, however, compared to respondents in the Nordic quartet, respondents in the Anglo-Saxon countries more often prefer to work and earn more. This outcome thus goes hand in hand with the higher work mobilization rates in the latter countries.

There are two possible interpretations of people's answer that they want to work longer hours and increase their income. Both are fully compatible with each other. One is that many are more or less forced to work a great deal to make a normal living. It is costly to pay for food, clothes, housing, transportation, etc., and it is difficult to avoid these costs. The other interpretation is that individuals wish to improve their standard of living. Realizing that this can be done by an increased work effort, they may develop a positive attitude to supplying more of their time for working. In societies where consumption is becoming increasingly important there are many tempting ways of using extra money. Some may just want to work more so that they can buy more goods and services. Such an attitude is perhaps sometimes a corollary of necessity, but we should not exclude that it is based on voluntariness; it can then be fully in line with the idea of free will and consent (cf. Gallie et al 1998: 188).

The above reasoning may help us to understand why respondents in the Anglo-Saxon countries tend to be more willing to work and earn more. It seems likely that people in the market-oriented Anglo-Saxon world are more heavily dependent on a paid job. Consequently their consumption to a larger extent relies on what is available in the market. Large segments of the population with low income need to work a great deal to survive at some minimum standard of living. As mentioned before, there are vivid stories describing how low-income earners sometimes must even have two jobs to keep their nose above water (Ehrenreich 2002). In our dataset we find that the proportion willing to spend longer hours at a paid job to get more money is higher among working class respondents than among the other socioeconomic categories.

Asking whether or to what extent people are motivated to engage in paid work, we should not merely focus on the notion of non-financial employment commitment but rather on a wider concept, which can include financial factors as well. What is suitable is of course always a matter of what we are looking for, but a broader approach to people's willingness to work requires that financial motives are taken into account. This is not to say that the work-more-earn-more question is the best possible for that purpose. There is no doubt a need to develop other questions—or batteries of questions—to remedy the relative neglect of a financial dimension in many social science accounts.

6 Work Attitudes in Low-Status Occupations
More than Instrumentalism

Ylva Ulfsdotter Eriksson

Some people are employed in intriguing and fascinating occupations with challenging daily tasks and ongoing opportunities to progress in their professions, which allows for self-actualization at work. Others have less stimulating jobs that are more standardized, repetitive, and afford little opportunity for either professional or personal growth in the work setting. These images roughly correspond to more qualified white-collar occupations, on the one hand, and low-status white-collar and monotonous blue-collar work, on the other hand (Morgan, Alwin and Griffin 1979). In addition to possibly vague images of what different occupations actually involve in terms of tasks and assignments, occupations also involve actual persons practising them. And based on the occupations people hold, others ascribe various characteristics to them, perhaps including stereotypes, that can entail personal traits, lifestyles, attitudes and so forth (Rothman 2002; Gesser 1977). These pictures have an empirical bearing and are not just reflections of lively imaginations (Bourdieu 1989). But it is important to acknowledge the fact that they might just be stereotyped images and a result of categorizations and classifications of individuals.

A consequence of categorical thinking is that it serves as a mechanism of reproduction. For instance, a common assumption is that employees in blue-collar jobs work only for the money, implying a weak engagement in tasks and assignments. The image of the instrumental worker involves the idea that holding a less challenging job leads to an attitude where work is seen as just a means to earn money, while self-actualization occurs outside work settings. This is described in *The Affluent Worker* by John Goldthorpe, David Lockwood, Frank Bechhofer, and Jennifer Platt (1968) alongside two further ideal types. Some studies contradict the ideal type of instrumental worker, stating that these workers in some respects are engaged (Eriksson 1998) or even altruistic (Berglund 2001). Even though different studies of the topic find contradictory empirical results and explore new theoretical explanations, the concept of the instrumental attitude held by workers in monotonous jobs is widely accepted and often used in research within the social sciences (MacKinnon 1980).

The aim of this chapter is to show how employees in low-status occupations express complex and varied attitudes to work. As we will see, employees actually convey several, sometimes contradictory, attitudes to work and their own occupations. In elaborating this, I also take a closer look at how instrumentalism is expressed and differentiated.

The ideal types of Goldthorpe and colleagues have been used as analytical tools and as a sounding-board to recognize attitudes to work and occupation. They can be helpful in describing the meaning that people attach to different situations and in revealing paradoxes and equivocations. A point of departure in this chapter is that it might be difficult to distinguish workers' attitudes toward any fixed points, and that attitudes are more blurred and less easy to tell apart. Whether or not employees reckon work as a means to an end, a role to perform or a part of their identity might not even be a result of a certain standpoint, but may instead vary according to how the employee relates to the organization or company and relationships with co-workers, assigned tasks, etc. A point of departure is that individuals are influenced by what they do and that these doings interact with experiences from past and present, and with their current settings. For these reasons it ought to be difficult to separate attitudes from roles and questions of social identity.

The different conditions people experience at their jobs and in workplace settings may cause varying degrees of job satisfaction or dissatisfaction. When required qualifications are low and people feel they have little room to act, scholars have spoken of 'passive' jobs. In these jobs the workers are assumed to be drained of creativity and, furthermore, to become inactive even in their leisure time (Karasek 1979; Karasek and Theorell 1990: 53–54; cf. also Kouvonen et al. 2005). Low-status occupations are often seen as examples of that kind of work. Such 'truths' form a rather poor image of the workers in low-status occupations and of the working classes in general. It may be that commitment to one's work in low-status occupations takes a different form than in high-status occupations, and therefore is not acknowledged or recognized (Becker 1998). For this reason it is important to listen to the voices of individuals in low-status occupations and take into account their own descriptions of their work settings and situations.

MATERIALS AND METHODS

This chapter is based on qualitative interviews in a Swedish research project funded by the Swedish Research Council.[1] The main purpose of the study is to examine how employees in low-status occupations relate to occupational prestige in their current occupations and how occupational status is perceived. Occupations with low status share the same characteristics as working-class jobs. Incumbents usually have a low level of education, few if any opportunities for a career and relatively low wages (Reiss 1961; Ulfsdotter Eriksson 2006; Svensson and Ulfsdotter Eriksson 2009).

According to Blumer (1986: ch. 4), people's attitudes to work are not something they 'have' but something they constantly create in relation to their practices and surroundings. Following this line of argument, I draw on qualitative data to grasp not just mere attitudes, but how employees in a wider sense relate to their occupation, to try to understand the complexity of how people reason about their occupation and work situation. The aim is to show that attitudes can be contradictory, spontaneous and well-considered at the same time, thus breaking the frame of ideal types and stereotyped categorizations.

We have conducted 39 interviews with a total of 78 individuals: 13 focus group interviews, 23 individual interviews, and three informant interviews. The interviewees are men and women from six different occupations and they range from 20 to nearly 65 years of age. The majority were born in Sweden, but some originate from other countries. The selected occupations are stockroom workers, waiters/waitresses, refuse collectors, caregivers for the mentally handicapped (habilitation trainers and home attendants), security guards and workers in the food industry. These occupations reflect a wide spectrum of working conditions and tasks and can be defined as having low status according to a Swedish prestige-ranking scale from 2002 (Svensson and Ulfsdotter Eriksson 2009; cf. Treiman 1977).

In the interviews we asked questions about, for example, the best and worst aspects of the occupations, attitudes toward wages and working hours, relations to co-workers and managers and treatment by others within and outside work settings. The stories and images they shared with us are not possible to combine into a single clear-cut attitude, but compose a kaleidoscope of experiences, emotions and events.

In analyzing the data, the transcripts were coded and findings that expressed attitudes were organized thematically. Two major categories that capture different aspects of approaches and attitudes were distinguished: *instrumental expressions* and *committed expressions*. Furthermore, within each of these categories I found a wide range of nuances that provide rich descriptions of how low-status occupations are experienced by the actual employees.

ATTITUDES, CLASSIFICATIONS, AND OCCUPATIONAL IDENTITY

Goldthorpe et al. (1968) constructed three ideal types of attitudes to work. They stated that workers in the industrial sector tend to hold an instrumental attitude to work, which means that these employees are primarily working for the money. The other two types of attitudes, the solidaristic and the bureaucratic attitudes, can be seen as contrasting with the instrumental one, but also as a complement to it. A solidaristic attitude is held by workers who are more engaged in their jobs and for whom work plays a larger part in life than just being a means of earning a living. Work is seen as a goal in itself and the employee can express loyalty to both work colleagues and the organization. An employee with a bureaucratic attitude is committed to the organization and pursues a career within it. These two latter types of attitudes are supposedly held by employees with more interesting, qualified or in other ways challenging work (cf. Morgan et al. 1979).

Even though the ideal types play a significant part in the analysis in this chapter, the foundation of this research lies within the sociology of occupations. Occupation is an excellent tool for conceptualizing an individual's social identity (Krause 1971: 3). Occupation, and perhaps even a job, contributes to more than just income, both on an individual and on a collective level (cf. Hall 1969: 5f.).

Occupations as Classifications

Occupations are categorized in different ways and we often use occupational labels to classify other persons and their social standing (Krause 1971: 58ff; Bourdieu 1989; Rothman 2002: 116; Crompton 2008). They are a means to classify tasks and serve as a basis for organizational structure as well as social stratification in society. With regard to social stratification, they make up one of the most essential aspects of the definition of class affiliation. People are classified by their occupational belongings in accordance with which they obtain differing incomes and opportunities in society.

Classifications of occupations provide a framework for popular representations, not only of the position but of the incumbent as well. We assume we know something about a person in a specific job that goes beyond the mere job description (Gesser 1977; Rothman 2002). For example, we do not expect a worker on an assembly line to enjoy the task, but we suppose that a child-minder likes the children and joyfully fulfills the tasks in the vocation. Perceptions of occupations may shape images and expectations in role performances and role behaviour as well as attitudes to work. Using occupations as a tool, people construct perceptions of the values of work – rewards and privileges as well as efforts and constraints.

Occupations as Roles and Social Identities

The analyses in this chapter start from the attitudes people hold toward their own occupations and thereby explore orientations to work in a wider sense. To ask for people's attitudes to their low-status occupations is partly to ask for their social identities, since they reveal how they relate to their occupations when talking about their work in general. The occupational role is a link between the individual and his or her position in the work organization and, as such, is part of his or her social identity (Krause 1971: ch. 2) Hence, for this statement to be relevant one should ask what the occupation means to the individual. According to Hall (1969: 5f.) an occupation is a social role performed by adults and an important part of life, with both financial and social consequences. A role can be defined as a set of activities performed in a given position (Katz and Kahn 1978: ch. 7). And, as stated in Hall's definition, an occupation is more than just a bunch of tasks. Or as Hughes (2008: 339) puts it, and on a more personal level, '[A] man's work is one of the more important parts of his social identity, of his self, indeed, of his fate, in the one life he has to live.' Occupations are social roles loaded with cultural meaning expressed for instance by language, uniforms, objects and symbols, as well as by acting and posing, and which can be expected to influence the incumbent (Krause 1971; Joseph and Nicholas 1972; Isacson and Silvén 2002; Svensson 2003).

When acting out a certain occupational role, the individual takes notice of expected behaviours and norms placed upon the role. These behaviours become predictable to others and form a familiar pattern. Expectations of others regulate to some extent the performance, and a role-sender is evaluated and judged by how well he or she orchestrates the role-set. The concept of role indicates that it is something from which a person more or less easily can withdraw. But as Katz and Kahn (1978) point out, there are other factors involved in role-taking which make the concept less static. In their exposition, the role performance takes on attributes of the specific individual, such as motives, values and personal traits that influence the behaviours of the sender. A social role also has an effect on the individual's personality. There is thus a two-way interaction between the individual and the environment.

An occupation can be understood as part of a social identity and as a central part of the self (Tajfel and Turner 1979; Ashforth and Mael 1989; Hughes 2008). A social identity consists of many different belongings, and is revealed on a surface level by statements such as 'I am a carpenter' or 'I am a woman.' Social identity in the modern Western world is fundamentally based on family, education, occupation, work and consumption, intersectionally constructed with age, gender, race, ethnicity and sexuality. As pointed out, the concept holds forth self-categorization and group formation as a basis for identity (Tajfel and Turner 1979; Oakes, Haslam and Turner 1994). It is a means for 'self-definition in a social context' (Oakes, Haslam and Turner 1994: 81) linking the self to the group, and pointing out values held therein. In acknowledging a group belonging, an individual is motivated to evaluate the group positively.

The importance of occupational identity has been questioned by researchers who claim that this kind of identification is more or less irrelevant in contemporary society. It is sometimes assumed that labour market flexibility is on the increase, leading to greater workplace and even occupational mobility and thus reducing the bonding between an individual and a specific position (Casey 1995; Sennett 1998; Isacson and Silvén 2002). Still, our occupations play a significant part in our lives, since we spend much of our waking hours working within the scope of a certain occupation, together with co-workers performing the same or similar tasks. The 'doings' are of importance in understanding social identities and it is somewhat difficult to distinguish between what we are and what we do.

Our 'doings' and 'beings' are intertwined – they nourish each other, as has been recognized by, for instance, Katz and Kahn (1978). Bourdieu (2000: ch. 4) has introduced the concept of *habitus* as a tool to reconcile the concepts of social identity and social role; it captures how specific individual dispositions are always connected with social structures. According to Bourdieu (2000: 156f.), we should treat habitus as having both an individual and a collective aspect. Structural similarities in people's lives, influenced by gender, class, or ethnicity, are defined as class habitus (Bourdieu 1989: 101ff). But habitus is also unique for each individual and can change with new social experiences, environments and settings. Complex and contradictory attitudes to work and occupation, and collective similarities and individual differences, can thus be interpreted as resulting from class habitus. Professional practices give rise to the same habitus as attitudes are a part of. What we are thus depends not only on what we do, but also what we think.

INSTRUMENTAL EXPRESSIONS

According to Goldthorpe et al. (1968), an instrumental attitude toward work implies that the individual relates to work basically in terms of earning income, and other values that might be associated with work are less articulated and less important. The interviewees sometimes reasoned in a way that can be interpreted as an instrumental attitude to work. This is further explored below.

Homo Economicus

An instrumental attitude is seen as an argument for being in a specific job position when it does not relate to aspects of occupational identity. Sometimes the incumbents stressed that their wages were reasonable, and even good in some cases, given the nature of the work, the qualifications required and the effort needed to fulfil the tasks. In the quotation below, a worker in the food industry maintains that the wages are fairly good considering the circumstances. He states that 'The pay is reasonable . . . I mean, I have no education.' A similar attitude is expressed by a male security guard when relating wages to the low level of dedication and involvement requested.

> I don't think that this is a lot of fun, no, I don't. As I already said, the basic wage is rather good. I think. . . . At least for the job we do. To be honest—it's pretty easy money. (*Security guard, male*)

An instrumental attitude is also expressed by a waitress who says she needs her wages to be able to provide for basic costs of living such as food and rent, and maybe some occasional luxury consumption (cf. Lamont 2000: 76). Her occupation differs from the others because of tips. Personnel in the catering trade have the benefit of making extra tax-free money. The interviewees in this occupation stress these extra earnings as an important reason for being in the business (Paules 1991: ch. 2).

> I don't work here because it's so much fun. I'm here to pay my rent, and besides I have the chance to earn some extra money to buy a nice pair of shoes. (*Waitress*)

For these workers the job is not a source of personal satisfaction or self-actualization, and they call attention to the fact that they do not enjoy their work very much. Their present job situation is a means to cover, as effortlessly as possible, the costs of living. The occupation is not something that contributes to a sense of self or impinges on questions of identity. Dull work is bearable if the investments are low with regard to the payoff in terms of providing for a reasonably good life. The occupations at hand, and the fact that they exist in the welfare regime of Sweden, enable the employees to make a rather good living from their earnings. These are not poor workers like the working poor in hamburger bars in the US described by Newman (2000), even if their wages are low in comparison with other more prestigious and privileged employees in Sweden.

Stories emphasizing aspects of economic rationality are sometimes referred to as narratives of 'homo economicus.' They can be seen as tools to delineate a line of reasoning that captures the relationship between investment and outcome. But using such labels can be dangerous since labels tend to simplify the reality and complexity of life (Blumer 1986: ch. 4; Dahrendorf 1969: 21). If instrumentalism is expected, then perhaps the individual will also display such an attitude, since expectations from others and social conventions make all of us play different roles (Katz and Kahn 1978). According to Hochschild (2003), such behaviours are consistent with special conventions, emotional scripts or 'feeling rules', which instruct us how to feel, and therefore act, in different social settings. Like roles, ideal types can give rise to expectations about how to act and feel

(Dahrendorf 1969). As a result, categorical representations of low-status occupations as monotonous, passive and lacking self-development may become self-fulfilling prophecies; the individual conveys an image of his or her work in accordance with the conventional images.

Identity Detached from Work and Occupation

Goldthorpe et al. (1968) make the assumption that the affluent worker with a rational attitude to work strives for personal fulfilment outside work and that the income acquired by working makes it possible to live a richer life. An opposing image is presented by Karasek and Theorell (1990) who point out the risk that passive jobs may make workers inactive in their spare time. Our interviews found attitudes and arguments that partly support the assumption that creativity starts after the working day is over. A stockroom worker says that his work is not a challenge at all, and that if you are interested in some kind of self-actualization this must be done in your spare time. An industrial worker states that he prefers to stand at his machine, doing an easy job that demands nothing of him, to be able to have a good time and do what he wants after working hours. None of these workers expresses any regrets about getting so little out of their work. This is even more clearly expressed by another interviewee, a refuse collector, who depicts a person living only for his or her work as a rather sad figure. He points to the danger of letting your work become the only thing of value in your life.

> Lots of people live for work. They go to work and 'Well now, let's do this and then do that' and then they come home and just sit down doing nothing and have a beer. Totally wasted after a day at work! They haven't got a clue what to do. Then they retire and 'Well, I can't go to work, so what do I do now?' Then they die. (*Refuse collector, male*)

The quotation above seems to express an attitude that self-actualization is not to be done at work but in one's spare time, which is consistent with having an instrumental approach to work. Life is viewed as being private, outside the workplace, and that is where one should engage in self-development of any kind.

The workers in this study describe how their current employment makes it possible to devote themselves to other activities since advantageous working hours and a good schedule enable parallel engagements. Working intensive shifts makes it possible for a young male security guard to take courses as a means to strive for a higher education and a better job in the future.

Some statements about self-actualization relate to leisure-time pleasures and enjoyments, primarily sporting activities. These are activities done just for fun. A female stockroom worker was interested in horses and her dog, and devoted her spare time to these commitments. A man in the same line of work stressed that it was life outside work that was significant for who he was—not his work. In his spare time he played floor ball and went to soccer games. A waitress, employed in a rather fancy restaurant, stated that the tips and the working hours enabled her to travel a lot, travel being her passion in life. The extra money coming in from tips allowed her longer vacations. This waitress worked four nights a week and had the possibility to choose when to work, which also gave her spare time for short trips.

Some aspects of self-development and self-actualization concern family. The interviewees stress that family life and social relations are of central importance to them, and that one essential aspect of their current work and occupation is that it is easy to let go after working hours. A male industrial worker claimed that 'it is good to get home and let go of everything when I know I can relax and be with my kids', in contrast to a situation 'when I must think about work all the time . . . that will keep me from being with the family.'

Without Ego Involvement

A person expressing an instrumental attitude sees neither the occupation nor the tasks as a significant part of his or her identity. A point to be made is that the workers strive to leave work behind after a working day and thereby uphold a boundary between private life and working life. This attitude is expressed by workers from different trades, by stockroom workers as well as caregivers. A female stockroom worker said that 'the moment you punch the clock you forget about work.' An attitude similar to this was expressed by a caregiver who stated:

> When I walk out through the gates, it's almost as if I can push a button and it [work] goes away, I don't think about work at all. I just let go. (*Caregiver, female*)

Not all caregivers can withdraw from work that easily, and some of them even express a longing for such an approach. They would like to be able to separate their work from their private life. They articulate an aspiration to have a clearer boundary between the spheres since they assume that a weaker distinction can have serious negative consequences. Because of colleagues' experiences they imagine that if you cannot keep the spheres separate there is an overwhelming risk for burnout syndrome.

> I have seen so many colleagues crack up under the strain and they become all . . . gone. Then you know that if you are going to make it, you must let everything go when you leave work. (*Caregiver, female*)

A demand for empathy and a sense of vocation is related to images of people employed in caregiving occupations (Skeggs 1998). This is also stressed in the interviews. It is stated that to be a suitable caregiver for the mentally handicapped, one must be able to see the needs of the client. The caregivers whom we have interviewed are exceptionally aware of the fine line between caring and getting emotionally involved. Not only do they strive for professional distance in relation to their clients—they are also aware of the necessity of it. As expressed in the quotation above, some mention the risk of burnout if one gets involved on a personal level, but the major reason for professional distance, they claim, is that it is required to do the job well. They consider themselves to be a tool, and therefore it is important to distinguish between their own emotional reactions and empathy for the client in order to maintain a sense of perspective. As one interviewee put it:

> 'Why am I going to work today? What is my role?' In this way, I don't get involved in this, because when I am here I carry out work. (*Caregiver, female*)

An interesting aspect of this awareness of role performance, as distinct from their own feelings, is that the caregivers often receive coaching from psychologists. In these sessions they discuss their relationships with clients— how to relate to them and learn to distinguish between their own emotional reactions and the requisite understanding and empathy for the client.

Burnout syndrome is assumed to be more common in occupations where one engages with other persons, as caregivers for mentally handicapped children do, and where social interactions of any kind are present but feedback is absent (Maslach 1982). In this view, there is no risk of such symptoms in occupations with little or no social interaction. For instance, a refuse collector ought to be at little risk. But even so, interviewees in this trade maintain that it is important to keep the spheres separate, since too much engagement in the work could lead to problems. Work and work roles should be separated from the private personality:

> Some men identify themselves with their work nearly one hundred percent. I guess I've learned from them to relax when I'm out of here, to relax and do something that I'm interested in. (*Refuse collector, male*)

COMMITTED EXPRESSIONS

In this section expressions of more personal commitment to work tasks and of a loyal attitude toward colleagues and clients are explored. In relation to the ideal types, the attitudes revealed in this part are a combination of the solidaristic and the bureaucratic. The definition of the bureaucratic attitude to work holds that workers' commitment to the organization is associated with the ambition to strive for a career (Goldthorpe et al. 1968: 39–40). The occupations in this study do not offer career openings and possibilities of advancement, but are rather so-called dead-end jobs. Even so, there is evidence of a willingness to carry out assignments in a responsible and con-scientious manner. Since there is little personal and financial gain in these occupations this ought to be understood as an expression of loyalty and com-mitment to the organization, and/or the work group, but also as an ambition to perform good work and to seek out some sort of self-development and satisfaction. These findings relate to the ideal type of the solidaristic attitude held by employees who consider work to be a goal in itself and a means for self-fulfilment (Goldthorpe et al. 1968: 40–42). A solidaristic attitude toward work implies that the separation between work and leisure is less distinct and that a job is seen as a central part of the worker's identity.

The following subsections illustrate how employees make use of their personalities in their current occupations and how work is not separate from life, but part of it. The theme of loyalty and commitment is divided into three sub-themes covering different aspects of a committed attitude. There is an underlying tone in the themes that leads to a more integrated approach in how the interviewed employees relate to work.

Being Oneself

> One thing that happened here at the disposal plant, actually just a min-ute ago. The supervisors weren't there / . . . / Some guys were throwing plastic among garbage to dump in the incinerator / . . . /. We're doing all this recycling and then we just dump it anyway? So what should we do? I put out some new bins. We had to solve this somehow, act, do something! / . . . / I mean, it's our business concept to recycle. (*Refuse collector, male*)

The incident described above was interpreted by the refuse collector himself as a reflection on his taking responsibility when needed, for the purpose of resolving a situation on behalf of the company and the company's business idea. Acts of responsibility have come up in other interviews as well, and are also mentioned by other refuse collectors, saying things like:

> We are the kind of people who want to take responsibility. We want to be our own bosses and to do a good job but without having the man-ager looking over our shoulders. (*Refuse collector, male*)

The employees often mentioned necessary and suitable traits for con-ducting the occupation at hand. They recognized that they used certain personal traits in carrying out work tasks in order to do a good job. A male caregiver emphasised that it is necessary to have empathy and that 'if you lack a sense of empathy you shouldn't be in this business.'

Making use of one's personality in performing an occupational role brings together the concept of roles and the idea of occupational identity as being part of a social identity. Katz and Kahn (1978) acknowledge the influence of personality on roles and vice versa. The effect of role upon personality was recognized by a waitress who thought she had learned a lot from her occupation, that she had become more socially competent, organized and structured, and better able to cope with stress. When work becomes more of an integral part of who you consider yourself to be, it is more than a just a means for meeting basic needs. The occupational role and personal life become intertwined. The quotation below, in which a security guard reflects on how his personal traits correspond with the suitable traits necessary for the occupation, provides a further example.

I think I can be myself when I'm working, as well. I suppose I can. I'm one of those people who like things to be orderly. (*Security guard, male*)

Another example is provided by caregivers who emphasise vocation. Vocation in caregiving occupations is part of a stereotyped image (Skeggs 1998) and has been discussed earlier in this chapter to illustrate the complexity of caregiving. It is expressed in a straightforward way by a female caregiver who simply states 'This is my vocation.' The urge to help sometimes also goes beyond the employment relation and the current job, and is perceived as a personal trait constantly present, as a willingness to lend a hand in all kinds of situations. In the quotation below, a caregiver explains this urge to be helpful and to express an altruistic personality and to 'make a difference' in people's lives.

I like helping people. I want to do that, but I don't have to be here, and with these people. But I like to be . . . to make a difference. (*Caregiver, female*)

Hochschild (2003) claims altruism to be a false self. Being altruistic is not a genuine expression of a personality, but a result of the commercialization of emotional work. Bolton (2005: 97f.) perceives it differently and claims that emotion management can be philanthropic, implying that it is possible to be sincere and genuine when doing emotional labour. Hochschild (2003: 195) also argues that women, to a larger extent than men, are at greater risk of developing this sort of false self because of the fact 'that they have traditionally been assigned the task of tending to the needs of others.' Holding an altruistic attitude toward work is, in any case, more common among female than male workers. Such an attitude is widespread among women in the public sector (Berglund 2001: 185). It is reasonable to assume that people working in the public sector and in caregiving occupations must deploy emotional labour and in doing so they set up expected attitudes to work (Eriksson 1998; Skeggs 1998; Hochschild 2003). Most of the employees in sectors engaging in emotional work (caregiving, service, nursing) are by tradition women, which probably can be explained with reference to habitus. But when men enter the field, they must make use of emotional capital as well. Berglund (2001: 204) argues that the greater frequency of altruistic attitudes among workers employed in the public sector might be due to work settings rather than gender (cf. also Eriksson 1998).

Engaging with Clients

Meeting clients and customers is highly valued by the workers we have interviewed, and is described as an aspect of the job that can actually provide enjoyment and self-development even if it is sometimes experienced as hard and draining work. A male security guard expressed his fascination over meeting people from all walks of life—from a nice old lady to an angry drug user. The diversity of encounters was seen as charming and was also acknowledged by other employees in other occupations. To experience satisfaction and recognition from customers and clients made interviewees feel good about themselves and proud of the tasks they performed. A waitress described her work like this:

> But it's fun, lots of music, lots of people, lots of stress, lots of joy. You're working with people who are happy all the time. Everyone's grateful. I'm rather nice, I come with good food and I come with good wine, so in this way it's a lovely atmosphere to be in. There's a lot of love, warmth, and people like you. You bring those things that make people happy . . . / . . . / There is so much love among the guests, and people are happy and come up and say 'thank you' with tears in their eyes sometimes. (*Waitress*)

This waitress portrays a friendly milieu promoting well-being for both customers and personnel. But she has also experienced the opposite: customers describing her as the nastiest person they ever met. So, even if meeting customers is usually a source of joy, there is also a downside. Nevertheless, the interviewees working in restaurants find setting the scene and using their acting talents to be a fun and satisfying part of the job (cf. Mulinari 2007). To satisfy customers and provide good service even to the most annoying customers is seen as a challenge that the waiting staff embrace with the ambition to do a good job and probably also as an act of loyalty to their employer. Acting skill is also seen as a self-developing aspect of work since it calls for self-control. But the satisfaction that comes from the everyday meetings can also result in stress and an urge to perform well all the time. A waitress describes that making use of her own personality at work is strenuous and that she needs her time off just to recover from a hard day's work.

> You expend yourself so much at work. You use your personality. / . . . / I was very mentally tired after work and it just spilled over. . . . I was really very inactive in my spare time. (*Waitress*)

In her narrative it was not a passive work situation that made her inactive in her leisure time; quite the contrary, it was devotion to work that made her passive. A food industry worker shows his commitment to the organization when he describes that he sometimes cannot sleep because his thoughts are occupied with problems and possible solutions related to work—a nightly cognitive dilemma in order to take care of a job that he wants to be well done. Dedication to work is expressed by employees in other lines of business as well. A female stockroom worker enjoys working with clothes, saying that 'I really find this kind of work interesting; picking up and folding. . . . I really think it's fun.' A male industrial worker claims that cleaning machines is more fun than operating them:

> I still find cleaning to be the most fun part. Me and my blow gun . . . you have one of those things with compressed air. I find it quite fun to go around and blow air and get things tidy. And it's the same when we clean with water. (*Industrial worker, male*)

As shown in these quotations, an employee may find a rather dull task amusing and, above all, enjoy the results of contributing. This relates to a person's deeper satisfaction and engagement with work.

Colleagues as a Source of Social Support and Joy

The relationship to a customer or client is fragile, ambiguous and somewhat of a balancing act. In this regard, relationships with colleagues are more stable, and work teams and workmates can generate trust in uncertain situations (Aurell 2001). For instance, it is a matter of course to be there for one another in difficult situations and show integrity toward the group and not involve management in group-related issues. Solidarity and loyalty within a group are expressed through norms of behaviour toward each other (Tajfel and Turner 1979). In the theory of instrumental attitudes, affiliation with co-workers is characterized as weak (MacKinnon 1980). But the employees in this study witness how colleagues and workmates contribute to making work more meaningful and enjoyable, implying that loyalty is highly valued. A dedicated attitude to work can therefore involve a reliance on colleagues.

> If something happens to a colleague, I don't care about the rules. A colleague is everything / . . . / I think of my colleague first. (*Security guard, male*)

This security guard conveys that his colleagues are of great importance. He claims that a colleague in need of help is prior to any other tasks. It may not be surprising that a security guard expresses himself in this way since a strong *esprit de corps* might be present, as is the case in the police force (cf. Björk 2008). More unexpectedly, a stockroom worker describes a similar team spirit when she states that conflicts ought to be resolved between the employees. She has seen, and disapproves of, situations where co-workers take issues concerning relationships within the team to the managers.

> I think it's so ridiculous. / . . . / I don't understand why they should know everything that happens between us when it's not about the job. I only hope that we can resolve conflicts between employees. (*Stockroom worker, female*)

Other stockroom workers describe how cordial relations in the workplace can make even the most tedious tasks enjoyable. Laughter, too, seems to give rise to a strong sense of community in the workplace by generating commitment and devotion. One waitress puts it as follows: 'A positive thing for me is that I work with great people. Those I work with are amazing persons and you get to laugh a lot at work.' Although the work in itself and the tasks performed do not entirely give rise to joy and satisfaction, friendly relations at work can change this.

> With the right co-workers you can work with dull and boring tasks / . . . / With the right workmates everything flows along. It's that simple. (*Industrial worker, male*)

In the interviews, and as illustrated in this section, work has been described as a place for fun and joy, a place where the employees like to spend time with co-workers. It has also been depicted as an activity that demands commitment and involvement—both in performing tasks and in social relations.

DISCUSSION

In this chapter, various expressions that reflect the attitudes held by employees in low-status occupations have been presented. The empirical analysis suggests that the theoretically ascribed instrumental attitude is common among employees in low-status occupations. Even so, there is also evidence of non-instrumental attitudes which seem to be more related to the occupation, and to occupational identity, than to work in general.

On Keeping Distance

Some attitudes expressed by the interviewees can undoubtedly be labeled instrumentalist. In this connection we find many shades of meaning and rather different arguments. A few workers claimed it was necessary to have a clear distinction between one's work and private life for health reasons, because strong involvement was seen as putting one at risk of burnout. Others stressed the importance of keeping oneself intact through a separation between the private self and the job. Some of the arguments relate to an understanding of identity as being only personal, therefore not including social aspects of the construction of identity such as those connected with the workplace or the occupation, which implies that these respondents lack an occupational identity.

The unequal evaluation of occupations is an effect of stratification and is related to positions, roles and individuals (Davies 1942; Treiman 1977; Ulfsdotter Eriksson 2006). In previous studies an instrumental attitude has been described as a defense mechanism for dealing with the ambivalence of being in a subordinate position. To adopt a rational attitude to one's work and occupation, and to describe one's current situation as self-chosen, can be seen as a strategy to manage subordination. It can thus be interpreted as a way of enhancing agency and counteracting the image of a subordinate position (Berglund 2001; Flisbäck 2008).

Consequently, there might be logical reasons to emphasise a withdrawal from occupational belonging because of the fact that the occupations at hand have low status and might therefore have low intrinsic worth (Ashforth and Mael 1989; Flisbäck 2008). But even if someone maintains a sharp demarcation line between his or her private and working life, withdrawing from any sense of belonging to a less desirable occupational category in order to protect one's self-value, the incumbent's value is judged by others in terms of how well the occupational role is performed: '/f/or he is judged also by the way in which he fulfils the requirements of his positions, i.e. by his roles' (Davies 1942: 312). This implies that meeting others, and performing an occupational role, contributes to an ambition to perform well and convincingly (cf. also Katz and Kahn 1978; Hochschild 2003). Hence, even if a person expresses an instrumental attitude to work, it might be hard to maintain such an attitude, since performance and outcomes are evaluated by others and the employee for these reasons also nurtures an ambition to do a good job.

Loyalty and Commitment in Demanding Jobs

Berglund (2001) presents statistical findings showing that employees in subordinate positions are less loyal than employees in superior positions. He explains this as a logical consequence of differences in working conditions: an instrumental attitude correlates with a lower degree of loyalty since working conditions are poor and the tasks are uninteresting and lack independence. He also found that persons with an instrumental attitude often exhibit less identification with the employing organization.

Among our interviewees, commitment, responsibility and accountability were frequently mentioned, thus revealing attitudes of loyalty, engagement and a willingness to take pride in one's work (cf. Eriksson 1998). If a person feels loyal to the employer, the organization or the clients, he or she probably develops and/or deploys some kind of responsibility and willingness to perform well. The empirical data show how the workers use personal traits and qualities to perform work in a satisfying way, and that they reckon this to be an important aspect of their work situation. This reveals a commitment to work that goes beyond providing for necessities as effortlessly as possible, and instead also involves one's personality. Work becomes a context where the individual can form and express a social identity and make use of personal characteristics (Hall 1969).

As was previously pointed out, it has been remarked that regardless of the performance, everyone likes to perform well. This can also be related to Davies's (1942: 312) writings on esteem and individual expressions of occupational roles and commitment: 'Esteem is thus always related to the expectations of a position, yet it is attached not to the position itself but to the success or failure in carrying out the duties and obligations.' Individuals strive not only for survival, but also for feelings of well-being, self-esteem and recognition from others (Skeggs 1998; Sennett 2003). A committed attitude to work and to performing tasks in a satisfying manner might serve as one way of building up one's own intrinsic worth.

NOTES

1. Professor Lennart G. Svensson and Marita Flisbäck, Ph.D., at the Department of Sociology, University of Gothenburg, are part of the project team. Many thanks to Marita Flisbäck for contributing to developing the idea behind this chapter and to sorting out the empirical data initially. Also, thanks to Lennart G. Svensson, Bengt Larsson, Micael Björk, Tomas Berglund, Anette Karlsson and the editors of this book for valuable comments.

7 Administrative Service Work, Occupational Identity and Work Orientations

Much-discussed Problems and Underrated Strengths

Anette Karlsson

The subject matter of this chapter is occupational identity and work orientations in two administrative service occupations: occupations which are since long female-dominated, have undergone more or less dramatic rationalization and other changes during the last few decades, and are generally not conceived to be characterized by strong work-related identities.[1] Empirically, the chapter draws on qualitative data from a study focusing on medical secretaries and post-office cashiers in Sweden.[2]

A characteristic of administrative service occupations is that they have a fuzzy or contradictory position both in the practical world of work and from the standpoint of most theoretical and ideological perspectives. Practically, they are often treated as ancillary functions more or less peripheral to the core operations of the organization; an issue that will resound throughout the chapter. Theoretically, they are notoriously difficult and sometimes outright controversial to define, whether it comes to class position, gender connotations or their place in the development of work or modern society (for different standpoints as well as broader overviews, see, e.g., Braverman 1974; Conradson 1988; Crompton and Jones 1984; Felski 2000; Kanter 1993; Karlsson 2009, 2010; Lundgren 1990; Pringle 1988). This general fuzziness is one reason why they—at least compared to 'classic' professions, crafts, industrial work and other more 'clear-cut' occupations—are seldom thought of in terms of occupational identity. But this also makes it interesting to raise questions precisely about the practisers' (work-related) identity.

One general conclusion from the larger study (Karlsson 2010) was that both occupations seem to be characterized to a high degree by occupational identities that can be described as distinct and strong *within certain limits*.

Even if the occupation is not 'all there is' in life, it typically stands out as either constituting an important and highly valued *part* of life, or as something that may not be very important in one's life taken as a whole but that one nevertheless engages in quite whole-heartedly *during the time spent at work*. That it is relevant to speak of *occupational* identity in this context is, among other things, supported by the finding that there is a distinct core of tasks, competences and ethical norms—particularly related to the multifaceted and intertwined themes of 'carefulness' and 'service'—that practisers of the respective occupations recurringly refer to (in similar although at the same time occupationally specific ways) and that plays a central role in their individual and collective identity work.

This chapter develops these findings further. Its overarching aim is to contribute to a more nuanced understanding of work-related identity and occupational solidarity in low- to middle-status occupations. To do this, the focus is on the interplay between different sources of identification (work-related and other), work orientations and collective occupational identity. Work orientation is here conceived of as a facet of individuals' work-related identity, in the sense that 'identity' implies something more deep-rooted and thorough-going than 'orientation.' The aim is also to discuss some theoretical and practical implications of 'strong but delimited' occupational identities, in terms of their both promising and problematic features, but with an emphasis on their strengths since these, as will be shown, are often underrated. The chapter is outlined as follows. The next three sections describe the theoretical perspective, some facts about the two occupations and the methods and material used. They are followed by three sections presenting results regarding (a) the importance of work in people's lives; (b) carefulness and service as central concepts (or rather competences) shaping meanings and identities in these and other administrative service occupations; and (c) the tendency to underestimate administrative service work(ers) and its consequences. Finally, the main points of the chapter will be summarized and developed.

THEORETICAL STARTING POINTS

The concept of *identity* has been widely discussed and debated since the 1980s (Bradley 1996; Jenkins 1996). Besides an interest in 'identity politics', it has been held that the conditions necessary for the existence of stable identities—individual or collective—are no longer present because of increasingly far-reaching technological, economic and cultural changes. These changes have also been associated with an 'identity crisis' in the world of work (du Gay 1996: 1ff). Not surprisingly, there are many theoretical approaches to identity, some of which contain strong assumptions of the modernity, form or content of identities. From the perspective of this chapter, a more modest and open-ended version is preferable.

Richard Jenkins (1996, 2000) offers such an approach. According to him, it is somewhat misleading to understand identities as an exclusively modern phenomenon insofar as people have always reflected on who they are. Neither does he assert their impending dissolution. He further argues that identities are always established in a social context. This establishing involves 'to classify things or persons and to associate oneself with something or someone else' (Jenkins 1996: 4; italics removed). Individual and collective identities are seen as closely related. Both are constituted through a dialectic of the *external* (classifications by others) and the *internal* (identifications by a person or group itself). Jenkins (1996: 24) also makes a distinction between *nominal* and *virtual* identity, where '/t/he former is the *name*, and the latter the *experience* of an identity, what it means to bear it.' For one thing, this clarifies that the same nominal identity—like a title or a diagnosis—can have very different meanings and implications for different persons. Another possibility is that a name can stay the same while the actual experience of bearing it changes over the years. Above all, it directs the attention to the practical consequences of the labels and descriptions people attach to themselves and others. Jenkins acknowledges the fact that identities exist in a material context, restricting the options available to a person or group at any given time. At the same time, he emphasises the potential for coexistence (harmonious or not) of many different identifications, for an individual as well as for a collectivity.

Importantly, he also underlines the role of formal organizations in contemporary societies, as arenas for the formation of individual and group identities and for the categorization of people. While my interest focuses on occupational as different from organizational identity (cf. Aurell 2001: 24ff), organizations constitute a medium of existence for all occupations. In the language of Jenkins, occupational positions and titles are nominal identities to a high degree institutionalized in and through work organizations but also professional organizations, unions and the like. While this perspective does not specifically centre on working life, it is well suited for such studies. One advantage is that it makes it possible to locate work-related identity within a wider theoretical frame where paid work, the organization or the occupation is not 'all there is.' Identity processes are operating across all spheres of life and through all its stages. And notwithstanding how central work-related identities may be for some people they are basically to be understood as secondary identities, that is, the result of secondary socialization (Jenkins 2000: 16f).[3] These are important points since they help to avoid tendencies to treat work too easily as people's—particularly men's—only or totally predominant base of identity (cf. Musson and Duberley 2007; also Brown et al. 2007).

Hitherto, I have spoken rather generally of *work-related identity* and hardly at all of *work orientations*. Before going on to the methodological and empirical parts of the chapter, something will be said in more detail about my use of such concepts. First, while I do not always uphold a strict division between the two terms, as mentioned earlier I basically conceive of work orientation as a facet of individuals' work-related identity in the sense that 'identities' implies something more deep-rooted and thorough-going than 'orientations.' How one identifies oneself—as a result of the broad social processes discussed above—is likely to colour one's orientation toward specific phenomena. Second, and in line with the main analytical strands of this book, it is useful to keep in mind a distinction between people's attitudes or orientations toward *work in general*, their *specific tasks* or *occupation*, their employing *organization* (which may be very large), their specific *workplace* (which may be a small entity within a big organization, as in the case of post offices and hospital wards), the various categories of *people* with whom they come into contact during work, and also toward *work in the context of life as a whole* (that is, 'work centrality') with family, friends, leisure activities, etc., entering the picture. All of the above can serve as bases of identity, a concept which here refers to everything that can be a source of identification—positive or negative—for an individual or group, as well as a source of categorization of others. The focus has been on bases of identity that (a) are clearly relevant given the research subject and earlier studies not least of administrative services (besides occupation and other work-related phenomena it was particularly gender, class and modernity that stood out as salient in this respect); and (b) have come out as important during the analysis of the empirical material. Whereas everyone who has an occupation can be said to have an occupational identity—since it unavoidably affects one's life and outlook in *some* way, however slight— the concept becomes meaningless if it is stretched too far. Being sensitive to other bases of identity helps avoiding this.

Finally—again in line with the main analytical strands of this volume— it is sometimes relevant to distinguish between an *absolute* stance toward work-related phenomena (when they are considered 'in themselves') and a *relative* stance (considered in relation to other areas and aspects of life such as family/friends and leisure activities/interests).

Discussions of work-related identity naturally touch upon and partly overlap those of work orientation. According to a line of research not least inspired by John Goldthorpe (cf., e.g., Berglund 2001; Eriksson 1998; and several contributions to this volume), in ideal-typical terms you can distinguish between an *instrumental* orientation where work is mainly a means to earn money to attain goals outside the sphere of work, and a *committed* orientation where work in itself is ascribed a value. The committed orientation, in turn, can be of different varieties: *career-oriented* where the main interest is to advance—which can entail substantial sacrifices for the sake of the organization but is in turn expected to 'pay back' in monetary and status-related as well as more personal terms (if the expectations are not met, however, the loyalty toward the organization will probably decline and be replaced by a more individualistic approach); *solidaristic* where work surely is important for economic reasons but where community with the colleagues and/or the workplace is at least as important and very well may be put before economic values; or *altruistic* where it is central that the work one performs is important for other people or society as a whole. Also, Berglund (chapter 4, this volume) identifies an *autonomy* orientation—quite individualistic but still fitting among the committed ones—where the room for self-direction in one's work is highly valued.

Other approaches or orientations toward work have above all been discussed in women's studies. Building on, among others, Sörensen (1982), Ve (see Gunnarsson 1994: 29ff), and Waerness (1984), it is possible to distinguish between an approach that is based on a *technical limited rationality* and another one based on a *rationality of responsibility or caring*. The first means an instrumental orientation and goals-means-thinking based on strict technical/economic criteria of efficiency—in other words, something that is generally encouraged in modern work organizations. In contrast, the second entails a comprehensive view regarding work that includes and emphasises human relations and the feelings, views and life situations of other people (colleagues, clients, etc.). Ewa Gunnarsson (1994: ch. 9) extends this to include also care for material things: machines, products and the physical workplace itself. Another development of this theme—actually based on studies of office occupations—is Päivi Korvajärvi's (1998: 113, 120) discussion of a reproductive work orientation where one takes responsibility for the continuity of everyday work which also can include seeing to the best of the whole organization. Perhaps the whole thing is best formulated by Berenice Fisher and Joan Tronto (1990: 40; my italics):

> *Caring about* involves paying attention to our world in such a way that we focus on continuity, maintenance, and repair. *Taking care of* involves responding to these aspects—taking responsibility for activities that keep our world going. *Caregiving* involves the concrete tasks, the hands-on work of maintenance and repair. / . . . / The caring process, as these categories suggest, *may be directed toward things and other living beings as well as toward people.*

Finally, in her study on women in knowledge companies, Martha Blomqvist (1994: 161ff) emphasises a third rationality that has become encouraged in working life over the last few decades: an *economic rationality of relations* where personal traits and, above all, relations, are seen as means to attain economic and organizational goals. It combines elements from the other two rationalities although with a 'bias' toward the technical limited variety.

The technical limited rationality has often been associated with men and the rationality of caring with women, while the economic rationality of relations has been rather ambiguously judged on this point (e.g. Blomqvist 1994, 2001; Peterson 2005). My point of departure is that all work orientations can be held by women and men alike (cf., e.g., Sörensen 1982;

Crompton and Jones 1984: 150; Eriksson 1998) but that there are reasons—socialization, gender segregation, etc.—why expectations of, as well
as actual, gender differences can develop here.

To summarize: the theoretical point of departure is *a pluralistic identity perspective* that facilitates recognizing many aspects of 'identity' while
avoiding strong presumptions of its form and content. This perspective is
further related to *various types of work-related identities and orientations*
that are relevant here. Finally, I want to emphasise the usefulness I have
found this approach to have for undertaking a balanced analysis of occupations that are low or relatively low in status. It is important not to underestimate the possibility that persons in such occupations (a) have chosen this
path deliberately for one reason or other (while recognizing that occupational choices are *always* to *some* extent influenced and circumscribed by
factors like class, gender, contemporary ideals, etc.); and (b) on the whole
like their occupations although these do not fit neatly into commonly held
pictures of what constitutes a 'good' or desirable job/occupation (cf. also
Flisbäck 2008, 2010; Gaskell 1992: 67ff; Ulfsdotter Eriksson, chapter 6,
this volume). In other words, it is crucial to be able to capture both positive
and negative aspects.

THE TWO OCCUPATIONS: SOME IDENTITY-
RELEVANT BACKGROUND

This chapter focuses on two administrative service occupations: medical
secretaries and post-office cashiers. Typically for such occupations, both
have a large majority of women, and the existence of both has repeatedly
been questioned during the last decades. One important difference between
them is that in the latter respect, the outcome has been very different. The
medical secretaries have so far kept their place in Swedish health care and
have seen a successive expansion of tasks as well as possibilities for education and training. The occupation of post-office cashier, on the other hand,
has gone from expansion of the work content in the 1980s and 1990s to
dequalification, splitting between two different types of workplaces (postal
service centres [PSC]) and the separate organization Swedish Cashier Service [SCS]), and finally to being abolished.[4]

A common denominator is that both the health and the postal sectors in
Sweden have been subject to similar reforms. These include deregulations
and introduction of more market-like conditions, customer orientation,
new forms of control systems and individualization of pay. The Swedish
Post Office was transformed from a public utility to a state-owned business enterprise in 1994, but already from the mid-1980s onward it adopted
strategies directly aimed at transforming what was increasingly described
as an old-style bureaucracy, hampered by a rigid work culture, to a modern
enterprise fit for the information age (Löfström 2003; Nissen and Olsson

1996; Karlsson 2010). This included the transformation of cashiers 'from tellers to sellers' (Regini, Kitay and Baethge 2000) typical for many countries at the time. The cashiers were expected to take an active role in selling a widening range of bank services and postal products, and to promote various self-service solutions. Although followed by the above-mentioned organizational split and cut-down of services, the managerially prescribed 'seller' identity was a ubiquitous part of the cashiers' working life and occupational training for a considerable time.

For medical secretaries, the situation has been quite different. In the health care sector, quality assurance systems became compulsory in the 1990s. This and other developments have required an increasing amount of documentation which often became the secretaries' responsibility. While large-scale reforms and reorganizations (not to mention computerization) have impinged on their working conditions, employers' and public sector reformers' attention to this occupational category has often been limited (something that is not specific to the Swedish context: cf., e.g., Armstrong, Armstrong and Scott-Dixon 2008; Davies 1995: 55f.). Accordingly, the most conspicuous 'identity' initiative has come from within the secretaries' own ranks. From the office computerization debate of the early 1980s onward, the medical secretaries' occupational association has worked not only for better pay and better education but also for a thoroughly renewed secretarial role, far from monotonous typing of medical records and stereotypes of feminine submissiveness. Having a university education and an interest in constantly developing her/his competence, the new medical secretary (who may not have this title at all) is not only a reliable expert on administrative routines and the proper use of written language. S/he is also quick at adopting new technology and finding creative solutions to administrative problems, not hesitating to take on new qualified tasks if necessary. Being in what is often termed a 'spider-in-the-web' position, s/he will actively strive to make the ensuing broad knowledge useful to the organization. This new role is often simply discussed in terms of 'the medical secretary of the future.' While no specific label is consistently used among its proponents, I will sometimes use the term 'the expert administrator' since this rather well captures its content.[5]

Which occupational identities and identity narratives were salient in the two occupations in the beginning of the 21st century, and which were their backgrounds? As we have seen, for the *cashiers* the 'official' identity narrative was developed by management in the 1980s and 1990s against the backdrop of time-typical bureaucracy critique and market orientation. The new prescribed 'seller' identity was met with everything from rejection to reformulation attempts to enthusiastic embrace, but practically lost its relevance around the millennial shift because of the restructuring of the Swedish Post. Since the occupation was split in two as well as emptied of much of its former content, the 'seller' identity hardly got any replacement from management. However, cashiers themselves substituted for it disillusioned labels such as 'living teller machines' (SCS) and 'janitors' (PSC) while their alternative ways of telling the history of the Swedish Post became more pronounced. The latter entailed critical evaluations of managerial and political decisions and, above all, a widely embraced emphasis on and identification with a never altogether forgotten image of a democratic and broadly competent service provider that partially drew on an older postal ideal of the 'public servant' (cf. Lundgren 1990).

As regards the *medical secretaries*, the predominant 'official' identity narrative discussed above emphasises the development from underestimated typists, personal 'maids' of the doctors or workplace 'mothers' serving others with the most trivial of tasks, to well-educated professional(izing) experts finally standing the chance, as a group, to gain their proper place as financially and socially recognized co-workers. This account was shared in large part by many of the interviewees, although several of these personally held less critical views on typing or on what constitutes an acceptable service role for a secretary. Beside this narrative, a rather pronounced alternative was also found to exist, describing instead a gradual degradation and status loss of the occupation since the time that it had a glamorous aura of novelty—particularly the 1950s and 1960s—and when status mainly derived from association with prominent physicians. Which narrative was embraced to a large extent seemed to depend on when, where and how a person had entered the occupation. However, the 'spider in the web' metaphor is common for both types of descriptions, indicating a relatively resilient point of reference of the same kind as the cashiers' public service ideal.

Finally, in both occupations broader narratives of later decades' technological and social development (inexorable computerization; less authoritarian social relations) were found to generally play an important part in reflections on one's work and occupation but also on other aspects of life and society.

METHODS AND MATERIAL

This study uses interviews as a main source of data in combination with various types of text material. Interviews were carried out by the author in 2004–2005 with a total of 22 medical secretaries and 17 post-office cashiers. The overarching criterion was that they should have at least a few years of occupational experience. For the cashiers, who by this time worked and had their employment in either SCS or PSC offices, it was additionally important that their experience included some period *before* the organizational split. Individuals from a variety of different workplaces were interviewed, since the research interest concerns occupations rather than particular organizations or sites of work. In all, 28 individual interviews and 4 group interviews with two or more participants were conducted.

Five of the individual interviews were with men—two secretaries and three cashiers—while all participants in the group interviews were women. Their occupational experience ranged from 2–3 years to around 40. The interviews were semi-structured, using a written guide with a limited number of questions and themes, also leaving some space to explore other themes emerging during the talk. Typically they lasted between 1 and 1 ½ hours.

The text material includes the yearbooks of the employee club of the Swedish Post and the membership journal of the medical secretaries' association from the early 1980s to 2005. It also includes memories written by post-office cashiers and medical secretaries, collected by White-collar and Professionals' Archival Institution and the Swedish Postal Museum, respectively. Interviews and other materials are analyzed using common qualitative methods, including sensitivity for the use of discourses and narratives. In the search for salient themes and relations between these, attentive listening through the audiotapes has been combined with close readings of transcripts and texts. The various themes are then further explored in the light of theory, earlier research and relevant research questions.

THE IMPORTANCE OF WORK IN LIFE

> /W/hen I'm at work, that is important. [*laughs a little*] And then . . . my friends at home and my family are important. And when I'm at work, that is important. Yeah . . . that's how it is. (*SCS cashier, woman*)

In this section, the most salient orientations among the secretaries and cashiers toward their work and occupation—as a part of their life and identity as a whole—are presented. Two common stances found among both medical secretaries and cashiers, which both can be summarized with the help of the quotation above, are the following. The first is work as an important and highly valued *part* of life which the person in question would not want to be without, but neither is it all there is in life and it should not be allowed to take over. The second is work as something that is not seen as very important in one's life taken as a whole but that one nevertheless engages in quite whole-heartedly *during the time spent at work*, when it becomes important to fulfill one's tasks and occupational role in a satisfactory way. The following answers to my interview question about how important work is and has been, compared to other things in life are illustrative:

> /I/t has been . . . quite important, but there's been much that has been just as important. That's what I think. You know, I have quite a lot of interests, I have many friends and . . . but yet I've thought that the job has been very important, because I've really thought it has been fun. Actually, I still think so! [*laughter*]. (*SCS cashier, woman*)

Very little. But then again, at the same time . . . I am very committed . . . to everything I do. So even if I don't think that the work is important in itself or the tasks are important in themselves—when you are at work, you still want it to function. (*Medical secretary, man*)

It's important, but it is not . . . that important. [*laughs a little*] Actually, I really protect my leisure time. I . . . want to be able to engage in my children and I want to be able to engage in different activities, so . . . But the job is an important part, for sure. And a fun, important part. (*Medical secretary, woman*)

'Purely' instrumental or committed orientations are, taken together, not common in my interview material. One explanation could be the obvious one that ideal types seldom match what is found in real life. Another one might be that it is not felt appropriate to voice 'too extreme' work orientations in an interview situation. More interesting, and looking at what the cashiers and secretaries actually express themselves, the mixed character of these occupations—always entailing some combination of 'paperwork' and interaction with service recipients—also seems to have a good deal to do with it. There seems to be a space for variation that does not favour the development of the more extreme orientations. From this perspective, it is not surprising that among the interviewees the cashiers are leaning somewhat more toward an instrumental stance than the secretaries because of the last decade's drastic cut in the range of postal tasks and services. However, even under these circumstances there is some variation to be found, as will be returned to below. In both occupations different forms of *strongly* committed orientations seem to have been more common earlier according to older written memories and studies, supporting the idea that under contemporary conditions (paid) work may well hold an important place in people's lives but nevertheless has to compete to a greater extent with other commitments, interests and identity bases.

Different kinds of interests in career and development are surely present among the interviewees (as in other material). At the same time, many also describe themselves as uninterested in a traditional career or emphasise the negative sides of having a position in the middle of a formal hierarchy—not least that work responsibilities then easily invade too much of one's life. The ambivalence is particularly well illustrated by some of the cashiers who have formerly been postmasters or at least have had formal supervisory and/or economic responsibility for a smaller post office for some period.

In the late '90s, I realized that there is a life outside the Post too. That's how it is, of course. A private life that you had to neglect a lot. Because as a manager, you had to work at home too, in principle, you had to bring the problems home with you. / . . . / It was stressful, really—I realized that if you don't do something about it, then something else will probably happen to you, that you . . . burn out. But I managed it—I got away in time. [*Tells about the return to mainly cashier work.*] And that is something I don't regret . . . because I realize that [*emphatically*] this is my thing—to sit at the counter, to meet customers, be service-minded toward customers. This is my job! (*SCS cashier, man*)

If I had only worked at the counter all the time—well, you shouldn't say 'only', it's to depreciate the job I suppose—then I might had got tired of it. . . . But since I worked with education for about one year and did different things, I could develop myself so to speak, I learned to do more things. And that's why I stayed, and why I'm still here. [*Further on in the interview:*] To be honest, I think everything stands a bit still today. But on the other hand . . . there are two sides to it. Because when I was responsible for staff and everything, I was never really free from work. But now when I go home, I'm free. That's the advantage even though I sometimes feel that . . . I don't make enough use of my head. / . . . / And at the same time, it's almost never boring, because, for one thing, our tasks are varied, and for another thing, something happens all the time when you have customers. (*PSC cashier, woman*)

The following excerpt from an interview with a medical secretary exemplifies a stance where one's job or occupation is seen as satisfactory and engaging for the time being but where one might consider leaving it if, for example, the overall conditions would deteriorate or tasks become too repetitive.

AK: How important is work in your life compared to other things, like leisure-time activities or . . . ?

I: [*thoughtfully*] It's important. I wouldn't be happy if I could not go to my job. But . . . I didn't have to be a medical secretary as long as I had some other . . . job that I like or that suits me. *AK asks what she sees as important in a job.*

I: I like to work! [*laughter, followed by a thoughtful pause*]. I can't answer—I don't know! I would not be satisfied if I couldn't work—I have to work with something . . . and I prefer it to be something that develops . . . that something happens to it.

AK: Is it important to have career opportunities and the like, or . . . ?

I: No, not really, actually—I don't need to rise 'up the ladder' or something like that . . . it doesn't matter much to me. But I don't want to stagnate at work, I want things to happen around me.

AK: Do you mean in the workplace, or more in the occupation as a whole, or both?

I: Both of them.

To problematize or downplay the importance of managerial/supervisory work in the manner above is discussed by Flisbäck (2008) as a strategy for people in low-status occupations to gain recognition by emphasizing their own relative freedom, their concern for family and friends and more generally the advantages of their own work. But in contrast to her study, quite a few of my interviewees are persons with their own experiences of managerial responsibilities, who thereby could make an actual comparison. To be able to leave work behind, physically and psychologically, after the working day is also something that many cashiers and secretaries without experiences of managerial work both appreciate and find relatively easy. It is interesting to note that the quotations not only show a concern for freedom *from* work when the working day is over, but there is also a concern for freedom and choice *at* work and *of* work, again something that is echoed in several other interviews. Perhaps this could be interpreted as a type of autonomy orientation.

Of course, the view of the place of work in life, as well as the more specific orientation toward work, is also affected by how satisfied one is with the occupation as such (or one's workplace, colleagues, family situation, etc.), and more generally by which bases of identification stand out as important. Gender is an aspect here; for example, many of the women interviewed had typically prioritized husband and children not least in the choices they had made regarding their working life (in both occupations it has usually been easy for women to get part-time employment). On the other hand, some women also emphasised their job as offering valuable variation and community in times when private life is troublesome. It is also clear that class background and conceptions of status have had an impact upon how people originally chose or got into their occupations. Several of the somewhat older cashiers (both men and women) mentioned the status, the comprehensive paid cashier courses and the employment security once associated with the Post Office. Likewise, several (female) medical secretaries had held an image of the occupation as glamorous and relatively status-filled for a woman. While many of the interviewees had had quite a clear picture of why they wanted this particular job, several had also entered the occupation by chance or as a second-best option. However, at least at the time of the interviews this factor did not seem to have much to do with the development of occupational identities that are 'distinct and strong within certain limits.' This is, of course, not to deny that people's views and priorities may change substantially over time, affecting the evaluation of both the occupation/work and its place in life.

Looking at which aspects of their work the cashiers and secretaries identify with and find satisfaction in, we can note some occupationally specific differences that I will shortly mention. The cashiers often emphasise the contact with the customers: partly because of the variation it automatically entails, partly because of the possibilities—in spite of all the cut-downs—to help people not only with purely postal tasks but also with small 'extra' services like taking some minutes to listen to an old person's problems, thus upholding a social function. As the aforementioned 'public servant' ideal implies, the identification with the Post as a reliable and valuable *social* institution is (was) long-lived and conspicuous. Both in the interviews and other material many cashiers further mention fellowship with colleagues. The medical secretaries often emphasise the constant learning taking place in their occupation (although many would like to see better formal opportunities and payoffs here) through their position in the organizations and their handling of a wide variety of medical and administrative documents. Many also refer to the enjoyment in carrying out the documentation tasks well, producing documents that are both formally correct and aesthetically satisfactory. And, from a broader point of view: being a part of the health care environment as such (more often than the particular workplace/organization even if the latter also occurs). This typically entails seeing oneself and one's occupation as fulfilling crucial functions in the health care system—the 'spiders in the web' being important for individual patients, for the work of the strictly medical occupations and for society at large. To sum up, one thing that is clear is that altruistic but also solidaristic orientations are of importance in these occupations.

In the next section, I take up two aspects—already implicit in much of what is recounted above—that more than anything else seem to hold the two respective occupations together across the many different bases of identity mentioned here. They constitute a valued core that is often present even beneath apparently instrumental orientations or weak work orientations.

THE COMMON CORE: CAREFULNESS AND SERVICE

This section discusses and develops what makes it plausible to speak of *occupational* identity, focusing on the finding that there is a distinct core of tasks, competences and ethical norms—particularly related to the intertwined themes of 'carefulness' (in Swedish *noggrannhet*) and 'service.' Practisers of the two occupations recurringly refer to these aspects in similar, yet occupationally specific ways. The word *noggrannhet* has hardly an exact counterpart in English, but its various meanings include accuracy, orderliness, thoroughness, conscientiousness and, not least, carefulness. From the interviews and other material, it is clear that while one of the most salient significations of *noggrannhet* is about keeping up high standards of correctness, an equally salient one is about being careful in the *literal* sense of the word. It simply means taking a caring stance toward other people—thus providing a bridge to the likewise central theme of 'service.' In the interviews, carefulness and service were conspicuously often mentioned when I asked about occupational knowledge. They were also often spontaneously mentioned in other contexts, as important but complex and sometimes contradictory competences having to be professionally balanced in the daily work. The following quotations are typical:

AK: What would you say is important occupational knowledge in this work?

I: Well . . . carefulness is very good I think, and a social ability to be able to communicate with customers . . . to have, as it were, a feeling for how customers should be treated. Hmm . . . to have the attitude that you should try to help . . . that you care enough to make that phone call [*even if it goes beyond one's regular tasks; my comment*] if necessary. And then you probably need some kind of . . . logical thinking so you can solve problems when they arise, that you can get round difficult issues and do things in a different way or . . . Hmm, but carefulness, that's really good I suppose. A certain courage is also needed, I think, a certain amount of integrity / . . . /, for example when you have to refuse somebody who wants to get money without an ID card or so. (*SCS cashier, woman*)

AK: What is important occupational knowledge?

I: It's the language. Definitely. And carefulness—we simply mustn't write anything down incorrectly. / . . . / And then it's secrecy, that we treat our information securely / . . . / also the computers, that we make sure to turn them off when we go out and. . . . You could imagine for yourself, if one's own medical record was shown there when the patients were passing by. / . . . /

AK: Is there an occupational pride? [Yes.] That has also to do with identity.

I: Yes. There is, because so many people see our work, so you want it to be well done. Correctly edited and spelled, and that you don't . . . it's much . . . that you don't write down a medicine that doesn't fit the disease—you have to go to the physician several times each day and ask 'should it really be like this?' They are of course very happy that we pay attention. (*Medical secretary, woman*)

I1:   You are a service person, that's what you are. If you say that's a kind of identity—then you are . . .
Participants agree that the cashier job today is simply and basically a service occupation.

I2:   For some time, your part was to be a seller / . . . / but now it's service—you could say that.
As a typical service task, participants talk about giving the right amount of money to the right individual.

I1:   . . . careful service person! You have to be careful.

I3:   Yes—that's the part we play. (*Group interview with SCS cashiers, women*)

Much earlier research on administrative service—including studies referred to in this chapter (e.g., Armstrong et al. 2008: 19–32; Conradson 1988; Korvajärvi 1998; Lundgren 1990; Salzer 1995)—support this picture of an emphasis on carefulness and service, and the ensuing dilemmas of having to balance their sometimes incompatible aspects, as characteristic of such occupations. Of the two themes, however, the focus of empirical studies is most often on the well-established subject of service, leaving the equally complex theme of carefulness (*noggrannhet*) less explored. The close connection between carefulness in its different forms, service and occupational ethic is therefore seldom at the centre of attention (Lundgren's historical study [1990] is a partial exception) but stands out as one of the most important focal points in the secretaries' and cashiers' individual and collective identity work. One dilemma or contradiction that asserts itself more than others is between a rationality of caring and more technocratically or instrumentally coloured rationalities. For example, my material contains rich examples of how many cashiers felt uncomfortable when they were suddenly expected to act in line with an economic rationality of relations. Different conceptions of service and carefulness easily clash at this point. In both occupations, alternative identities exist that more—or in other ways—than the 'officially' promoted ones emphasise care(fulness) and a general social responsibility that can be directed at individual customers/patients as well as the public; they also entail care about the workplace, the colleagues and—particularly for the secretaries—people with other occupations with whom one works (cf. Fisher and Tronto 1990; also, e.g., Kennelly 2006; Lundgren 1990). Many of these caring concerns shine through in the interview quotations. Put in other words, it is above all the altruistic but also the solidaristic orientations that come to the fore here and offer resistance.

In any case: the competent exertion of carefulness and a service role—however these are conceived and combined—stand out as central components of what makes people in administrative service occupations value their job, either highly as one among several important parts of life, or, more prosaically, only during the time the work is performed. As such, they serve as a base for ethical concerns that has the potential to give strength and direction not least to collective occupational identities.

THE PROBLEM OF UNDERESTIMATION—
OTHERS' AND OWN—AND ITS CONSEQUENCES

This section deals with two phenomena that complicate the picture of relatively strong and distinct occupational identities given in the last two sections, but that—as I will argue—may not preclude or weaken identity in these occupations as much as work to *conceal* it in different ways. The first phenomenon is that people on the 'outside' often undervalue and depreciate administrative service work(ers), for example, by seeing it as superfluous or soul-deadening or by simply taking it for granted. The second one is that people inside the occupations seemingly have a tendency to undervalue their own (collective) strength.

As for the first phenomenon, there are many sides to it. Occupations of the administrative service type, as well as their practisers, have a long history of being negatively depicted in fiction and popular culture. Also in research there is a tendency to emphasise various negative traits (Conradson 1988; Felski 2000; see also Karlsson 2010), from Robert Merton's classic description of 'bureaucratic personalities' (Merton 1964: ch. VI) to newer studies treating administrative service jobs as not much more than dead-end traps for women. This is echoed by the fact that 'office secretary' and 'post-office cashier' both scored low (places 74 and 89, respectively) in a Swedish survey where a random sample ranked 100 occupations according to their perceived societal status (Svensson and Ulfsdotter Eriksson 2009: 40).[6] Why these negatively slanted, low-status images and stereotypes?

As previously mentioned, these occupations are difficult to define and pin down both in theoretical and practical terms. They are also often misunderstood or little known by persons outside the occupations. For example, medical secretaries almost unanimously hold that people that do not themselves work in health care do not know much, if anything, about their jobs—as these interview quotations exemplify:

> You say 'hospital' and people think of doctors and nurses. / . . . / that's what makes a hospital, so to speak. I don't believe that people ever think of medical secretaries at all, that they exist in hospitals. (*Medical secretary, woman*).

> I don't think they [*the public*] really know what you do. And then I think that they . . . 'well well, but you just type, it can't be very difficult.' (*Medical secretary, woman*)

Albeit the occupation of post-office cashier is (was) generally more well-known because of its higher visibility, it is not free from this problem. Many cashiers, at the time of my study but also in earlier text material when the occupation was more stable, express that other people often have an inaccurate image of their work and what it takes to do it properly. A report from 1995 summarizes a view I met in different versions among cashiers and others during the research process:

> At the same time as the Post is one of Sweden's most well-known companies, it is also very unknown. In fact, people on the outside know rather little of what it does or what happens inside the large 'Office.'

Stereotyped 'caricatures' of the Post are common (Salzer 1995: 14; my translation).

Experiences of lack of knowledge and recognition by others can be the case also in one's own organization. This is expressed by both secretaries and cashiers. Not least the cashiers who had started working in the postal service centres sometimes felt themselves in an organizational 'no man's land', being more or less forgotten by managers/supervisors and having no longer a clearly defined occupational role or title.

To continue, administrative service occupations are typically female-dominated, either created by work organizations with women directly in mind or having gone through a process of numerical and symbolic feminization (cf., e.g., Conradson 1988; Crompton and Jones 1984; Davies 1982; Lundgren 1990; Pringle 1988; Witz and Savage 1992). Therefore, they are easily treated as taken-for-granted service functions noticed only when problems arise. My material contains ample exemplification of that. Being somewhat diffusely expected to 'gatekeep' and ensure the smooth functioning of all kinds of postal services, Swedish post-office cashiers have had to face customer criticisms both for the mistakes of others and, increasingly, for controversial management decisions over which they have had no say at all. As for the medical secretaries, a laconic, quite representative quotation is that 'We're just supposed to be there.' Anne Witz and Mike Savage (1992: 25) put the classic predicament succinctly:

> /W/omen both outside *and* inside bureaucracies / . . . / are engaged in similarly gendered modes of acting, ones which order the materiality of the everyday world, be this a kitchen or an office. They are facilitating, cleaning, tidying, bolstering, soothing, smoothing over, sustaining etc. Women's housekeeping and caring activities are fundamentally geared towards relieving men of having to bother with the messy, untidy, unpredictable bodily modes of existence, but equally women are concerned with the concrete underbelly of conceptual activities when these are located within bureaucratic administrative organizations, by doing the clerical work and 'tidying' the information flowing through the office.

Much as a consequence of the women-concentration, they are also comparatively low-paid and often lacking career and development opportunities. To get employed, there are usually no formal demands of higher (college/university level) education. Finally, they are vulnerable to introduction of new technologies aimed at reducing staff, and to the concomitant labeling as outdated.

As for the second phenomenon, a strong awareness of others' ignorant or one-sided negative images of the occupations and tasks is often present in my material, sometimes to the point of incorporating aspects of these views in individual or collective occupational identities (cf. Aurell 2001; Flisbäck 2010). There is also the idea of women-as-a-group as quite powerless, *both* because of low estimates of women's commitment and solidarity when it comes to strive for better working conditions (that family goes first; that many women together means a lot of 'bitching' [cf. Pringle 1988], etc.) *and* because of awareness or expectations of discrimination against women in work organizations and unions as well as in society at large.

> We are a small group, and we're only women, and we're not committed ourselves . . . we're really not good at that. (*Medical secretary, woman*)

This quotation is rather typical for the medical secretaries' view of their power to make themselves heard when I asked about trade unions[7], but it also captures a broader conception common for both occupations. In both, several interviewees emphasised their small numbers compared to other occupational categories in their union as well as in the work organization.

However, there is more to be said about this. As mentioned at the start of this section, the phenomena discussed above may not always preclude or weaken identity in these occupations as much as work to *conceal* it in different ways. This is not as contradictory as it might sound. While negative depictions are often loudly expressed, it is likely that delimited occupational identities are normally not much noticed precisely because of their limited character, and the strong occupational focus on carefulness-plus-service is of an 'everyday', non-spectacular sort that for a long time has been all too easy to overlook. But this is obviously not the same as not being present. I will now turn to this topic, discussing potential consequences of strong but delimited identities in the context of devalued, relatively low-status occupations—with an emphasis on positive consequences and underrated strengths.

To start with the problematic side: besides the commonplace that all occupational identities can entail hampering one-sidedness and conformity pressures, some more specific issues need to be addressed. One has to acknowledge the potential collective weakness stemming from the fact that both types of occupational identities discussed here *are* to a high degree characterized by competing sources of identification outside work. For example, if the employing organization withdraws its support for the occupational group, a lack of coherence or unity may result: there is vulnerability here because of a potential lack of interest. First from those who see doing a good job as important when at work but do not think the work/occupation is important in itself or in life as a whole. Second from those who are committed to the occupation as a component of their life, but mainly 'as it is' and therefore might be ready to move on if its original character deteriorates (which can include diminishing of all kinds of work-related bases of identity, such as personnel cuts affecting colleagues or the breaking up of established work units). In this context, collective weakness may be particularly detrimental to interests of developing or professionalizing the occupation.

On the other hand, to return to the more constructive side: The 'common core' of carefulness and service constitutes what could be described as an underestimated occupational ethic. While it is consistent enough to serve as a focal point for ethical and competence-related considerations in the two occupations, it is also broad enough to serve as an 'identification umbrella' under which different bases of identity, different work orientations, etc., can coexist (more or less easily and temporarily). Clearly, such an identity resource should have the potential to strengthen people in the occupations both individually and—not least important with regard to power relations in the world of work—as a collective. Here, it is important to take into consideration how identities are collectively articulated.

For one thing, various articulations can be more or less consistent with contemporary strong ideals and discourses and so have different chances of being widely accepted. There is no doubt that the medical secretaries' officially promoted 'expert administrator' identity has had easier to win institutional acceptance than the 'public service' identity embraced by many cashiers.[8] A complication is that administrative service occupations generally have to dissociate themselves—at least outwardly—from certain types of carefulness and service to get this broad acceptance, which may cause strain on the occupational ethic. In line with widely embraced ideals and narratives of the last decades' development toward a high-technological as well as non-hierarchical, (gender-)equal working life, everything that smacks of old-fashioned technology, paternalism or submissiveness needs to be avoided. Some aspects of carefulness and service, associated with dull routine work and femininely gendered 'everyday' maintenance or people-supporting tasks, are notoriously difficult to accommodate with such ideals (cf., e.g., Pringle 1988). However, despite the old-fashioned connotation of 'public service' at least for the time being, it seems unlikely that this concept or ideal has lost its force once and for all. Perhaps Ivy Kennelly's (2006) suggestion could be a part of the solution: to start recognizing and rewarding the public service ethic, the willingness to contribute to society through a caring—largely altruistic—orientation that she found in private-sector secretarial work, much like I (and many other researchers of administrative service) have found in the occupations studied here.

For another thing, it is important to consider the possibility that the (ethically) strong but partial and/or delimited character of the occupational identities and work orientations discussed here can serve as *alternatives* and correctives to today's dominating economic priorities and tough efficiency ideals in the world of work. Thereby, they can be a potential source of solidarity, resistance and promotion of wished-for changes from both employee and client/customer perspectives that otherwise are easily overlooked. From this perspective, to identify with the 'wrong' kind of occupation or tasks, as well as drawing a clear limit between paid work and other areas of life, does not have to be attempts to compensate for a devalued job or some other lack in one's life (cf. Flisbäck 2008, 2010; du Gay 1994; Hasselbladh 2002; Lindgren 1999; Lysgaard 1967; Sennett 1998).

Finally, experiences of devaluation, technological and economic threat and more or less badly implemented changes can actually be conducive of a more positive assessment of—and a willingness to defend—one's competences, tasks and whole occupation (cf. Aurell 2001; Flisbäck 2010; Fältholm 1998: ch. E; Lysgaard 1967; O'Connell Davidson 1994). The contributions of one's work/occupation to the organization and society may then come to the fore more clearly. As expressed by one or two of my interviewees, one's role and identity become more clear-cut under 'threatening' circumstances. Even though people and groups often have a propensity to overstate their own importance,[9] others' negative views of an occupation can cause a reaction among its practisers that pinpoints and possibly helps ward off negative consequences of insensitive change initiatives. However, this process should be easier if there is already a lively identity discussion in the occupational collective about ideals, ethic and competences. Of the two occupations studied here, this has more been the case among the medical secretaries than among the cashiers. Such discussions would probably also benefit from a growing awareness of different work orientations and the reasonable limits of commitment.

CONCLUDING DISCUSSION

As is strongly implied in classical and more recent studies of work orientations (e.g., Eriksson 1998; chapters 2, 5, and 6, this volume), there can be much more to work orientations primarily labeled as *'instrumental'*—based either on expectations of the type of occupation or on answers to some standardized survey questions—that is, if one takes the time and effort to look beneath the surface. This chapter has explored this possibility further, since it stands out as salient in my material, fleshing out some of its expressions and consequences against the backdrop of an identity perspective.

One conclusion is that a basically instrumental orientation—where one's work is not described as an important part of life—does not preclude taking pride in doing a good job during the time spent on work. This orientation can have many sources (related to gender, class, the organization, the workplace, etc.) but first and foremost seems to get its particular form from the occupation and the ethical norms that come with its exertion. These norms are in this case highly related to carefulness and service, which together serve as a focal point for the development of occupational identities.

Another salient phenomenon that has been described and explored is the possibility of some sort of basically *non-instrumental* work orientation (emphasizing for example the socially valuable, organizationally important and/or personally enjoyable character of one's job/occupation) coexisting with a general orientation where the job is one of several, more or less equally appreciated parts that together make up one's life as a whole.

The first variety above is primarily about the job's relative importance in a time (and place) perspective. In other words, the instrumental orientation 'contains' a more committed orientation restricted to a particular time and place. To describe it like this does more justice to the empirical material than seeing it only as expressions of people's 'absolute' stance toward their work, since this type of answers and reflections sometimes came up precisely when I asked about work in *relation* to other areas of life. The second variety is primarily about the job's relative importance in a 'total life' perspective (and thus corresponds more closely to the established concept of relative attitude). At the risk of being somewhat banal, all of this underscores the capacity of humans to compartmentalize their lives and identities in time, space and any other way. Less trivially, it also underscores people's potential to keep clear of exaggerated work ideals and find alternative ways to negotiate a balance between paid work and the rest of life. In terms of work orientations, it is particularly altruistic, solidaristic and autonomy orientations that are actualized here.

It is also of interest to delve deeper into and underscore the main dimensions involved here and their possible combinations. For one thing, it makes sense to distinguish between *the centrality of work in life relative to private/leisure time*, and *work commitment*. Both of these can vary from low to high. If a person is low on both, it roughly corresponds to an ideal-typical 'instrumental' work orientation. The other way round, being high on both dimensions corresponds to an ideal-typical 'committed' orientation. The two stances I have explored here, however, can best be described as occupying a space in between. The first stance certainly implies being low on work centrality, but it is reasonable to describe it as leaning toward the middle when it comes to commitment since work is actually seen as engaging and/or important when it is performed. The second stance implies being in the middle on the work centrality dimension—since other areas of life are also central—and leaning toward a relatively high score on the commitment dimension.

From a slightly different angle, it also makes sense to distinguish between (A) *an inclination to draw a clear line between one's job and private life* as different from (B) not considering this separation important at all; and (1) *an inclination to see one's job as a totally uninteresting means to attain non-work-related goals* as different from (2) seeing one's job more in terms of its innate values or even a goal in itself. The combinations A1 and B2 are the most 'logical' ones, again corresponding to ideal-typical instrumental and committed work orientations while the combination B1 is rather improbable (and at least not salient in my material). Nothing in principle speaks, however, against the possibility of the A2 combination where one appreciates and protects the separation between work and other areas of life at the same time as the job is valued. Precisely this combination is also salient in my material.

All the above is basically another way to conceptualize what I have described as occupational identities that are distinct and strong within certain limits. To develop conceptualizations is, I hope, one step toward getting a more nuanced understanding of identity work in low- to middle-status occupations. In the preceding sections, I have also fleshed out some strengths and weaknesses of such identities, particularly for the occupations as collectives. The type of work-related identities discussed here has, as this chapter has tried to show, both problematic and promising consequences for working life.

NOTES

1. The concept of administrative service is used to refer to work and occupations which include *both* an administrative component (to handle some kind of day-to-day monetary, paper or electronic routines) *and* a service component (to 'serve' other people inside or outside the organization, or both).
2. The research project was funded by the Swedish Council for Working Life and Social Research (FAS). Thanks to Ylva Ulfsdotter Eriksson, Gunnar Gillberg, the editors of the book (particularly Bengt Furåker who offered help with the text at some critical moments) and all others who have contributed valuable comments during the writing of the chapter.
3. The existence of strong political and cultural norms regarding paid work in contemporary 'Western' societies should not be underestimated here—nor should the existence of class-based patterns (cf. Eriksson 1998: 50f, 105, 168; also Furåker, chapter 2, this volume). That people are unavoidably exposed to ideas and practices regarding 'work' from early childhood is not, however, tantamount to being born into predetermined, practically non-negotiable occupational positions. If the latter situation was the rule, it certainly would be warranted to speak more of primary socialization.
4. The last SCS offices were closed in autumn 2008, while the closing of the PSCs—later called 'company service centres'—was announced in January 2010.
5. In the terminology of Jenkins, these are primarily *collective* identities. Being conceived and promoted from inside the occupation, 'the medical secretary of the future' is primarily a *group identification*. Being initiated and promoted mostly from outside the occupation, the 'seller' is primarily a *category*. To the extent that it was accepted by the cashiers, it was also a group identification. As labels, both are also *nominal* identities that are filled over time with experiential, emotional, embodied (that is, virtual) content.
6. 'Medical secretary' was not included as an option in this survey, which was distributed in 2002.
7. Cf. also Hertting et al. (2003: 166): 'the medical secretaries also reported difficulties being heard in the trade union since they belong to an underrepresented female occupation in public sector.'
8. I would not go so far as to say that the eventual disappearance of the cashier occupation was a direct consequence of weaknesses in the collective

occupational identity. A strong collective identity /strategy/ might very well have steered the changes in another direction, but complex political, technological and economic factors also played a part in the developments.

9. In other words: occupations are not entities beyond critique that should necessarily be defended or preserved at *any* cost.

8   The Development of Attitudes to Work in Sweden

Birgitta Eriksson, Jan Ch. Karlsson and Tuula Bergqvist

All work tasks, Aristotle (2006: X: VII: 7–8) says, 'are in themselves unpleasant and trying, but they are of use. We do not try to attain them for their own sake, only for the purpose of the income or other advantages that we get from them.' The term 'joy in work' would be self-contradictory to Aristotle. Not so for Jean Lacroix (1952: 10), who says: 'There is no work without joy: it is born from the transforming activity, from the completed oeuvre, from what is created.' In the terms of our days, we would call the Aristotelian view on work an instrumental or a non-committed attitude and the Lacroix one an engaged or a committed attitude.

The dissemination of engaged and instrumental attitudes to work has been studied and discussed by many researchers. To mention a few, during the 1960s John H. Goldthorpe et al. (1968) argued that the instrumental attitude to work would probably be increasing, especially among unskilled workers. However, some years later Walter Korpi (1978) stated that there was no evidence for a widespread instrumental attitude in Sweden. In the 1990s a number of studies concluded that a sense of attachment and solidarity to one's work organization was a common attitude (e.g., Applebaum 1992; Eriksson 1998; Halvorsen 1997; Johansson, Isaksson and Sjöberg 1996).

What has happened since then? The aim of this chapter is to examine attitudes to work today and how they have changed during recent years. We want to find out if there is variation in attitudes to work among different groups of people, as well as if the change in attitudes is similar within these groups. Our data concern the Swedish labour market. A first study was conducted in the middle of the 1990s and it was repeated in 2010. The first investigation was based on data from a questionnaire sent to a random sample of employees and among other things contained questions about attitudes to work and questions on different types of jobs. The questionnaire was answered by 1,928 employees, which means a response rate of 68 percent. A replication of the study was carried out at the end of 2010. This questionnaire was answered by 1,482 employees, representing a response rate of about 62 percent.

We begin this chapter by presenting some theoretical ideas concerning the dependent variable attitudes to work and the independent variables sex, age, class, work life balance and work environment in order to establish our research questions. Thereafter, we describe the measures that we use to answer these questions. Then the empirical results are presented, first descriptively and subsequently by a logistic regression analysis. Finally we draw some conclusions concerning attitudes to work.

FACTORS RELATED TO ATTITUDES TO WORK

When studying attitudes, we have to consider the distinctions that can be made between different kinds of objects of the attitudes (cf. Johansson, Isaksson and Sjöberg 1996), like work in general, one's own work and one's own workplace—the last type is often called organizational commitment (e.g., Allen and Meyer 1996). Furthermore, the attitudes to work can be investigated in an absolute or a relative sense (Johansson, Isaksson and Sjöberg 1996; Eriksson 1998). In the case of absolute attitudes, work is studied without relating it to anything else; relative attitudes to work are regarded in relation to other important aspects of life, such as family, friends and leisure activities. We combine these two dimensions, type of object of the attitude and absolute and relative attitude, when analyzing attitudes to work.

With this wider perspective on attitudes to work, we also need to test some other factors previously known for their influence. The difference between women and men is a factor with such a general power that it must be included. However, there is no consensus regarding the results; some findings (e.g., Johansson 1991) show that women express a more non-work oriented attitude, while other studies (e.g., Ellingsæter 1995; Eriksson 1998; Hult and Svallfors 2002; Svallfors, Halvorsen and Andersen 2001) indicate that men have a more non-work oriented attitude than women. There are also some empirical doubts that gender has any strong impact at all on attitudes to work (Gallie et al. 1998; Marsden, Kalleberg and Cook 1993; Tolbert and Mohen 1998).

Attitudes to work can also be expected to vary between age groups, especially regarding the young compared to older groups, since they are often found at entry-level jobs in the labour market (Hult and Svallfors 2002). According to Johansson, Isaksson and Sjöberg (1996) young people deviate more from the general pattern than do other groups by reporting that the salary is their main reason for working; they feel less attached to their workplace and less loyal to their employers. In contrast to this, other studies have found that the youngest are more committed than those aged

25 to 34 (Esser 2005) or that the differences between age groups are very small (Svallfors, Halvorsen and Andersen 2001).

As class positions generally tend to have an effect on attitudes (Wright 1997: ch. 14; Johansson 1991), class is another factor that can be expected to correlate with attitudes to work. For 'class' we use the Socio-Economic Classification, which is rather common in Sweden. A first classification is between employees and self-employed, but that does not concern us here, as the present study is limited to employees. Employees are first divided into white- and blue-collar workers, and then according to the qualifications of the work tasks. Among employees we find the following categories: unskilled blue-collar workers, skilled blue-collar workers, lower white-collar workers, intermediate white-collar workers, and higher white-collar workers. It is important to note that this is a classification of positions, not of individuals; individuals in an 'unskilled' position can be very skilled. Earlier research is unequivocal when it comes to the relation between class and attitudes to work: blue-collar workers tend to be less committed to work than white-collar workers (e.g., von Otter 1978; Eriksson 1998; Svallfors, Halvorsen and Andersen 2001).

As mentioned earlier, relative attitudes to work are regarded in relation to other significant aspects of life, such as family, friends and leisure activities. Much attention, both in the popular and academic press, has recently been given to work-life balance—individuals' ability to successfully pursue their work and non-work lives without undue pressures from one undermining a satisfactory experience of the other (Warhurst, Eikhof and Haunschild 2008). What makes up a satisfactory balance varies from person to person, reflecting a wide range of circumstances and preferences: work-life balance can mean different things to different people, depending on their work and their non-work circumstances. Imbalance between these two spheres could, in principle, take two forms: pressures of work making it difficult to fulfill responsibilities in non-work spheres or non-work pressures making it difficult to carry out work obligations (Noon and Blyton 2007: 355–356).

When studying attitudes to work we must of course take into account variables associated with work itself. The experience of the work environment is one such variable. 'Work environment' is defined by using a model developed by Robert Karasek (1979; Karasek and Theorell 1990). It is built up by three dimensions: the demands that work makes on the worker, the control the worker has in and over work and the extent to which the worker gets social support from others. Each dimension can be attributed the values 'high' and 'low.' The correlation between work environment and attitudes to work seems rather evident: Good work environments tend to lead to committed views on work, while bad work environments tend to lead to instrumental views (Halvorsen 1997; Berglund 2001).

Based on these theoretical ideas we formulate the following research questions: What is the general attitude to work today in Sweden? Do sex, age, class position, the way people manage work-life balance and finally work environment have an influence on attitudes to work? As for the development of attitudes to work, are there any changes between 1994 and 2010?

MEASURES

In reference to the operationalisation of the main concepts included in our analysis we can start with the dependent variable—attitude to work (Table 8.1). About the absolute attitude to work in general, people were asked to consider the statement: 'Work is a dull necessity. If I didn't have to I would not work.' The absolute attitude to their own work was measured by a choice between two opposite statements. One was: 'This job is just like any other—one does one's job and the only thing that matters is the salary.' The other was: 'There is something special about this job. Apart from the salary it gives me a sense of personal satisfaction.' To answer the question about the absolute attitude to their own workplace, the respondents were asked whether they felt a sense of attachment to their workplace or not. With the relative attitudes, the respondents were asked to choose and rank the three most important factors in life from the following: being healthy, spending time with family and friends, having an interesting job, making money, pursuing meaningful leisure activities, having a good place to live, being able to make an active contribution to society and being able to enjoy good food and drink. To find out how people valued their own jobs in relation to life outside work, they were asked to answer this question: 'What do you value most—the time you spend at work, the time when you are not working, or do you value both equally?' The sixth field, the relative attitude to one's own workplace, was not examined.

Table 8.1   Operationalisations of Different Kinds of Attitudes to Work

	Work from a general perspective	*One's own work*	*One's own organization*
Absolute attitude	Is work a dull necessity that you would rather be without?	Do you only work for money or because there is something special about your work?	Do you feel a sense of attachment to your workplace?
Relative attitude	Is an interesting work one of the most important factors in life?	What do you value most—working hours or non-working hours?	

As mentioned before, our measure of 'class' is constructed in accordance with the Social-Economic Classification. Regarding work-life balance, the respondents answered the question: 'How do you manage combining work and life outside work?' and the answering alternatives were very good, rather good, rather bad and very bad.

In the operationalisations of the dimensions included in the work environment, those for whom there is not enough time to perform the work tasks, those who suffer physical symptoms or those with repetitious work have high demands; others have low demands. Work with a high level of control is characterized by making personal development possible; the worker can use his or her own ideas, knowledge and skill (skill discretion) and decide how the work tasks are to be performed (decision authority). Otherwise the workers' control is low. Appreciation and feedback from colleagues and management and concrete cooperation in work mean a high level of social support; if not, social support is low. Thus, to be located in the category of high work demands, it is enough to satisfy one of the demand criteria, while several requirements need to be fulfilled in order to be placed in the categories of high self control and high social support.

RESULTS

With the distinction between absolute and relative attitudes in mind, let us start the presentation of the results by looking empirically at the absolute attitudes to work in Sweden 2010. In Table 8.2, we find that 85 percent, a significant majority of the responding employees, would work even if they did not have to. In other words, they express a committed absolute attitude to work in general. Several studies have been carried out in which people were asked whether they would continue working even if they received a large sum of money (e.g., Gallie and White 1993; Halvorsen 1997; Harpaz 2002). The results show that only a minority would stop working. A criticism of these studies is that they are based on a hypothetical question. In recent years, however, it has been examined how people actually act when they win large sums of money, and the results confirm that most people continue to work as before (Hedenus 2011). Our result is in this respect in line with these studies.

When it comes to the employees' own work in an absolute perspective, 76 percent do their job also for other reasons than the salary. Here too, the committed attitude is strong. Finally, 67 percent feel attached to their workplaces. In sum, the results show that large majorities of more than two thirds up to 85 percent of Swedish employees show committed attitudes to work in terms of an absolute perspective on their workplace, their jobs and work in general.

We turn now to the relative attitudes, whereby we find a different pattern, although it is quite as distinct as in the case of absolute attitudes. As

Table 8.2   Attitudes to Work, 1994 and 2010. Percent

	1994	2010	diff. 1994–2010
Absolute perspective			
Work is a dull necessity. If I didn't have to work I would not.			
Agree	9	15	6
Do not agree	91	85	-6
This job is just like any other—one does one's job only for the salary.			
Agree	23	24	1
Do not agree	77	76	-1
I feel attached to my workplace.			
Agree	69	67	-2
Do not agree	31	33	2
Relative perspective			
An interesting work is one of the most important factors in life.			
Agree	46	36	-10
Do not agree	54	64	10
What do you value most?			
The time spent at work	8	4	-4
The time spent not working	43	52	9
Both equally	49	44	-5

far as the attitude to work in general, two thirds do not agree that work is one of the most important factors in life, which means that they report a non-committed work attitude. Furthermore, a bit more than half of the answering employees say that the time they value most is when they are not working; more than 40 percent value work and non-work equally, while only 4 percent rank work at the top. The relative attitude to work, that is when work is compared to other times or other activities, is clearly dominated by non-committed perspectives.

We now come to the change in attitudes to work in Sweden during the period 1994 to 2010 (the percentage differences in Table 8.2). In all cases there is an unequivocal, although sometimes rather small, development in favour of a non-committed attitude. In the absolute sense, the growth is 6 percentage points when it comes to work as such; 9 percent in 1994 and 15 percent in 2010 say that they would not work if they did not have to. The change concerning the employee's own job and workplace is more modest, 1 and 2 percentage points, respectively. The biggest changes can be found, however, concerning the relative attitudes. When it comes to the general relative attitude to work, measured by the statement 'An interesting work is one of the most important factors in life', the non-committed attitude (stated by those who did not agree) expanded with 10 percentage points. The relative attitude to one's own work had a similar development, in which putting a higher value on time spent outside work than on working—showing a non-committed attitude—grew with 9 percentage points. In conclusion, the non-committed attitude to work has expanded in Sweden when we consider the way of looking at work in a relative sense.

Our first research question concerns the empirical pattern of attitudes today (2010) among Swedish employees. This pattern is a very clear duality of work orientations: The absolute perspective is dominated by committed attitudes, while the relative perspective is dominated by non-committed attitudes. Second, the pattern of change in attitudes is quite unambiguous: A non-committed attitude is held by growing proportions of Swedish employees in the absolute sense as well as in the relative sense.

Let us go on to factors influencing attitudes to work—factors related to sex, age, class and work life balance, together with such organizational characteristics as the work environment. The results are presented in Table 8.3 in which the outcome of each variable can be seen. We limit, however, the presentation to the non-committed attitude since this is the expanding one; the empirical pattern of the committed attitude is, of course, the mirror image thereof. The absolute non-committed attitude concerns, then, employees who work only for the salary; the relative non-committed attitude concerns those who value the time off work more than working hours. The argument for choosing these variables is that they are focusing on the employee's own work and are therefore the most concrete ones for those who answered the questions about them.

Let us first look at the factors and the absolute and relative non-committed attitudes, respectively, in 2010. There is a difference between the sexes, implying that it is more common among men than women to have a non-committed attitude to work. This is in line with Ellingsæter's (1995) and Eriksson's (1998) results. One explanation for this could be that women work more with people in health care and education, while men work more with objects. Also Furåker (chapter 5, this volume) found that the female non-financial employment commitment is high. The differences between men and women are, however, small, but they exist in both the absolute and the relative perspective. In the latter sense there is a similarity to the age pattern, showing the same tendencies in both perspectives: The higher the age group, the smaller the proportion holding a non-committed attitude. At the same time the proportions are about doubled in the relative sense compared to the absolute one.

Class appears to be one of the most important variables when it comes to explaining attitudes to work and our data verifies earlier results (e.g., von Otter 1978; Eriksson 1998; Svallfors, Halvorsen and Andersen 2001), concluding that there are large differences between classes; the higher up

Table 8.3   Proportion of Employees with a Non-committed Attitude to Work by Sex, Age, Class, Work Life Balance and Different Aspects of Work Environment, 1994 and 2010. Percent

	Absolute non-committed attitude			Relative non-committed attitude		
	1994	2010	diff. 1994–2010	1994	2010	diff. 1994–2010
Sex						
Man	26	26	0	49	53	-4
Woman	19	20	1	39	50	11
Age						
16–30	34	31	-3	59	69	10
31–50	21	25	4	43	55	12
51–65	18	21	3	32	46	14
Class						
Unskilled blue-collar workers	35	45	10	47	58	11
Skilled blue-collar workers	29	31	2	52	57	5
Lower white-collar workers	27	30	3	42	53	11
Middle white-collar workers	12	16	4	40	52	12
Higher white-collar workers	6	12	6	30	45	15
Work-life balance						
Good	22	22	0	42	51	9
Bad	29	35	6	53	64	11
Work demands						
High	24	26	2	44	53	9
Low	16	11	-5	43	45	2
Self-control						
High	7	8	1	37	43	6
Low	34	40	6	49	62	13
Social support						
High	18	17	-1	39	49	10
Low	32	42	10	53	61	8

in the class hierarchy, the greater proportion of people with a committed attitude, and the lower down in the class hierarchy, the greater proportion of people with a non-committed attitude.

Among employees who have problems balancing work and life outside work, there are bigger proportions that hold non-committed attitudes to work—which is in line with what could be expected. The work environment variables also follow the predicted pattern, showing that bad conditions lead to larger proportions of employees holding non-committed attitudes. Work environment also has a great influence on the attitudes. The aspect of self-control seems to be of particular relevance. A comparison between those with high self-control and those with low self-control shows that the absolute non-committed attitude may be observed among 8 percent of the former and 40 percent of the latter. This is the largest difference that can be found in Table 8.3. A similar pattern exists concerning the relative non-committed attitude. Furthermore, social support functions in an analogous way: High support paves the way for a committed attitude to work and low support for a non-committed one.

The factors influencing attitudes to work seem on the whole to follow the expected pattern. The proportions vary between the absolute and the relative attitudes as the former are not as widespread as the latter, but they follow the same pattern. Let us therewith go to the changes between 1994 and 2010. The overarching picture is that the non-committed attitude to work is growing. There is, however, a smaller growth in the absolute than in the relative attitudes. In the first perspective there are even a few cases of no difference at all between those two years (men, aged 16–30, good work-life balance) and expansion of committed attitudes (low work demands, high social support in work). The non-committed attitude is not as common and it does not expand as easily in the absolute sense. It is when work is compared to other spheres of life that the non-committed attitude not only is more frequent, but also expands more at the expense of the committed one.

In reference to the different factors, we find that there has hardly been any change at all between women and men concerning the absolute non-committed attitude; its relative counterpart has, however, expanded among both sexes, but more among women than men. As for age, we find that it is only the absolute non-committed attitude in the youngest cohort that has not grown; especially the relative attitude has expanded, the more so the older the group.

Table 8.3 also illustrates that the proportion of employees working just for the salary has increased in all classes and most among the unskilled blue-collar workers. The attitude of valuing non-work more than work has also expanded all over the class schema, but most among the higher white collar workers. What is not shown in the table is that there have been major changes in class structure since 1994. This is evident in our material by a decrease of the proportion of blue-collar workers and lower white-collar workers from overall 62 to 44 percent, while the proportion of middle and higher white-collar workers has increased from 38 to 56 percent in total. This development indicates that the changes in attitude to work between the two years would be much more apparent if the class variable were held constant; parts of the changes toward a more non-committed attitude are thus hidden by the fact that the class structure has changed.

When it comes to work-life balance, there is no change in the absolute non-committed attitude to work among those who succeed in keeping such a balance, but this attitude is growing among those who are not doing as well in this regard. The relative non-committed attitude has, however, expanded in both those groups.

Finally, we come to the work environment variables. In the absolute perspective, two instances of the non-committed attitude are diminishing; in other words, the committed attitude has expanded. The first one is among employees with low demands in work, the second among those who enjoy high social support. In Karasek's model low work demands is a negative trait, which might contribute to an explanation of this pattern, while high social support from workmates and managers could contribute to an absolute committed attitude. There is also a considerable growth of the non-committed attitude among those who experience low social support. The relative non-committed attitude has expanded in all instances of the work environment, especially among employees with low control in work and with high support.

Up to now we have analysed the connection between attitudes to work and separate variables. A supplementary question is whether the connections remain when all variables are analysed together. This is done through logistic regression analyses and the results are presented in Table 8.4. The results show that most of the correlations found in the bivariate analyses presented in Table 8.3 persist. In the absolute non-committed attitude, exceptions are the age group 31–50, middle white-collar workers and work demands. However, sex, other age groups 1994 and age as such 2010, class in 1994 and other classes than middle white-collar workers in 2010, work-life balance as well as the work environment aspects self-control and social support are related to the absolute non-committed attitude to work.

In reference to the relative non-committed attitude, we find that sex is not significant in 2010, and perhaps equally surprising is that neither is class. At the present phase of the investigation we can only state this result, not explain it. Furthermore, work demands show the same pattern as in the case of the absolute perspective, namely that it is not statistically significant. This is less surprising as both high and low demands can be both good and bad in Karasek's model, depending on with which other aspects of the work environment it is combined. The relative non-committed attitude is correlated with sex 1994 but not 2010, age, class 1994 but not 2010, work-life balance both years, control and social support at work both years.

Finally, Model 2 in Table 8.4 shows that the change in the absolute non-committed attitude as well as in the relative non-committed attitude is statistically significant.

Table 8.4   Factors Impacting on Having a Non-committed Attitude to Work, 1994 and 2010. Logistic Regression. Odds Ratios

	Absolute non-committed attitude			Relative non-committed attitude		
	Model 1		Model 2	Model 1		Model 2
	1994	*2010*	*1994 and 2010*	*1994*	*2010*	*1994 and 2010*
Sex						
Man	2.04***	1.60**	1.83**	1.59***	1.23	1.41***
Woman (ref.)	1.00	1.00	1.00	1.00	1.00	1.00
Age						
16–30	2.22***	2.01*	2.28***	3.24***	2.75***	3.02***
31–50	1.31	1.53**	1.42**	1.79***	1.52***	1.64***
51–65 (ref.)	1.00	1.00	1.00	1.00	1.00	1.00
Class						
Unskilled blue-collar workers	4.96***	3.22***	3.54***	1.75**	1.29	1.45***
Skilled blue-collar workers	4.18***	2.16**	2.76***	2.19***	1.33	1.71***
Lower white-collar workers	4.60***	2.75***	3.17***	1.64*	1.24	1.39*
Middle white-collar workers	2.09*	1.31	1.49*	1.63**	1.30	1.43**
Higher white-collar workers (ref.)	1.00	1.00	1.00	1.00	1.00	1.00
Work-life balance						
Good (ref.)	1.00	1.00	1.00	1.00	1.00	1.00
Bad	1.56*	1.56*	1.60**	1.50*	1.58*	1.55*
Work demands						
High	1.20	1.70	1.30	0.93	1.06	0.97
Low (ref.)	1.00	1.00	1.00	1.00	1.00	1.00
Self-control						
High (ref.)	1.00	1.00	1.00	1.00	1.00	1.00
Low	5.11***	5.57***	5.41***	1.58***	1.97***	1.75***
Social support						
High (ref.)	1.00	1.00	1.00	1.00	1.00	1.00
Low	1.79***	2.92***	2.20***	1.66***	1.46**	1.57***
Year						
1994 (ref.)			1.00			1.00
2010			1.67***			1.89***
R^2 (Nagelkerke)	0.26	0.31	0.28	0.11	0.09	0.11
n	1,817	1,408	3,225	1,834	1,402	3,236

*** $p<0.001$; ** $p<0.01$; * $p<0.05$.

CONCLUSIONS

The empirical results of our study show that work is a central feature in most people's lives and that work gives them personal satisfaction in addition to the salary. In absolute terms the committed attitude is dominating. In relative terms, however, the non-committed attitude is the most comprehensive. Regardless of the perspective, the tendency is quite clear: the non-committed attitude is increasing. It is especially prevalent among blue-collar workers, those who have difficulties combining work and life outside work, those whose work environment is characterized by low self-control and low social support.

The increase is not a dramatic one, but there is a clear tendency for this over the past 16 years. One explanation to this development is probably the insecurity of the labour market. Since 1994 we have experienced worldwide financial crises at two different time periods (see also Bjarnason, Chapter 10, this volume). The unemployment rate in Sweden has grown several percentage points since the 1980s and especially young people have difficulties finding an entry to the labour market. Also the fact that the sense of attachment and solidarity to one's workplace has decreased supports this interpretation. If you are prepared to leave your job for a better one, you do not really need to get attached to the workplace or the employer you have for the moment. To escape unemployment you may have to keep an unappealing and/or low-paid job (Burchell 1993). It is also reasonable to consider the effect of temporary agency work on our attitudes to work that Håkansson and Isidorsson discuss (Chapter 11, this volume), even though this kind of work constitutes only a minor part of the labour market.

So what does the increase of non-committed attitude imply? An increase of 'bad jobs'? Not unexpectedly, in looking at work itself, our results show that work environment has great influence on people's attitudes. The employees' self-control—their autonomy and the level of qualification of their work tasks—and the social support they receive from their employers and workmates, play an important role. According to our results a lack of self-control and social support has a significant effect on the attitude to work toward a non-committed direction.

In sum, the answers to our research questions are as follows: The general attitude to work in Sweden today (2010) differs depending on whether it is regarded in an absolute or a relative sense. When work is looked at in itself, the committed attitude dominates strongly, but when it is compared to other spheres of life the non-committed dominates almost as powerfully. There are a number of significant differences between groups of employees. Men are more non-committed to work than women, younger than older, employees lower down in the class hierarchy than those in higher positions, those who do not succeed in balancing work and the rest of life and those with a bad work environment more than employees who enjoy a good environment. In the relative sense, that is, when work is compared to other parts of life, the picture is similar in many ways, but there are two important exceptions: neither sex nor class differences are statistically significant. Finally, the changes we find between 1994 and 2010 indicate a clear trend toward growing instrumental and non-committed work orientations. When it comes to the absolute attitude the increase is only 1 percentage point, but it is statistically significant. It is also interesting in that it is part of a trend, witnessed by the much more evident growth of the relative non-work orientation.

9 Employee Satisfaction, Exchange Paradigms and Community versus Autonomy in Employment Relations

Dan Jonsson

The term satisfaction has its roots in the Latin word *satisfacere*, which literally means to *do (facere) enough (satis)*; to satisfy came to mean basically to do enough to meet a need or demand. Two meanings of 'satisfaction' given by the *American Heritage Dictionary* are 'the fulfilment or gratification of a desire, need, or appetite' and 'pleasure or contentment derived from such gratification.' In other words, satisfaction (or frustration) presupposes human aspirations which are satisfied (or not satisfied), so any theory of satisfaction must be explicitly or implicitly connected to theories about individual motivation and social values.

This chapter deals with employee satisfaction. By that we mean satisfaction that employees receive in connection with their work and employment. Somewhat more specifically, employee satisfaction is seen as satisfaction with elements and aspects of an employee's work and work contexts. The term job satisfaction is generally used in a similar sense.

It is obviously possible to distinguish many different subtypes of employee satisfaction, corresponding to different elements and aspects of employees' work and work contexts. Terms such as 'job satisfaction' or 'work satisfaction' sometimes refer to satisfaction with the *work itself*, independent of work contexts. The border between 'work' and 'work contexts' is, unfortunately, rather fuzzy, but nevertheless it makes sense to make an analytical distinction between satisfaction with the work itself and satisfaction with the physical, interpersonal and organizational environment within which the work is performed—what one could call the *workplace*. One additional type of employee satisfaction of interest here concerns the *employer and the employment relation*. This could be related to aspects such as wage policy, employment security and management styles. Accordingly, we shall consider three broad types of employee satisfaction in this chapter: namely, satisfaction with 'the work', 'the workplace' and 'the employer'.

Much research has been devoted to the determinants of employee satisfaction (or job satisfaction). Since satisfaction depends on both individual motivation and common values, explanations of employee satisfaction should ideally take individual differences and differences between jobs simultaneously into account (Kalleberg 1977). In practice, however, research contributions have tended to focus on variation in either individual characteristics (e.g., Judge and Larsen 2001; Strümper and de Bruin 2009) or job characteristics (e.g. Herzberg 1966; Hackman and Oldman 1980; Karasek and Theorell 1990).

This chapter, like the studies just mentioned, presents data and theory relating to determinants of employee satisfaction, but the present contribution has a broader scope than either one of the two traditions just delineated. In the present approach, certain fundamental aspects of employment relations are seen as shaping work and work contexts, and while job characteristics are recognised as proximate causes of employee satisfaction, the basic nature of the exchange relation between employer and employee is seen as an ulterior cause. Thus, empirical research concerning employee satisfaction will be reported here, but, equally important, the results presented will be linked to a new theoretical framework, centred on the notion of different *exchange paradigms in employment relations.*

EMPLOYMENT RELATIONS AS EXCHANGE RELATIONS

For Nisbet (1993: 47), '[t]he most fundamental and far-reaching of sociology's unit-ideas is *community*' (italics added). In the history of sociological thought, the notion of community is most closely associated with Tönnies (1887), who contrasted *Gemeinschaft* and *Gesellschaft*—the former regulated by common mores and marked by a 'unity of will', the latter maintained through individuals acting in their own self-interest. Tönnies was not alone in drawing attention to this contrast, however. For example, Durkheim (1964) introduced a similar dichotomy between 'mechanical' and 'organic' solidarity, and in terms of Parson's (1951) 'pattern variables', social relations which are characterised by ascription orientation, diffuseness, particularism, affectivity and collective orientation are contrasted with relations which are characterised by achievement orientation, specificity, universalism, instrumentalism and self-orientation.

For the purpose of the analysis in this chapter, employment relations are regarded as exchange relations, where work is directly or indirectly exchanged for money and other rewards. In other words, employment relations will be analysed as exchange relations. One possible interpretation of the *Gemeinschaft-Gesellschaft* dichotomy is that it concerns the prevalence of exchange relations in a social group. That is, *Gesellschaft*-type social groups are dominated by exchange relations (cf. Asplund 1991), while *Gemeinschaft*-type social groups are dominated by more intimate social relations, not exchange relations. It is also possible, however, to relate the *Gemeinschaft-Gesellschaft* dichotomy to differences between *different*

Table 9.1   Specific versus Generalised Exchange Relations

	Specific exchange relation	*Generalised exchange relation*
Scope	Narrow	Broad
Directness	Direct	Indirect
Duration	Non-permanent relation	Long-term relation
Orientation	Achievement orientation, instrumentalism, self-orientation, weak trust, weak sense of obligation	Ascription orientation, affectivity, collective orientation, strong trust, strong sense of obligation

kinds of exchange relations rather than differences between exchange relations and other social relations. Social relations that differ from narrow economic exchange relations can nevertheless be seen as 'generalised exchange relations.' In this vein, Blau (1967: 93), drawing on Malinowski's (1922) and Mauss's (1923–1924) analysis of 'primitive', *Gemeinschaft*-type societies, argues:

> Social exchange differs in important ways from strictly economic exchange. The basic and most crucial distinction is that social exchange entails *unspecified* obligations. The prototype of an economic transaction rests on a formal contract which specifies the exact quantities to be exchanged. . . . Social exchange, in contrast, involves the principle that one person does another a favour, and while there is a general expectation of some future return, its exact nature is definitely *not* specified in advance (italics in original).

While I prefer to speak about 'generalised' versus 'specific' exchange relations rather than using the somewhat vague expression 'social exchange', a distinction similar to Blau's is used in the analysis below. Somewhat schematically, generalised and specific exchange relations differ in four respects, as summarised in Table 9.1.

A TYPOLOGY OF EXCHANGE PARADIGMS
IN EMPLOYMENT RELATIONS

While it provides a useful perspective, the contrast between specific and generalised exchange relations cannot be directly translated into a classification of employment relations regarded as exchange relations. In fact, specific and generalised exchange should not be seen as the components of a dichotomy, but as theoretical ideal types at opposite ends of a continuum. Below, I will present three, rather than two, exchange paradigms that may characterise employment relations and employees.

Work-Time Sellers and the Struggle over Time

Generally speaking, conventional employment relations regarded as exchange relations occupy an intermediate position between generalised and specific exchange relations. Exchange relations between a company and its employees bear some similarity to specific exchange relations between a company and its suppliers, but there are also significant differences between these two types of exchange relations. A company does not usually buy specific services from its employees in the same manner that it buys specific services from suppliers. It is more accurate to say that a company buys some of its employees' *time*, and only indirectly buys services—that is, work—performed by employees during this time—the working time. This kind of exchange may be called *time-for-pay* exchange; the corresponding types of employment relations and employees will be referred to as *time-based employment relations* and *work-time sellers*.

The fact that in a conventional time-based employment relation the employer buys services from employees not directly but indirectly by buying their working time justifies the employer's exercise of authority over employees. Since the employer pays for the employee's time, the employer needs to ensure that this time is used efficiently to create something of economic value for the employer. From the point of view of the employee's self-interest, on the other hand, no incentive exists to work either harder or smarter in order to maximise the economic benefit reaped from the employee's work by the employer. In employment relations based on time-for-pay exchange, employers and employees thus tend to be engaged in a 'struggle over time'; there is a built-in conflict of interests about how the working time should be used.

Given the struggle over time between employers and employees, employers have an incentive to supervise and regulate the employees' work. This is facilitated by a Taylorisitic work organization, with standardised, fragmented, repetitive work, where work tasks are pre-designed by the employer. However, such a system impoverishes work and can be used not only as a tool to guarantee that the employer receives his due, but also as a tool for exploitation of employees. It is thus highly likely to create collective resentment and 'passive resistance' from employees (cf. Lysgaard 1967). This, in turn, may motivate increased efforts by employers to design, supervise and regulate the work process, leading to a further deterioration of the employment relation.

It is thus argued that time-based employment relations contain a potential for escalating conflicts between employers and employees. At best, this may lead to an uneasy compromise; at worst, it could lead to a situation where the employees have been subjugated, where the employers dictate the work conditions and where employees are treated as machines, which means not only that employees suffer but also that employers fail to benefit from harnessing the employees' intellectual, creative capabilities.

Trusted Employees

It may be objected to the analysis above of time-based employment relations that the conception of employees' self-interest used is too narrow. It can be argued that employees tend to have some sense of obligation to reciprocate the pay received, so that employers need not supervise and regulate their work closely and the vicious circle sketched above need not start. That employees can have such motives is obvious, but in this case we are no longer dealing with a pure time-for-pay exchange, but with a more generalised, *Gemeinschaft*-type exchange relation.

In relations of this kind, individuals contribute loyalty to an organization or a social group and receive attention to their needs in return. As a consequence of the individual's loyalty to the organization, he or she will spend time to support it; the organization, on the other hand, will give money or provide other rewards as a consequence of its attention to the individual's needs. A specific period of time contributed by the individual is not necessarily coupled to a specific reward from the organization, however, so time is exchanged for money or other rewards only indirectly.

In general, we may distinguish a type of employment relationship where the employee is not motivated by narrow self-interest. When the employee wants to 'do his best'—because of loyalty to the employer, loyalty to co-workers, loyalty to customers, dedication to the work or some other 'intrinsic' reason—and employers take advantage of this sense of responsibility by giving employees greater autonomy, an exchange paradigm somewhat different from the time-for-pay exchange paradigm exists. It may be said that the employee provides commitment to the employer's economic goals and receives trust from the employer in return; conversely, the employer gives commitment to the employee's well-being and receives trust from the employee in return. We may speak about *commitment-for-trust* exchange, *trust-based employment relations* and *trusted employees*.

Employed Suppliers

Although the terminology may be new, work-time sellers and trusted employees are old acquaintances in working life research. For example, the distinction between the time-for-pay and commitment-for-trust exchange paradigms is quite similar to the labour contract versus service contract dichotomy suggested by Erikson and Goldthorpe (1993: 41–42):

Employment relationships regulated by a labour contract entail a relatively short-term and specific exchange of money for effort. Employees supply more-or-less discrete amounts of labour, *under the supervision of the employer or the employer's agents* in return for wages which are calculated *on a 'piece' or 'time' basis*. In contrast, employment relationships within a bureaucratic context involve a longer-term and generally more diffuse exchange. Employees render service to their employing organisation in return for 'compensation', which takes the form not only of reward for work done, through a salary and various perquisites, but also comprises important prospective elements—for example, salary increments on an established scale, assurances of security both in employment and through pensions rights, and, above all, well-defined career opportunities (italics added).

A close reading of this quotation suggests, however, that an additional distinction can be made, roughly corresponding to the difference between wages calculated on a 'piece' basis versus a 'time' basis. The fact that employees are not trusted employees does not imply that their *work process* necessarily has to be subjected to 'the supervision of the employer or the employer's agents.' It is also possible that there is a direct exchange of services from employees for payment from employers, where employees are paid for the services performed during their working time rather than for their working time per se, using some kind of payment-by-result wage system. In this kind of exchange relation, the employee's self-interest dictates that he or she should use the working time efficiently in order to maximise the monetary reward received. Conversely, there is no need for the employer to supervise and regulate the work process, though monitoring of the *work output* is of course required, since pay is based on performance. Thus, such relations differ from time-for-pay relations in a way which allows the struggle over time between employer and employee to be mitigated.

Furthermore, in trust-based employment relations the employer has to trust the employee to choose the best way to perform the work and exert reasonable effort in his work, but in the third kind of exchange relations trust is not as necessary, since employees' work performance can be monitored directly and linked to remuneration. Moreover, in this alternative type of exchange relation, work performance is more important both for the employer and for the employee than commitment to the work or the work organization. The exchange paradigm sketched here thus differs from both time-for-pay exchange and commitment-for-trust exchange. We may speak about *performance-for-pay* exchange, *performance-based employment relations* and *employed suppliers*.

Prerequisites of Employment Relations
According to Exchange Paradigm

It should be noted that different kinds of employment relations have different prerequisites. For example, it is easier to create commitment to work, workplace and employer if the work is attractive and interesting than if it is not. Employment relations of professionals are thus frequently trust-based.

Performance-based employment relations also have specific prerequisites. For example, it is not possible to pay an employee according to performance unless there is some way of defining, isolating, observing and quantifying that employee's performance. In addition, the performance measured must depend mainly on the employee's own work. For example, if the employee's output is determined by the pace of a machine, or the work-pace of co-workers, a performance-based pay such as a piece-rate based on the number of units produced does not make sense. As an illustration, an operator at a paced assembly line cannot produce more products than brought to him or her by that assembly line and cannot (except temporarily, while filling up buffers) assemble more products than other operators at the same assembly line.

The assembly-line example also illustrates the fact that while the nature of the work process helps to shape the exchange paradigm, the work process is in turn shaped by other conditions, some of which can be changed at will. While the production task—to assemble a particular product—may be pre-determined, the work organization or production system is not strictly determined by the production task. For example, there are equally efficient alternatives to manual assembly lines where operators can work independently of each other (Engström 1983; Engström, Jonsson and Medbo 1996), creating one prerequisite for a performance-based exchange paradigm.

Conclusions about Exchange Paradigms

The discussion of exchange paradigms in this section is summarized in Table 9.2, which is based on but much more elaborated than Table 9.1.

At this point, a new theoretical problem needs to be addressed. The performance-for-pay and commitment-for-trust paradigms have been conceived as opposite ideal types with regard to the theoretical dimension summarised in Table 9.1. Yet, they are, as discussed below, quite similar in certain respects—*les extrêmes se touchent*. This apparent inconsistency derives from the fact that the two tables are structured so as to reflect the *community* dimension of employment relations, while the work-related *autonomy* of the employee, with regard to which employed suppliers and trusted employees are in a similar situation, is not emphasised. Therefore, it is useful to bear in mind the very simple model in Figure 9.1 which relates the three exchange paradigms to the two dimensions just mentioned.

Table 9.2 Typology of Exchange Paradigms

Exchange paradigm	Performance-for-pay	Time-for-pay	Commitment-for-trust
Employee status	Employed supplier	Work-time seller	Trusted employee
Type of employment relationship	Performance-based	Time-based	Trust-based
What the employee sells to the employer	Services	Time	'Oneself'
Relation between employees' and employers' interests	Complementary interests	Contrary interests	Aligned interests
Employees' sense of responsibility for the company	Low	Low	High
Employers' sense of responsibility for the employees	Low	Low	High
Attractive, interesting work	Not required	Not required	Required
The employee is motivated to use the working time efficiently	Yes	No	Yes
The employee is given responsibility for using the working time efficiently	Yes	No	Yes
Pay	According to performance	According to work role (job designation)	According to qualifications
Job security	Possibly precarious	Not necessarily high	Generally high
Pre-defined, observable, quantifiable work output	Yes	Not required	No
Autonomy regarding work goals	Low or nonexistent	Low or nonexistent	Some
Autonomy regarding work methods	High	Low	High
Autonomy regarding work scheduling	Moderate	Low	Moderate

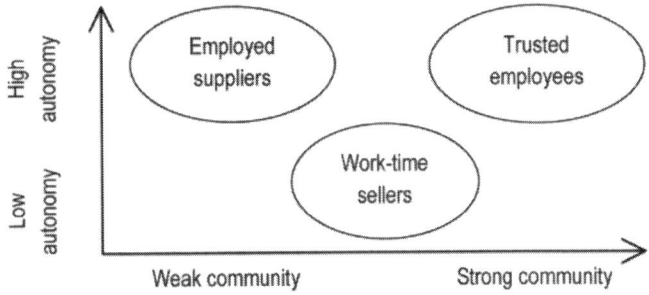

Figure 9.1   Three exchange paradigms in relation to community and autonomy.

EXCHANGE PARADIGM AND EMPLOYEE SATISFACTION

What can be predicted about employee satisfaction among employed suppliers, work-time sellers and trusted employees? Generally speaking, it is to be expected that strong-community employment relationships will be characterised by higher employment satisfaction than weak-community employment relationships. *Gemeinschaft*-type relations built on community are usually associated with more positive attitudes than are looser relationships, and this should be true of relations between employees and employers (or employing organizations) as well. This is consistent with classical sociology's interpretation of community, and also with more recent theories about social relations in general and exchange relations in particular, as summarised in Table 9.1. The positive correlations generally obtained between, on the one hand, attitudinal variables such as job satisfaction and, on the other hand, variables more related to the organizational integration of employees, such as organizational commitment and organizational citizenship behaviour (Bjarnason 2009), also suggest that employee satisfaction is associated with what Nisbet refers to as community.

As made explicit by Figure 9.1, however, the three employment paradigms differ not only with regard to the community dimension but also with regard to the autonomy dimension, and there are reasons to believe that employee satisfaction is influenced also by autonomy. First, there is reason to believe that autonomy per se is rewarding, and therefore conducive to positive attitudes (Jonsson 1980); this supports the notion that autonomy in work tends to produce high employee satisfaction. As discussed above, low autonomy is also a characteristic feature of time-based employment relations, and in this type of employment relations there is a basic conflict of interests between employees and employers. The latent hostility and distrust between employees and employers described by Lysgaard (1967) will of course hurt employees' attitudes toward employers and this would tend to negatively affect employee satisfaction in general. Furthermore, the Tayloristic work organization that tends to characterise low-autonomy, time-based employment relations is certainly conducive to poor employee satisfaction. Specifically, traits of Tayloristic work organization such as close monitoring of employees, unskilled, repetitive work, exchangeability and little opportunity for competence development, can be expected, based on both theoretical arguments and empirical research, to lead to poor employee satisfaction.

Taking into account the expected effects of community, autonomy and the conflict potential of the time-for-money exchange paradigm, it is natural to propose the following three hypotheses regarding employee satisfaction:

Hypothesis 1: Employee satisfaction is higher among trusted employees than among work-time sellers because of stronger community, higher autonomy and an exchange paradigm with less conflict potential.

Hypothesis 2: Employee satisfaction is higher among trusted employees than among employed suppliers because of stronger community.

Hypothesis 3: Employee satisfaction is higher among employed suppliers than among work-time sellers, despite weaker community, because of higher autonomy and an exchange paradigm with less conflict potential.

DATA AND VARIABLES

The data reported in this chapter were collected by Statistics Sweden in 2002. Postal questionnaires were distributed to 3,000 respondents, making up a representative sample of subjects aged 25–64 in the agency's Employment Register. Questionnaires were returned from 1,936 subjects, corresponding to a response rate of 64.5 percent. Since the Employment Register was known to be not entirely reliable and up-to-date, a screening question was included in the questionnaire to be able to exclude respondents who did in fact not currently have an employment. 316 respondents indicated that they were not currently employed, so 1,620 respondents were included in the data set analysed.

Operationalisation of Exchange Paradigm

The first, crucial step in the analysis of data is the operationalisation of the theoretical ideal types: work-time sellers, employed suppliers and trusted employees. According to the theoretical discussion above, employed suppliers and trusted employees, on the one hand, and work-time sellers, on the other hand, differ with respect to the degree of autonomy that they enjoy in their work. Four aspects of autonomy were measured by the following question:

To what extent do you decide by yourself about the following in your work?
- *What work tasks to perform*
- *How to perform your work tasks*
- *When to start and end your workday*
- *When to take a break from your work*

The four response options for these items ranged from 'I decide completely' to 'I don't decide at all.' There were strong to moderate correlations between the four autonomy items. A factor analysis produced a one-factor solution (alpha = 0.74) with factor loadings ranging from 0.73 to 0.77. An unweighted additive index of the four items mentioned was used. This index ranged from 0 (lowest autonomy) to 12 (highest autonomy); its mean value was 7.2. Somewhat arbitrarily, values from 0 to 6 were designated as 'low' autonomy, whereas values from 7 through 12 were designated as 'high' autonomy. Using this dichotomy, the three exchange paradigms were defined operationally in the following way:

(1) *Employed suppliers* are employees with high autonomy who agree 'completely' or 'partly' with the assertion 'It is in my own interest to use my working time efficiently, since my wage is based on my work performance'.

(2) *Work-time sellers* are employees with low autonomy who agree 'completely' or 'partly' with at least one of the assertions 'My employer checks that I am using my working time efficiently' and 'I have to use my working time efficiently to be able to keep up with the work pace.'

(3) *Trusted employees* are employees with high autonomy who (a) agree 'completely' or 'partly' with at least one of the assertions 'My work is stimulating and interesting' and 'My employer supports me' and (b) do *not* agree 'completely' or 'partly' with the assertion 'It is in my own interest to use my working time efficiently, since my wage is based on my work performance.'

About 85 percent of the respondents could be classified into one of these three categories. Among the respondents matching one of these ideal-types, 19.2 percent were classified as employed suppliers, 33.3 percent as work-time sellers and 47.5 percent as trusted employees.

Other Independent Variables

In addition to exchange paradigm, eight other variables are used as independent variables in the analyses reported below. Information about sex, age, sector of employment, level of education and income for each respondent was retrieved from other registers available to Statistics Sweden and added to the dataset. Two items in the questionnaire provided information about tenure at workplace and whether the respondent had been assigned supervisory tasks. Finally, occupation was coded manually, based on two open questions where the respondents were asked to name their occupation and describe their main work tasks. By this procedure, each respondent was assigned to a three-digit occupational group according to the Swedish SSYK occupational classification system.

Dependent Variables

As described in the beginning of the chapter, employee satisfaction is conceived as including three main components: satisfaction with the work itself, satisfaction with the workplace and satisfaction with the employment relation and the employer. The questionnaire contained the following question, with five response options ranging from 'completely satisfied' to 'completely dissatisfied':

> *Generally speaking, how satisfied are you with the following?*
> * *Your work*
> * *Your workplace*
> * *Your employer*

These items are admittedly not ideal measures of the underlying theoretical constructs. For example, 'your work' can be interpreted as meaning the work itself, but this phrase can perhaps also be given a broader interpretation, corresponding to overall job satisfaction. With this caveat, the three items can nevertheless be used as complementary measures of employee satisfaction.

EXCHANGE PARADIGM VERSUS OCCUPATION AND OTHER EMPLOYEE CHARACTERISTICS

So far, exchange paradigms have been described in fairly abstract terms. Considering also that 'employed suppliers', in particular, is not a widely used concept, it may be useful to relate exchange paradigms to specific occupations. Table 9.3 shows occupational groups with above-average shares of employees assigned to one of the three exchange paradigms.

It is evident from Table 9.3 that the exchange paradigm taxonomy does not replicate the usual occupational hierarchy. While trusted employees are mainly found among white-collar employees with upper-middle and middle level occupations, work-time sellers include not only the expected blue-collar workers and service workers but also some professionals and semi-professionals. Similarly, employed suppliers include blue-collar and white-collar employees on all levels of the occupational hierarchy, from helpers and cleaners to managers.

Table 9.3   Exchange Paradigms by Occupational Group. Relative Frequencies (%)

Employed suppliers (19%)	*Work-time sellers (33%)*	*Trusted employees (48%)*
(131) Managers of small enterprises (41%)	(222) Health professionals (53%)	(213) Computing professionals (71%)
(122) Production and operation managers (38%)	(233) Primary education teaching professionals (60%)	(231) Higher education teaching professionals (75%)
(123) Other specialist managers (53%)	(323) Nursing associate professionals (57%)	(241) Business professionals (68%)
(214) Architects, engineers and related professionals (44%)	(422) Client information clerks (72%)	(245) Writers and artists (82%)
(235) Consultants/ educators (39%)	(513) Personal care and related workers (51%)	(249) Psychologists, social work and related profes- sionals (78%)
(341) Finance and sales associate professionals (40%)	(522) Shop and stall salespersons and demonstrators (54%)	(311) Physical and engineering science technicians (63%)
(713) Electricians, plumbers and related trades workers (28%)	(712) Building frame and related trades workers (63%)	(343) Administrative asso- ciate professionals (72%)
(714) Painters and related trades workers (30%)	(723) Machinery mechanics and fitters (78%)	(346) Social work associate professionals (83%)
(912) Helpers and clean- ers (47%)	(828) Assemblers (71%)	(411) Office secretaries (67%)
	(832) Motor vehicle drivers (58%)	(512) Housekeeping and restaurant services workers (71%)

Note: The number identifying each occupational group is Statistics Sweden's three-digit SSYK code. N=1,378.

One concern regarding the data reported here is that different response rates for different kinds of employees could have distorted the results. To estimate the magnitude of such possible effects, a comparison was made with data from Statistics Sweden's Employment Register for 2002 (Statistics Sweden 2010). This Register contains data reported by employers about their employees' occupations and can be regarded as accurate for present purposes. A comparison of the respondents' occupations with data in the Register revealed that, as expected, response rates differed significantly between occupations. For example, 22.2 percent of the respondents were manual workers, compared to 27.7 percent in the Register. Multiplying the raw frequencies in each cell with a correction factor, in this case 27.7/22.2, relative frequencies corrected for response rate bias were obtained, as shown in Table 9.4.

Table 9.4   Exchange Paradigm by Occupational Group. Response-rate Corrected Relative Frequencies (%)

	Employed suppliers	Work-time sellers	Trusted employees	Total
Manual workers	4.9	12.5	10.4	27.7
Service workers	3.9	13.7	12.2	29.7
Semi-professionals	3.9	4.8	10.5	19.1
Professionals	3.9	3.9	10.0	17.8
Managers	2.4	0.2	2.9	5.5
Total	19.0	35.0	46.0	100.0

Note that the marginal frequencies for occupations are by design equal to those in the Employment Register, while all other frequencies in Table 9.4 are hypothetical, corrected frequencies. It is noteworthy that as 19.2 percent of the respondents were identified as employed suppliers, 33.3 percent as work-time sellers and 47.5 percent as trusted employees according to the uncorrected estimates, a comparison with Table 9.4 reveals that estimates of these proportions are reassuringly robust. Table 9.4 also has intrinsic interest by providing a quantitative as well as qualitative map of the Swedish labour force in 2002, underlining its heterogeneity.

Five occupational groups are distinguished: manual workers (SSYK 6–9), service workers (SSYK 4–5), semi-professionals (SSYK 3), professionals (SSYK 2) and managers (SSYK 1). Three levels of education are also distinguished: low (levels 1–3 in the classification earlier used by Statistics Sweden), middle (levels 4–5) and high (levels 6–7).

Frequency distributions for background variables in the entire sample and within subgroups of employees representing particular exchange paradigms were calculated. A representative *employed supplier* turned out to be a semi-professional (25%) or professional (26%) who is 50 years old or more (42%), works in the private sector (62%) and has supervisory work tasks (58%). He or she may have short or long tenure at the present workplace. A representative *work-time seller* is a female (63%) service worker (37%) without supervisory responsibilities (68%) who has worked between 5 and 20 years at her present workplace (43%). She may work in the private or public sector and may be young or old. A representative *trusted employee*, finally, is a semi-professional (28%) or professional (27%) who works in the private sector (56%) and has supervisory responsibilities (55%). She or he may have short or long tenure at the workplace and may be young or old.

The effects of background variables on exchange paradigm were studied by means of a regression analysis. As shown in Table 9.5, factors that make it more likely that an employee is a trusted employee tend to make

Table 9.5 Exchange Paradigm by Background Variables. Multi-linear Regression. Unstandardised Regression Coefficients

		Employed supplier	Work-time seller	Trusted employee
Sex	Male (ref.)			
	Female	-0.01	0.07*	-0.06
Age	25–34 (ref.)			
	35–49	0.03	-0.07*	0.04
	50–	0.07*	-0.11**	0.04
Level of education	Low (ref.)			
	Middle	-0.05	0.04	0.04
	High	-0.06	0.08	-0.08
Sector of employment	Private (ref.)			
	Public	-0.06**	0.07**	-0.05
Tenure at workplace	Less than 5 years (ref.)			
	5–19 years	-0.03	0.07*	-0.04
	20 years or more	0.03	0.08*	-0.12**
Supervisory work tasks	No supervisory tasks (ref.)			
	Supervisory tasks	0.04*	-0.14***	0.10***
Occupation	Manual workers (ref.)			
	Service workers	-0.02	-0.05	0.07***
	Semi-professionals	0.06	-0.23***	0.17***
	Professionals	0.07	-0.29***	0.22***
	Managers	0.26***	-0.37***	0.11
R^2		0.05	0.12	0.05

Note: Levels of significance: * = p<0.05; ** = p<0.01; *** = p<0.001. The range of both dependent variables is 1.0; the standard deviations are 0.37 for Employed suppliers, 0.45 for Work-time sellers and 0.49 for Trusted employees. N = 1,370.

it less likely that an employee is a work-time seller. Thus, male employees, older employees, private sector employees, employees with short tenure and employees with supervisory tasks are somewhat more likely to be trusted employees than employees with opposite characteristics. By contrast, female employees, younger employees, public sector employees, employees with long tenure and employees without supervisory tasks are somewhat more likely to be work-time sellers. The same pattern, where trusted employees and work-time sellers have opposite characteristics, is also very pronounced for occupation. For employed suppliers, however, there is no obvious pattern of association with independent variables, except that the regression coefficients are in general small and that managers are particularly likely to be employed suppliers.

EXCHANGE PARADIGM AND EMPLOYEE SATISFACTION

Reported employee satisfaction was in general high; 82 percent of the respondents were 'completely satisfied' or 'rather satisfied' with their 'work'; the corresponding figures for the 'workplace' and the 'employer' were 76 percent and 59 percent, respectively. Correlations between the three satisfaction items ranged between 0.40 and 0.51, indicating that the three items measure separate but related concepts.

A regression analysis was performed for each type of employee satisfaction. Since we are especially interested in the effect of exchange paradigm, two regression models were used for each dependent variable. Model 1 includes sex, age, level of education, income, sector of employment, supervisory tasks, tenure at workplace and occupation as independent variables, while Model 2 includes exchange paradigm as well. As usual in similar analyses, we are interested not only in the regression coefficients for exchange paradigm in Model 2, but also in how the regression coefficients in Model 1 change when we introduce exchange paradigm as an independent variable.

The data analysis is complicated by the fact that not all respondents could be categorised into one of the three exchange paradigms, and only respondents belonging to one of these categories can be used in a regression analysis according to Model 2. For a regression analysis according to Model 1, on the other hand, one can either use all 1,620 respondents in the dataset (Sample 1) or the same respondents as used in the analysis with Model 2 (Sample 2). While this complication is not expected to be a serious one, in view of the fact that some 85 percent of the respondents in Sample 1 belong to Sample 2, it is prudent to calculate regression coefficients according to Model 1 for both Sample 1 and Sample 2. If the regression coefficients for the same variable differ substantially between the two samples, there may be a problem; otherwise, it suffices to consider Sample 2.

Linear regression is used in all regression analyses presented. All independent variables are either dichotomous or have been transformed into sets of dichotomous dummy variables. While there are scale-theoretical arguments for dichotomising the dependent variables as well, it was deemed more important to prevent the loss of information that dichotomisation would entail. Thus, the original five-point Likert-scale structure of the dependent variables has been retained.

Satisfaction with Work

Results for regression analyses with 'satisfaction with work' as dependent variable are presented in Table 9.6. In general, the differences between

Table 9.6   Satisfaction with Work by Background Variables. Multi-linear Regression. Unstandardised Regression Coefficients

		Model 1, sample 1	*Model 1, sample 2*	*Model 2, sample 2*
Sex	Male (ref)			
	Female	0.24***	0.19**	0.17**
Age (years)	25–34 (ref.)			
	35–49	0.20**	0.18**	0.08
	50–	0.37***	0.39***	0.27***
Level of education	Low (ref.)			
	Middle	0.04	0.05	0.02
	High	-0.05	0.01	0.04
Income (SEK/month)	–15000 (ref.)			
	15000–25000	0.41***	0.42***	0.33***
	25000–	0.45***	0.44***	0.28**
Sector of employment	Private (ref.)			
	Public	0.01	-0.02	0.02
Tenure at workplace	Less than 5 years (ref.)			
	5–19 years	0.06	0.09	0.08
	20 years or more	-0.02	-0.01	0.01
Supervisory work tasks	No supervisory tasks (ref.)			
	Supervisory tasks	0.25***	0.23***	0.12*
Occupation	Manual workers (ref.)			
	Service workers	0.29***	0.32**	0.21***
	Semi-professionals	0.25**	0.33**	0.17*
	Professionals	0.35***	0.35**	0.17*
	Managers	0.31*	0.35*	0.14
Exchange paradigm	Work-time seller (ref.)			
	Employed supplier			0.61***
	Trusted employee			0.50***
No-intercept R^2		0.63	0.67	0.70
N		1,620	1,378	1,378

Note: Levels of significance: * = p<0.05; ** = p<0.01; *** = p<0.001. The range for the dependent variable is 4.0; the standard deviation is 0.76.

Sample 1 and Sample 2 for Model 1 were small, so we can confidently use Sample 2 for a comparison of Model 1 and Model 2.

There are moderately strong effects of sex and age on satisfaction with work in Model 1 as well as Model 2. As discussed in the literature, there are many possible explanations of these differences. In both cases, the effects may be due to different work values, different levels of aspiration and self-selection through selective participation in the workforce. For example, it has been suggested (Clark 1997) that female employees have lower expectations and aspirations than male employees and therefore higher levels of work satisfaction, and higher work satisfaction among older workers could partly be attributed to dissatisfied employees moving on to more satisfying jobs or leaving the workforce early. With regard to age, additional causal links are possible. For example, cohort effects, organizational mobility, intra-organizational work careers and life cycle processes may also explain differences between old and young employees (Kalleberg 1983).

It is notable that level of education and tenure at the workplace have no effect on satisfaction with work. While it is reasonable to expect that employees with higher education and longer tenure have better jobs, the level of aspiration enters the equation again and may cancel out the effects of favourable job characteristics. It is also possible that there are effects of these variables, but that these effects are mediated by other variables in the regression models, so that the corresponding regression coefficients tend to vanish.

By contrast, income has an independent effect on work satisfaction. This is of course not unexpected, but it is also not unexpected that this association seems to be non-linear. In view of much previous research (e.g., Fredholm 1989) it is to be expected that perceptions of fairness and multi-faceted comparison processes mediate the influence of income on work satisfaction.

Finally, and most important, supervisory tasks and occupation have moderately strong associations with satisfaction with work, but the regression coefficients are generally much lower in Model 2 than in Model 1. On the other hand, the two regression coefficients reflecting the effect of exchange paradigm on satisfaction with work are quite high. The coefficients of 0.61 for employed suppliers as compared to work-time sellers and 0.50 for trusted employees as compared to work-time sellers both stand out as considerably higher than other regression coefficients in Table 9.6. This pattern suggests that the effects of supervisory position and occupation are to a large extent mediated by exchange paradigm. For example, the fact that professionals, semi-professionals and managers exhibit considerably higher satisfaction with work than manual workers can be partly explained by the fact that employees with these occupations are more likely to be employed suppliers or trusted employees than are manual workers.

Of the hypotheses stated above, Hypothesis 1 and Hypothesis 3 are clearly supported: satisfaction with work is higher for employed suppliers and trusted employees than for work-time sellers. Hypothesis 2 was not supported, however. Contrary to expectations, satisfaction with work was somewhat higher among employed suppliers than among trusted employees.

Satisfaction with Workplace and Employer

Results for regression analyses with 'satisfaction with workplace' and 'satisfaction with employer' as dependent variables are presented in Table 9.7. With regard to Model 1, regression coefficients for Sample 1 were again similar to those for Sample 2, so only results for Sample 2 are shown in this table.

In general, the results for satisfaction with workplace and satisfaction with employer were similar to those for satisfaction with work. For example, the effects of sex and age are very similar for all three aspects of employee satisfaction, and the associations can be interpreted as done above. There is overall also a close correspondence between regression coefficients for satisfaction with work and satisfaction with workplace. One reason for this may be that these two items were too similarly or abstractly formulated to discriminate well between different aspects of employee satisfaction.

On the other hand, there are some notable differences between effects on satisfaction with workplace on the one hand and satisfaction with employer on the other hand. Thus, level of education tends to be negatively associated with satisfaction with employer, and tenure at workplace is clearly negatively associated with satisfaction with employer. A natural interpretation of these results is that employees who have made significant 'investments' (Homans 1961) in terms of education or staying with the same employer for a long time, but feel that they are not rewarded accordingly in terms of wages, career, etc., tend to be dissatisfied, and it is natural that this dissatisfaction is directed at the employer.

While private or public sector employment does not affect satisfaction with work or satisfaction with workplace, public sector employees are significantly less satisfied with their employer than private sector employees. It is not easy to give a theoretically grounded explanation for this finding, and I shall abstain from speculative ad-hoc explanations.

We saw in Table 9.6 that satisfaction with work tends to increase with increasing income, although the relation is not linear. Similar non-linear associations with income exist for satisfaction with workplace and satisfaction with employer as well, again suggesting a level-of-aspiration effect.

With regard to differences between Model 1 and Model 2, the main results are similar to those in Table 9.6. Supervisory position and occupation are again associated with employee satisfaction in Model 1, but these associations are substantially reduced in Model 2, which includes exchange paradigm as an independent variable. The regression coefficients corresponding to employed suppliers and trusted employees in Model 2 range from 0.45 to 0.69. This confirms the interpretation that much of the effect of supervisory position and—in particular—occupation is an indirect effect via exchange paradigm.

Table 9.7 Satisfaction with Workplace and Employer by Background Variables. Multi-linear Regression. Unstandardised Regression Coefficients

		Workplace		Employer	
		Model 1, sample 2	Model 2, sample 2	Model 1, sample 2	Model 2, sample 2
Sex	Male (ref)				
	Female	0.21***	0.19**	0.24**	0.21**
Age (years)	25–34 (ref.)				
	35–49	0.21***	0.12*	0.15*	0.05
	50–	0.40***	0.29***	0.46***	0.33***
Level of education	Low (ref.)				
	Middle	0.03	-0.02	-0.12	-0.15
	High	-0.02	0.01	-0.16*	-0.13
Income (SEK/month)	–15000 (ref.)				
	15000–25000	0.29***	0.20***	0.26***	0.15*
	25000–	0.32***	0.16*	0.22*	0.04
Sector of employment	Private (ref.)				
	Public	-0.09	-0.07	-0.24***	-0.22***
Tenure at workplace	Less than 5 years (ref.)				
	5–19 years	0.05	0.04	-0.18**	-0.19***
	20 years or more	-0.02	-0.01	-0.27**	-0.26***
Supervisory work tasks	No supervisory tasks (ref.)				
	Supervisory tasks	0.18***	0.08	0.14*	0.03
Occupation	Manual workers (ref.)				
	Service workers	0.37***	0.27***	0.30***	0.18*
	Semi-professionals	0.36**	0.21*	0.44***	0.26*
	Professionals	0.27**	0.11	0.30**	0.10
	Managers	0.47**	0.27*	0.61***	0.37*
Exchange paradigm	Work-time seller (ref.)				
	Employed supplier		0.61***		0.69***
	Trusted employee		0.45***		0.55***
No-intercept R^2		0.53	0.56	0.27	0.33
N		1,374	1,374	1,370	1,370

Note: Levels of significance: * = p<0.05; ** = p<0.01; *** = p<0.001. The range for the dependent variables is 4.0; the standard deviations are 0.87 for satisfaction with workplace and 1.04 for satisfaction with employer.

Finally, employed suppliers showed higher employee satisfaction than trusted employees also with regard to satisfaction with workplace and satisfaction with employer. This confirms the conclusion from Table 9.6—Hypotheses 1 and 3 are supported, but Hypothesis 2 is not supported.

DISCUSSION

Based on a theoretical analysis of employment relations, three exchange paradigms, represented by employed suppliers, work-time sellers and trusted employees, were distinguished. The data presented in Tables 9.3, 9.4 and 9.5 suggest that the analytical distinctions summarised in Table 9.2 are empirically meaningful. It is possible to classify some 85 percent of the respondents as representing one of the three exchange paradigms. Some 20 percent of the categorised respondents fit into the theoretical ideal type of employed suppliers. This unorthodox category turned out to have interesting characteristics, different from those of the more familiar categories of work-time sellers and trusted employees.

The data reported suggest that exchange paradigm strongly influences employee satisfaction. Indeed, in Tables 9.6 and 9.7 the unstandardised regression coefficients measuring the influence of exchange paradigm are higher than all other regression coefficients. A comparison of Model 1 and Model 2 in Tables 9.6 and 9.7 shows that regression coefficients for other independent variables tend to decrease when exchange paradigm is introduced in the regression model. This tendency is particularly strong for occupation, so it appears that to a large extent the effect of occupational level on employee satisfaction is mediated by exchange paradigm. In other words, a mechanism is suggested which to a large extent explains the frequently observed influence of occupation on employee satisfaction.

A new look at an old subject has thus produced some new findings, but also a large number of new research questions. Methodologically, the operationalisation of exchange paradigm needs further validation and refinement. The simple operationalisation used here has been partly validated theoretically by the results obtained, but further research is obviously required. Empirically, a replication of the present study would be interesting, considering that the data was collected in 2002. Comparisons with other countries would of course also be interesting; maybe Sweden is an extreme case with regard to the emphasis on autonomy.

On the level of theoretical elaboration, I would like to mention two areas. First, a simplifying assumption has tacitly been made above, namely that employment relations are 'balanced' exchange relations, where employees and employers give and receive equally much, loosely speaking. This is obviously not the whole truth. While exchange always involves some reciprocity, it can also involve exploitation, and not only by the employer. The forms of such exploitation would depend on the exchange paradigm; for example, they might involve a breach of trust as well as insufficient remuneration. Second, in reality employment relations usually feature characteristics of more than one exchange paradigm. Nevertheless, each exchange paradigm has an 'internal logic', and the combination of elements belonging to different exchange paradigms may therefore have negative consequences. For example, the use of piece-rate reward systems in employment relations generally operating according to a 'time-for-money' or 'trust-for-commitment' logic may be dysfunctional. In both areas mentioned, many subtle complications await elucidation in the light of the theoretical perspective sketched here.

Finally, further theoretical development of the present approach should take note of its relations to some other well-known theoretical perspectives or traditions. Much of the theoretical reflection about employee satisfaction and related attitudes is rooted in the traditional white-collar versus blue-collar contrast. Erikson and Goldthorpe's (1993) distinction between labour contracts and service contracts falls within the scope of this theoretical approach. The problem here is obviously not that there are no theoretically significant differences in employee satisfaction and related attitudes between white-collar and blue-collar employees, or their theoretical counterparts. But as long as empirical research essentially operates within the confines of a traditional work-time sellers versus trusted employees dichotomy (or continuum), the effects of autonomy and community tend to be confounded, since strong-community, high-autonomy employees are compared to weak-community, low-autonomy employees. By contrast, the two-dimensional model of employment relations proposed in this chapter suggests new research questions which concern the relative importance of community and autonomy for employee satisfaction and other work-related phenomena. The unexpected finding that employed suppliers showed higher satisfaction with work, workplace and employer than did trusted employees suggests that autonomy is more important than community, but of even greater theoretical significance than this tentative answer is the question itself.

Also related to the theme of this chapter is the broad theoretical tradition dealing with fundamental questions about conflict and consensus in social relations (see, e.g., Bernard 1980; Burrell and Morgan 1979). In one perspective on employment relations, harmony of interests between employers and employees is emphasised. Employees, it is assumed, by innate nature want to do a good job, and by doing a good job they create value for both the employer and themselves. Conversely, employers who create work conditions that enable employees to do a good job benefit from this, so it is in their own interest to organise the work so that it becomes fulfilling for the employees. Subjectively, there is a natural tendency for employees to identify with the organization where they work, so there is a natural community of interests between employers and employees.

In another perspective on employment relations, conflict of interests is emphasised. The struggle over the value created through the work process is seen to be at the core of any employment relation. Employers try to extract as much work as possible from employees in order to maximise their profit; employees resist being exploited by their employers.

In the contingency perspective described in this chapter, though, neither harmony nor conflict of interests is seen as an essential characteristic of employment relations (cf. Goldthorpe 2000). Briefly, it is proposed that under certain circumstances employers' and employees' interests tend to be in harmony, under certain other circumstances they tend to be in conflict and under certain circumstances they tend to be neither aligned nor opposing but complementary. In fact, these three cases are hypothesised to correspond to the three exchange paradigms elaborated above: namely commitment-for-trust exchange, time-for-pay exchange and performance-for-pay exchange, respectively.

ACKNOWLEDGMENT

The author wants to express his grateful appreciation of a grant from the Swedish Council for Research in the Humanities and Social Sciences (HSFR F006/2000), which made the research reported here possible.

10 Work Attitudes in a Crisis

Tómas Bjarnason

In October 2008, the Icelandic bank system collapsed, starting a crisis that has been described as the 'deepest and most rapid financial crisis recorded in peacetime history' (Danielsson and Zoëga 2009: 1). The Icelandic currency lost nearly half of its value in an instant. Downsizing, layoffs and closures became rampant in the weeks and months following the collapse. It was in this environment that Capacent Iceland, a private research and consultancy company, surveyed employees of the Commercial and Office Workers' Union regarding their work environment, job satisfaction and pay.

This chapter explores the impact of the recession on employed union members by comparing results from 2008 before the recession hit Iceland with the 2009 results, a few months following the collapse of the bank system. It also examines the effects of various downsizing measures on employee attitudes and satisfaction with life. The analysis is based on survey responses collected in February 2009 from roughly 8,000 employed union members and on nearly 7,000 responses collected in February 2008. The questionnaire included questions about management, morale, pay satisfaction, flexibility, work environment, corporate image and job satisfaction. Because of the crisis, questions on wage cuts, job insecurity and downsizing were included in the 2009 survey. As the survey has been conducted in similar ways for several years, it offers unique opportunities for estimating the impact of the economic recession and various downsizing strategies on employee attitudes.

THE IMPACT OF THE CRISIS

By the end of 2007, Iceland was able to look back at a decade of remarkable economic growth and prosperity (Porter and Ketels 2007). Unemployment was low and all indicators pointed to a thriving economy (Statistics Iceland 2010). The collapse of the banking system in October 2008 changed all that. Because of the immense size of the financial system in relation to the Icelandic economy,[1] the fall of the financial system affected all basic institutions throughout Icelandic society.

The crisis was clearly noted in both economic and labour market indicators; GDP per capita dropped by almost 2 percent in 2008 and by almost 7 percent in 2009. Labour force statistics in early 2009 showed a sharp decrease in labour force participation and working hours and an increase in part-time work and unemployment. Unemployment more than tripled between the first quarter of 2008 and the first quarter of 2009, and real wages fell some 7 percent in the first year following the collapse (Statistics Iceland 2010). The cost of living increased as a result of skyrocketing prices of food, gasoline and other necessities (*Economic Indicators* 2009). In addition, many were hit hard economically as loans in foreign currencies almost doubled in value because of the devaluation of the Icelandic *krona*. Loans in the national currency also increased because of the rise of the consumer index.[2]

Accordingly, many families found it difficult to make ends meet. An analysis of household income and debt conducted by the Icelandic Central bank indicated that about 23 percent of all households were likely to have problems in paying their debts (*Fjármálastöðugleiki* 2010: ch. 2.2). A recent survey among the Icelandic population portrays a similar picture where a total of 27 percent of respondents said either that their debt was increasing or that they were using savings to make ends meet (Capacent 2009c). The same study showed that economic deprivation had tremendous impact on stress and psychosomatic symptoms. Almost half of those who were taking on increased debt said they had 'grave concerns' twice a week or more in the past six months compared to 6 percent in the group that had managed to put savings aside.

The situation for many businesses was similarly disastrous for much the same reasons as sketched above. Danielsson and Zoëga (2009) estimate that the share of non-financials being technically bankrupt ranged between 33 and 60 percent.[3] Many operations managed to stay in business, however. Some were already well consolidated, while others responded with various downsizing strategies—such as partial closures, layoffs, pay cuts or adjustments in working hours—and could thus maintain operation.

What followed was a period of both political unrest and social turbulence. Riots broke out, and protestors and riot police clashed together on several occasions.[4] This situation eventually led to a political crisis and then to the fall of the right-wing government and the formation of a left-wing government in May 2009.[5] Surveys revealed that trust in the main institutions and governmental bodies of Iceland had weakened (Capacent 2009a, 2009b).

EMPLOYEE ATTITUDES

As has been outlined above, the crisis has had various negative effects on the social, economic and political arena in Iceland. Families and employees were hit hard as a consequence of growing inflation and increasing debt.

At the time of the 2009 survey there was a real threat of income and job loss for the majority of employees in the private sector and it came on top of the already high flexibility of the Icelandic labour market (Ólafsdóttir 2008). Iceland deviates in important aspects from the Scandinavian labour market model (Ólafsson 1999). There is less protection against dismissals in the private sector, unemployment benefits are low and active labour market policies are fairly undeveloped, making job and income loss all the more serious.

Studies show that life satisfaction is affected by many factors, of which actual income and satisfaction with income have been found to be important. Another essential factor is 'agency', or feelings of control over one's life (Welzel and Inglehart 2010), which is likely to be severely compromised in this situation, affecting life satisfaction negatively.

A recent study confirms, accordingly, that economic crises have adverse effects on health and suicide rates (Stuckler et al. 2009). On the basis of data for 26 European countries from 1970 to 2007, it found that increased unemployment rates were associated with various negative health consequences. This relationship was, however, weaker among nations with higher levels of active labour market policies, indicating that welfare policies can diminish the blow of economic crises on individuals. Given the lower level of welfare expenditure in Iceland, with undeveloped labour market policies and low unemployment benefits, negative responses to the crisis should be expected, for example lower life satisfaction.

Yet another study shows that job factors are important for explaining declining well-being among employees in recessions (Tausig and Fenwick 1999). The recession which hit the US in 1974–1975, similar to the crisis in Iceland, marked the end of a prosperous period. As in Iceland, this recession was distinguished by increasing unemployment and rapid increase of the costs of living. Two waves of surveys were compared. The first survey was conducted in 1973, shortly after the onset of the recession, and the second was conducted shortly after its end. On comparison of the results the recession turned out to have had considerable negative effects on full-time workers. The most important factor for explaining the increase in distress and dissatisfaction with life was 'job restructuring', in particular intensified job demands and inadequate pay. Other important factors were the experiences of unemployment and changes in marital status from married to unmarried.

With regard to work attitudes, the approach taken here is to view the relationship of employees and their employing organization in terms of 'social exchange' (Blau 1967) or 'psychological contract' (Rousseau 2001), to use a more familiar conceptualization (see Chapter 2, this volume, for some further discussion on the concept of psychological contract). A key element in social exchange is that actors strive to maintain a balance in reciprocity. This means that the more employees receive from the organization, the more they have to give back to the organization to keep the equilibrium in the exchange. Under normal conditions, trust is extended if both parties prove to be reliable. Gradually a mental scheme develops about the exchange agreement between the employee and the organization. This agreement is promise-based and perhaps increasingly robust. It is then experienced as being mutual and binding (Rousseau 2001). The organization contributes various remunerations such as pay, supportive environment and recognition, which employees reciprocate with their efforts, performance, commitment, attendance, loyalty, etc.

Breaches in the exchange agreement are expected to negatively influence employee perceptions of the social exchange. A breach is likely to result in negative behavioural and emotive responses. Accordingly, contract violations have frequently been suggested to explain negative reactions from employees in a situation with downsizing (e.g., Greenhalgh and Rosenblatt 1984; Davy et al. 1997; Kets de Vries and Balazs 1997; Adkins, Werbel and Farh 2001).

To sum up, employees are expected to be negatively affected by the crisis, which will be reflected in more negative attitudes in the 2009 survey compared to the 2008 survey. The circumstances of many families worsened severely after the collapse of the banks, which is likely to be reflected in declining life satisfaction. The crisis is also assumed to have affected the workplace negatively. There was a concrete threat to job and income security for most employees; real wages declined and many workplaces took direct steps to cut costs, lay off employees and cut pay and bonuses. In accordance with the theoretical departure taken in the chapter, it is argued that employees respond to reduced benefits by decreasing their support to the organization. The following hypotheses are thus formulated:

> *Hypothesis 1:* Job satisfaction, pay satisfaction, morale, corporate image, attitudes to management, flexibility and attitudes to the work environment will be more negative in 2009 than in 2008.

> *Hypothesis 2:* Life satisfaction will be more negative in 2009 than in 2008.

In addition, we can expect a direct effect of various downsizing measures on employee attitudes. Organizations executed various downsizing strategies (layoffs, pay cuts, elimination of bonuses and reduction in working hours) in response to the crisis. These might be experienced as violations to the psychological contract between employees and their employer, causing a decrease in employees' support for their organization. The negative impact of various downsizing strategies on employees' attitudes, behaviour and health is well documented (Ashford, Lee and Bobko 1989; Davy et al. 1997; De Witte 1999; Erickson and Roloff 2007; Ferrie 2001; Hertting and Theorell 2002; Kivimäki et al. 2001). According to Erickson and Roloff (2007: 36), downsizing lowers productivity and increases absenteeism and its effects also include 'reducing organizational commitment, morale, job satisfaction, while increasing turnover intention and job stress.'

Job insecurity is an important negative consequence of various downsizing strategies for those remaining in the organization (e.g., Ferrie et al. 1998; Sverke, Hellgren and Näswall 2002; Østhus 2007; Cheng and Chan 2008). Examining several studies, De Witte (1999) reported that job insecurity has negative effects on job attitudes, well-being and diverse physical and psychosomatic areas. He further pointed out that these results have been confirmed through longitudinal research, thus indicating that a decline in job security initiates changes in attitudes and health. The negative impact of job insecurity on attitudes, behaviour and health has been verified in later studies (Adkins, Werbel and Farh 2001; Kivimäki et al. 2001; Sverke, Hellgren and Näswall 2002).

Research shows a strong negative effect of pay cuts on employee attitudes and particularly on pay satisfaction (Lovett et al. 2008). Pay equity has been found to strongly influence work attitudes and behaviours, such as organizational commitment (e.g., Mowday, Porter and Steers 1982; Cowheard and Levine 1992). Moreover, pay equity and pay satisfaction have shown to be better predictors of employee attitudes and behaviours than are levels of pay (Lovett et al. 2008).

According to the social exchange and psychological contract perspectives, downsizing and layoffs signal to the remaining employees that the psychological contract could be violated. Violations occur, 'when one party perceives another to have failed to fulfil promised obligation(s)' and a breach in the contract can create a sense of 'wrongdoing, deception and betrayal with pervasive implication for the employment relationship' (Robinson and Rousseau 1994: 247). Due to various downsizing actions, employees may experience declining morale, demotion, loss and the like—all of which are likely to influence the exchange with the employer negatively. Pay cuts create an imbalance in the reward-effort relationship which employees may consider unfair. Layoffs can be expected to create increasing job insecurity, which in turn implies an increasing disbelief in the reciprocity between employees and the organization and a fear that the organization will not or cannot fulfill its obligations. Layoffs, pay cuts and increasing job insecurity may signal to employees a possible breach in the contract which will cause them to decrease their support to the organization. Decreasing support is exemplified by more negative employee attitudes, in particular to the organization and its managers. It is also proposed that downsizing experiences will have a negative impact on employees' life satisfaction. The following hypotheses are therefore proposed:

> *Hypothesis 3*: Job satisfaction, pay satisfaction, morale, corporate image, attitudes to management, flexibility and attitudes to the work environment will be negatively affected by job insecurity, layoffs and pay cuts.

Hypothesis 4: Life satisfaction will be negatively affected by job insecurity, layoffs and pay cuts.

EDUCATION AND OCCUPATION AS MEDIATORS DURING DOWNSIZING

While most researchers propose that downsizing has direct negative effects on worker attitudes, some situations and/or individual characteristics can mediate the relationship between downsizing strategies and affective responses. Greenhalgh and Rosenblatt (1984) suggest that stronger negative reactions can be expected from those who are more dependent on their job than from those less dependent. In addition, they propose more negative responses from those who experience powerlessness in the downsizing process.

A number of factors can contribute to perceptions of dependency and powerlessness. Dependency is for example created by low employability, merely firm-specific skills, high unemployment levels and extensive debts. Powerlessness is likely to be influenced by lack of information and resources and inability to influence the downsizing process. 'Control' has accordingly been shown to be an important mediator between downsizing and workers' affective responses (Brockner et al. 2004). It has similarly been shown to be of key importance for explaining various individual outcomes—stress, well-being and health—in other work contexts (Karasek 1979).

Research is inconsistent regarding the impact of insecurity on attitudes within different educational categories (De Witte 1999). However, there are good reasons to believe that educational merits operate positively on attitudes and well-being when employees are facing downsizing, as more educated employees have higher employability and usually have access to more resources within the organization. Unemployment statistics strongly indicate that those with less education are more vulnerable to economic downturns than are those with more education (Eurostat 2011). Hence job insecurity, layoffs and pay cuts are expected to have more negative effects on attitudes among employees with less education.

In regard to occupation, it is argued that holding managerial positions within the organization indicates having more control over downsizing processes, more influence over decision making and greater access to valued resources. These factors are assumed to reduce the impact of downsizing and job insecurity through less stress, less insecurity and positive assessment of fairness. Some studies, accordingly, confirm that managers respond more favourably to layoffs than do other employees (Tourish et al. 2004). It has also been shown that mid-level managers present more negative reactions to downsizing than do executive-level managers (Moore, Grundberg and Greenberg 2006).

In contrast, some research suggests that managers respond more negatively to downsizing or threat of unemployment, because unemployment poses a bigger threat to their status than to that of other employees. Still other studies indicate that there is little difference between employee reactions across occupational strata (De Witte 1999; Sverke, Hellgren and Näswall 2002).

It is argued that powerlessness and lack of information are more likely to characterize those with less education and lower job positions within the organization. Consequently, it is assumed that these categories will react more negatively to downsizing than will categories with more education and more formal authority, and the following hypotheses are formulated:

Hypothesis 5: Employees with less education will be more negatively affected by downsizing (declining job security, layoffs and pay cuts) than will those with more education.

Hypothesis 6: Managers will be less negatively affected by downsizing (declining job security, layoffs and pay cuts) than will other categories of employees.

METHODS, DATA AND VARIABLES

The data come from two surveys, one carried out early 2008 and the other in early 2009 and both conducted on behalf of the Commercial and Office Workers' Union. Capacent was responsible for the data collection, analysis, and reporting.[6] The survey has been conducted in similar ways for several years and thus furnishes a rare opportunity for comparison and estimation of the impact of economic recession on employee attitudes. We can study the impact of the recession on the attitudes of the commercial union's employees toward their work and pay in the months following the collapse.

These data are, however, not representative for the Icelandic labour market in general. Rather, they describe the situation of employed union members in commerce, retail and office work. Through telephone calls, the Internet addresses of union members were collected for the distribution of the survey. Those not having an Internet address were sent a questionnaire by post. Most of the responses were collected via the Internet: 90 percent in 2008 and 93 percent in 2009. The questionnaire was available in two languages: English and Icelandic. Particular means were taken to ensure confidentiality throughout the data collection process and the analysis of the results. This was emphasized during the data collection. The response rate was 47 percent in 2008 and 55 percent in 2009. The present analysis is based on nearly 7,000 responses for 2008 and roughly 8,000 responses for 2009.

The questionnaire consisted of about 45 items. It included questions on gender, age, tenure, occupation and education as well as on work organization, leadership and management of the company that the respondent worked for. Both surveys entailed an item on satisfaction with life. In addition, the 2009 survey had questions on downsizing specially selected because of the crisis.

Attitudinal Measures

Most of the attitudes were measured on a five-point Likert scale. Items were grouped into factors by means of factor analysis: 'attitudes to management' was captured with five items, such as trust and support from management. 'Morale' was based on three questions on communication and perceived quality of interaction. 'Pay satisfaction' was measured by three items: overall pay satisfaction, fairness of pay and pay comparison. The 'work environment' factor had six questions on satisfaction with office-space, canteen, computers, air-conditioning, etc. 'Flexibility' came out of seven items on flexibility and work-life reconciliation. The 'corporate image' factor included three items on employees' estimation of how the corporate image is among customers and the public. Finally, 'job satisfaction' was measured by three items: global satisfaction, overall well-being and pride in the organization. It is defined as employees' overall affective response to the job situation. Table 10.1 reports reliability, means and standard deviations of the measures. All factors turn out to have good internal consistency making them attractive for further analysis.

Table 10.1   Measures of Attitudes: Reliability, Means and Standard Deviations

Variables	No. of items	Alpha*	Mean	N	Std. deviation
Attitudes to management	5	.88	3.87	15,803	0.90
Morale	3	.84	4.32	16,006	0.73
Pay satisfaction	3	.86	3.34	15,615	0.91
Work environment	6	.84	3.96	15.579	0.79
Flexibility	7	.83	3.92	15,791	0.75
Corporate image	3	.88	4.10	15,545	0.78
Job satisfaction	3	.90	4.28	15,688	0.79
Satisfaction with life	1	–	4.21	14,591	0.75

* Alpha is a measure of internal consistency. All items are measured on a 1–5 scale, 1 being lowest and 5 highest.

Measuring Downsizing

Three aspects of downsizing were measured: change in job security, whether there had been layoffs in the organization or not and whether the employee's pay had been cut or not. These measures were included only in the 2009 survey. They can be considered 'factual' rather than 'affective', that is, employees were asked if they had experienced each aspect of downsizing, but not how they felt about it. Moreover, all indicators of downsizing in this study were single-item measures. Both these features are likely to produce lower correlations with affective factors than would be the case otherwise (Probst 2003; Sverke, Hellgren and Näswall 2002).

Change in job security was measured with a single item on a five-point Likert scale and dichotomized into two groups (decline in job security and other responses). Layoffs in the organization were also determined by means of one item; it was asked whether there had been layoffs in the organization because of the crisis (yes–no). Pay cuts were similarly captured with one question, in this case on whether the employee had experienced pay cuts (yes–no).

RESULTS

High means are generally reported for the factors measured (Table 10.1). The highest means (most positive responses) appear for morale and job satisfaction and the lowest (most negative responses) for pay satisfaction. Inter-correlations between the factors are quite high and most of the factors are strongly correlated with job satisfaction, supporting the notion that this aspect is an overall affective response to the job situation.

Changes in Attitudes between 2008 and 2009

A comparison of the means from the two surveys surprisingly shows that three of the seven indicators for work-related attitudes improve between 2009 and 2008 (Table 10.2). The largest increase is found for attitudes toward management (+0.19). There is also improvement regarding the work environment (+0.10) as well as a small but significant upgrading in pay satisfaction (+0.05). Morale, corporate image and job satisfaction do not change significantly, and only one factor, flexibility, shows a decrease between 2008 and 2009.

Thus, unexpectedly, hypothesis 1 is rejected; no general decline in employee support is visible in the data. On the contrary, as we can see in Table 10.2, more positive work attitudes appear in 2009 than in 2008 on three of the factors measured. Hypothesis 2 is, however, confirmed. It is not shown in tabular form, but the comparison of the means for satisfaction with life reveals a significant decrease between 2008 and 2009.[7] Thus people were significantly less satisfied with their lives after the crisis. The change in this respect is also the largest of the attitudes examined.

Table 10.2 Comparison of Work-related Attitudes (Means of Factor Scores), 2008 and 2009

Factors	Mean diff.	P-value	Mean 2008	Std. dev.	Mean 2009	Std. dev.
Attitudes to management	0.19	0.000	3.76	0.93	3.95	0.87
Morale	0.01	0.462	4.31	0.73	4.32	0.73
Corporate image	-0.02	0.141	4.11	0.77	4.09	0.79
Work environment	0.10	0.000	3.90	0.82	4.00	0.77
Pay satisfaction	0.05	0.000	3.30	0.93	3.35	0.89
Flexibility	-0.05	0.000	3.95	0.75	3.90	0.75
Job satisfaction	0.01	0.660	4.27	0.79	4.28	0.79

Manova statistics: Pillais trace = 0.04; F=80; p<.000; N=15,065.

The presence of more positive work attitudes in 2009 than in 2008 raises fundamental questions regarding the impact of the crisis on employees. But before accepting these results as the correct description of reality, alternative explanations need to be considered. Three alternative explanations come to mind: (1) changes in the composition of respondents, that is, there was perhaps a larger proportion of affluent employees in the 2009 survey than in the 2008 survey; (2) selection effects, that is, companies may have dismissed their most negative employees and kept the most positive ones, resulting in more positive attitudes within the companies; (3) fear, that is, employees were possibly so insecure or afraid that they gave false positive responses. These three alternative explanations are discussed shortly below.

Concerning the first alternative explanation, almost no difference is found between the datasets with respect to personal and work-related characteristics. There is a slight increase in part-time work between 2008 and 2009, but as regards most other factors—such as gender, education and age—the distributions are almost identical. Response rates improved slightly between 2008 and 2009, but not so much that any larger differences in attitudes should be expected. Thus, it is argued that a change in participation or in the composition of the sample does not explain improvements in work attitudes between 2008 and 2009. The first alternative explanation is rejected.

On the topic of selection effects, research strongly suggests that layoffs have adverse effects on survivors for a considerable period of time, although some improvements in work attitudes can be noted as time passes (Allen et al. 2001). Even though some studies indicate that, under special circumstances, people work harder in response to layoffs (Brockner et al. 1988) and that some attitudes can actually improve (Allen et al. 2001), the good majority of research shows that survivors react negatively to insecurity and layoffs (e.g., Adkins, Werbel and Farth 2001). Furthermore, if more positive people were employed in the organization after the crisis than before, this would be reflected in positive developments in all of the factors examined and not in just some of them. Rather, there is improvement in some factors and no change or decline in others. Additionally, as we will see later, there is a clear negative impact of downsizing measures on employee attitudes. The second alternative explanation is therefore also dismissed.

Regarding the effect of fear, much the same applies as above. First, if people were fearful, it would be more reasonable for them not to respond to the survey at all rather than to give false positive attitudes. Second, fear should have elicited more positive responses across all factors, not just some of them. Third, if fear was an issue, the most positive attitudes should be found in organizations where there had been layoffs and where job security had declined the most. As we will see in the next pages, this is not the case. This alternative explanation is hence also rejected. It is therefore concluded that employee attitudes were more positive in 2009 than in 2008. Why it is so will be explored in greater detail in the discussion section.

The Impact of Downsizing on Employee Attitudes in 2009

Three indicators of organizational downsizing were examined: changes in job security, layoffs in the organization and pay cuts. More than half of the respondents said there had been layoffs in the organization; one quarter of them reported having their pay cut because of the recession, and roughly 40 percent felt a decline in job security.

The variable change in job security was dichotomized into two categories; those experiencing either no change (49%) or improvement (8%) were allocated to one category called 'no decline in job security', while those experiencing a decline in job security were allocated to another category called 'decline in job security' (43%). We then examined how this variable affected the work-related attitudes (Table 10.3). A strong and negative impact of perceived change in job security appears on all the attitudinal measures. In all instances those experiencing no decline in job security have more positive work attitudes than do those who report a decline in job security. The strongest effects are found on attitudes to management and job satisfaction. Lesser impact appears on flexibility and work environment, although these effects are significant as well.

Then the effects of pay cuts were examined. Respondents were divided into those who had experienced pay cuts (25%) and those who had had no such experience (75%). A strong negative impact of this factor was also found (not shown). Those experiencing pay cuts had more negative attitudes than did those who did not have such an experience. As could be expected, the clearest effect was noted on pay satisfaction. Similar effects were also observed on job satisfaction and attitudes to management.[8]

Table 10.3   Impact of Perceived Change in Job Security on Work-related Attitudes

Variables	Mean diff.	P-value	No-change mean	Std. deviation	Decline mean	Std. deviation
Attitudes to management	-0.38	0.000	4.13	0.77	3.75	0.93
Morale	-0.21	0.000	4.42	0.66	4.21	0.79
Corporate image	-0.33	0.000	4.24	0.70	3.90	0.84
Work environment	-0.22	0.000	4.10	0.73	3.88	0.79
Pay satisfaction	-0.33	0.000	3.50	0.86	3.17	0.88
Flexibility	-0.16	0.000	3.99	0.71	3.82	0.75
Job satisfaction	-0.37	0.000	4.45	0.67	4.08	0.88

Manova statistics: Pillais trace = 0.07; F=80; p<.000. Univariate F-test was significant for all variables. N=7,644.

Finally, the impact of layoffs in the organization was examined. Respondents were divided into those who had experienced layoffs in the organization (44%) and those who had not (56%). It turned out that this kind of experience had a negative impact on all the factors examined (not shown). The strongest negative effect appears on corporate image, but such strong effects were also revealed on pay satisfaction, job satisfaction and attitudes to management.[9]

In conclusion, the three indicators of downsizing (job insecurity, layoffs and pay cuts) had significant effects on all the work attitudes examined. Hypothesis 3 is thus confirmed. With respect to satisfaction with life, a similar picture emerged (not shown in tabular form) and hypothesis 4 is accordingly also verified.[10]

DOES THE EFFECT OF DOWNSIZING VARY BY EDUCATION AND OCCUPATION?

As a first step it was examined whether education and occupation had any effect on work attitudes. Education was divided into three categories: primary, secondary and tertiary. Occupation was likewise divided into three categories: managers, experts and others. Then mean differences in work attitudes were examined by educational and occupational attainment.

Education and occupation showed significant effects on work attitudes. Attitudes were found to be a little more positive among those with higher education than among those with lower education. The effects were largest on flexibility, morale and attitudes to management. With regard to occupation, similar results were found, although a little stronger than for education. More positive attitudes appear for those higher in the organizational hierarchy. The effects of occupation were particularly evident for pay satisfaction, flexibility and attitudes to management. The positive impact of job status on work attitudes is in accordance with numerous organizational studies (Bjarnason 2009).

It was then tested whether the effects of downsizing varied across educational and occupational groups. The analysis shows that, for the most part, different educational groups respond in similar ways to downsizing. This indicates that downsizing has negative effects on employees irrespective of their educational attainment.

In regard to occupation, it came out that downsizing affects the three occupational categories (experts, managers and other employees) differently. Results are, however, somewhat unlike what was expected. The least effect appears for experts and not for managers. The latter and other employees were affected in similar ways. This pattern was particularly evident in the analysis of the impact of layoffs, less so with respect to changes in job security, while no interaction effect was found as to pay cuts.[11] So for the most part, pay cuts and decline in job security have similar negative effects on all three occupational groups, while layoffs in the organization have less effect on experts than on other employees.

In Figure 10.1 we find that morale was only slightly lower among experts in those organizations that had experienced layoffs than among experts in organizations where layoffs had not occurred. The same comparisons for managers and other employees show considerably larger differences. Figure 10.1 also confirms, as expected, that other employees generally have more negative attitudes than do both experts and managers.

In conclusion, we find little or no support for hypotheses 5 and 6. Overall, those with less education are no more affected by downsizing measures than are those with more education, which means that hypothesis 5 is rejected. As to hypothesis 6, it surprisingly came across that experts and not managers were least affected by downsizing measures. Experts seem

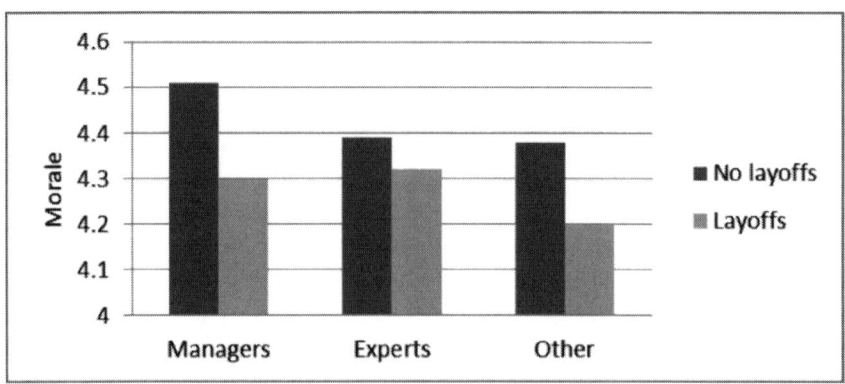

Figure 10.1   Morale by job position and layoffs, 2009.

to be relatively better off in downsizing situations than are other employees. Thus hypothesis 6 must also be rejected. For the most part, employees are negatively affected by downsizing, irrespective of their educational and occupational attainment.

DISCUSSION

The aim of this chapter was to explore the impact of the economic crisis in Iceland on employed union members. Changes in attitudes were examined by comparing survey data from the year before the crisis with data from a few months after the banks collapsed. It was expected that the crisis, which hit Iceland between the two measurements, would have strong negative effects on work attitudes and satisfaction with life. The impact of three indicators of downsizing on employee attitudes was also studied. It was assumed that downsizing would clearly influence work attitudes and satisfaction with life in a negative way. Finally, the effects of downsizing on attitudes were looked at by a comparison of educational and occupational categories.

The results presented here partly support and partly reject the main assumptions presented in the beginning of the chapter. Downsizing was found to have strong negative effects on employee attitudes, as anticipated. The negative impact of downsizing is suggested to be due to breaches in the exchange relationship with the organization or failures by the organization to fulfill promised obligations. As expected, the crisis and downsizing were also found to affect satisfaction with life negatively. This probably has to do with several factors: declining real wages; loss of 'agency' or feelings of being in control and having liberty of choice; increased debt; and increased job insecurity, factors which have all been found to be related negatively to life satisfaction.

Previous research on the influence of downsizing on attitudes across educational and occupational categories has shown mixed results. In this study, the initial impact of downsizing was for the most part experienced negatively irrespective of educational and occupational attainment. This probably reflects the fact that our data were collected in an early phase of the crisis in Iceland. The immediate effects were abrupt and not very selective in terms of the employees' education or occupation.

What is surprising is the positive development of some of the attitudes between 2008 and 2009. Why are employees more positive toward some aspects of their work environment in 2009 than they were in 2008 despite the collapse of the economy, the political crisis and the decrease in job and income security? Among the most astonishing aspects we find the more positive attitudes to management, the improvement in pay satisfaction and the more encouraging assessment of the work environment. What possible reasons could there be for this development? Is the answer that those employees who did not experience pay cuts, layoffs in the organization or decline in job security experienced increased benefits from their employment because of the crisis? Could it be that those employees considered their situation clearly advantageous in the light of what was happening generally in the labour market and therefore responded by increasing their support to the organization?

When examining the changes in employee attitudes between the two surveys, it is tempting to conclude that a positive development has taken place among those employees not experiencing declining job security. On attitudes to management (Figure 10.2) we see that employees reporting a decline in job security responded in a similar way in 2009 as employees in general did in 2008, whereas those with no experience of decreasing job security show much more positive attitudes in 2009.

It is suggested here that this 'improvement' in attitudes toward management is attributable to a perceived relative increase in rewards as decline in job security was a common experience after the crisis (43% reported this), and those not facing such a decline may have considered this as something extraordinary given what was happening in many organizations around them. More positive attitudes may have developed because employees felt their managers succeeded in steering through the crisis without being forced or tempted to lay off employees, cut pay, reduce working hours, etc. In contrast, those employees experiencing layoffs or pay cuts may have regarded such actions as 'normal', considering the acute situation of the economy.

With regard to the physical work environment, much the same applies. It is tempting to draw the conclusion that more positive opinions about the physical work environment in 2009 than in 2008 are due to a change among those employees still unaffected by various downsizing measures. For them,

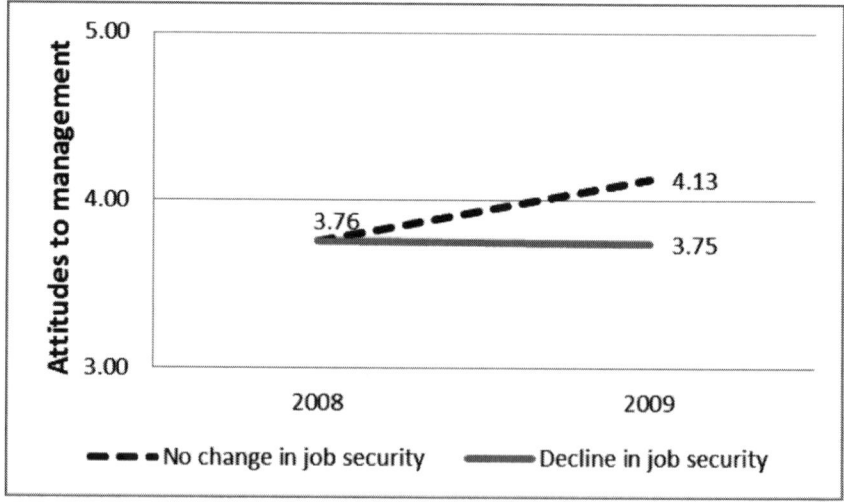

Figure 10.2   Changes in attitudes to management, 2008 and 2009.

making complaints about the work environment must have seemed a bit trivial at this time, considering the acute situation facing many employees, families and businesses. In contrast, the assessment of the physical work environment among employees experiencing a decline in job security in 2009 is about the same as for the total sample in 2008 (not shown). This also makes sense, as any larger changes in the physical work environment are unlikely to have taken place between the two measurements.

A somewhat different pattern appears regarding pay satisfaction (Figure 10.3). In contrast to the previous examples, those reporting pay cuts have a considerably lower pay satisfaction than employees generally had in 2008. This negative effect of pay cuts is understandable, given that employees experienced deprivation and inequity in comparison to their previous situation. Furthermore, pay cuts may have been issued for selected categories within the organizations, thus creating opportunities for negative comparisons among some individuals. As in the previous examples, the category not experiencing pay cuts expresses much higher satisfaction with pay compared to respondents overall in 2008. It is suggested that this 'inflation' in attitude is created by a favourable comparison with those subjected to pay cuts, within the employing organization as well as in the economy in general.

Research on the basis of equity theory gives some support for this interpretation. According to this theory, inequity results from input-output discrepancies relative to some reference group. Subjects tend to resolve such inequity through cognitive or behavioural means (Goodman and Friedman 1971). It has thus been shown that overpaid individuals raise their inputs by producing more as a way of reducing inequity. Not facing pay cuts or job insecurity

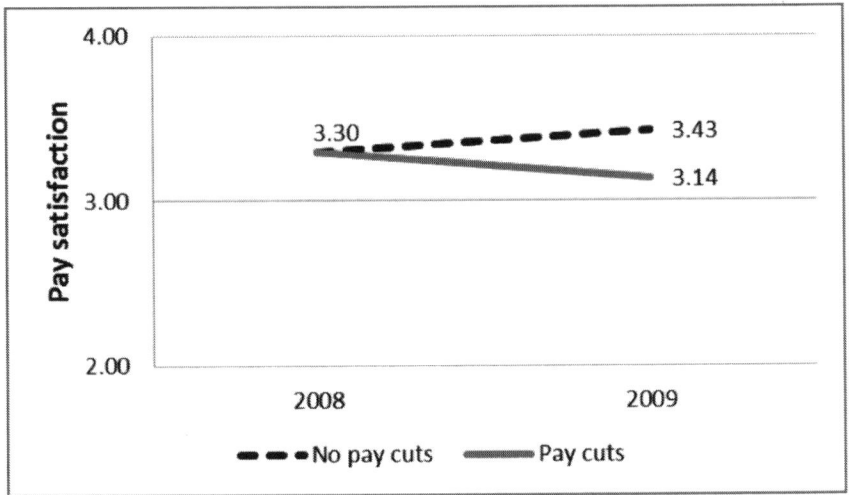

Figure 10.3   Changes in pay satisfaction, 2008 and 2009.

in a situation where many have had to do so could be interpreted as a form of 'overpayment' eliciting more positive responses among employees.

Brockner et al. (1988) similarly argue, based on equity theory, that layoffs may cause survivors to work harder in situations where employees believe they could just as well have been the victims of layoffs. The perception of 'random layoffs' can thus create 'guilt' or 'positive equity' among survivors. In some ways this may apply to the crisis in Iceland. Some organizations had to lay off people while others did not. If employees felt that organizational downsizing was somehow randomly distributed, employees in non-downsizing firms might have considered themselves fortunate in comparison.

Studies of value change show, in addition, that major recessions can shift values toward increased materialism in the short term because of an effect of 'scarcity.' Scarcity implies, in this case, that declining opportunities for gaining material rewards make people place a higher value on material factors such as work and pay (Inglehart 2008).

In the case of Iceland, this means that in light of the acute situation facing many individuals, families and businesses, employees may have reappraised some aspects of their lives. Not only did employees most likely find their work and pay to be more important than before because of the crisis, but in addition those employees feeling sheltered from various downsizing measures might have considered their situation particularly favourable. This situation was possibly viewed as an 'overpayment,' to which employees responded by increasing their support to the organization.

Such re-evaluation is likely to have taken place among employees in downsizing environments to some degree as well. This is what Rousseau (1996) calls 'transformation' of the psychological contract. As a result of the immense significance and impact of the crisis, there was probably a great readiness among employees to re-evaluate the contract they had with their employer. Employees experiencing downsizing may therefore have regarded many of the downsizing actions taken by their organization as justifiable, so that these actions may have had less effect on employee attitudes than would have been the case otherwise.

This chapter has several theoretical implications. First, as proposed in the beginning of the chapter, 'deprivation' theory would suggest that attitudes would become more negative as a consequence of the recession. It would for example predict a decline in pay satisfaction, not only among those who experienced pay cuts, but also among the overall sample because of the fall of real wages between 2008 and 2009. Deprivation theory therefore seems unable to explain the increased pay satisfaction found in the data. In contrast, a theory using social comparison as a point of departure can explain both developments: pay cuts initiate inequity (unfairness or underpayment) caused by changes in the reward-effort relationship and comparisons with more fortunate groups, while not experiencing pay cuts is associated with feelings of equity (fairness or overpayment) through comparison with less fortunate groups.

Second, we must take into account the economic and social context in which the downsizing takes place. Downsizing in a situation of economic meltdown is unlikely to be experienced in the same way as when an organization downsizes for internal (fiscal) reasons alone. Because of the crisis, employees most likely experienced downsizing as being more legitimate in light of the circumstances their organization was facing.

Third, viewing the employee-organization relationship in terms of social exchange—in which each party is obligated to reciprocate rewards brought to the exchange by the other party—offers a fruitful way for understanding how downsizing can affect employee attitudes. Equity theory adds to this understanding by highlighting 'cognitive re-evaluation' processes when employees have to adapt to rapidly changing environments.

A line of caution is in order. This chapter examines the reactions of employed union members to the crisis a few months after the collapse of an entire financial system. The economy, families and businesses were hit hard, but most of those who suffered had only just begun to deal with the aftermath of the recession. Despite all, at that point in time there might still have been a lot of hope and optimism amongst the population. What will happen in the months or years to come is still to be explored.

NOTES

1. By 2007 the financial system had grown to 873 percent of the annual domestic product of Iceland (Helgason 2010). In order to put the bankruptcy of the three largest banks in context, Baldursson and Zoëga (2011) point out that this would rank as the third largest bankruptcy in the US ever.
2. This is one peculiarity of the Icelandic economy, in which the value of loans is generally tied to some index of prices or currencies, thus safeguarding the lender from any possible loss because of inflation and devaluation of the Icelandic currency.
3. The term 'technically bankrupt' refers to business organizations that are still operating but have more debt than assets and are unlikely to be able to fully pay their debts. Some are however in operation, because they manage to pay off some of their debt, or because they are undergoing re-negotiations regarding terms of payments or they have been taken over by their creditors.
4. E.g., http://news.bbc.co.uk/2/hi/7744355.stm.
5. http://www.island.is/endurreisn/stjornvold/upplysingamidlun/frettir/nr/836.
6. Special thanks to Kristín Sigurðardóttir at the Commercial and Office Workers Union who gave her kind permission to use these data in writing this chapter.
7. Mean differences between 2008 and 2009 on life satisfaction = -0.21; $F=277$; $p<.000$; $R^2=0.02$.
8. Manova statistics: Pillais = 0.03; $F=35$; $p<.000$. Significant negative effect of pay cuts was found for all the attitudes examined; $N=7,690$.
9. Manova statistics: Pillais = 0.04; $F=44$; $p<.000$. Significant effect of layoffs were found for all the attitudes examined, $N=7,590$.
10. Significant effects were found for job insecurity on satisfaction with life, $F=240$; $p<.000$. Significant effects were also found for pay cuts, $F=76$;

p<.000; and finally, for layoffs, F=81; p<.000. R^2 for the three independent variables = 0.04; N=7,431.

11. Manova statistics for occupation and decline in job security: Pillais = 0.003; p<.05. The largest interaction effects were found for flexibility (p<.000); work environment (p<.001); morale (p<.05) and job satisfaction (p<.05). Manova statistics for occupation and layoffs: Pillais = 0.01; p<.000. The largest interaction effects were found for flexibility (p<.000); work environment (p<.001); morale (p<.01) and corporate image (p<.01).

11 Temporary Agency Workers and Organizational Commitment

Kristina Håkansson and Tommy Isidorsson

Research on organizational commitment has developed over several decades and is now quite extensive. In general, conceptualizations of commitment include a bond to the organization, a readiness to stay with it (Allen and Meyer 1990; Meyer and Herscovitch 2001). Most research on organizational commitment is based on traditional workers, that is, employees with one employer and open-ended contracts. Theories are thus built on employees' identification with, and engagement to one organization—a single employment relationship where the employer and the workplace coincide.

This chapter deals with a group of workers who have a rather different work situation—temporary agency workers. The basic idea of temporary work agencies is to provide workplaces with staff for a limited period. The agency worker does not have one fixed workplace, but has to be mobile, moving between different workplaces depending on the needs of user firms. The hiring periods can range from hours to several years. Theoretically the most important feature of temporary agency work is the temporary agency worker's dual relationship with the agency and user firm. This is illustrated in Figure 11.1.

The formal employment relationship is with the temporary work agency. However, the work is performed and managed/supervised in the user firm; therefore one can talk about a quasi employment relationship. Swedish legislation differs from that of most other countries in that the agency worker can have an open-ended contract with the temporary work agency.

The aim of this chapter is to investigate whether temporary agency workers are organizationally committed and if so whether they are committed to the temporary work agency or to the user firm and to explain why. By studying temporary agency workers' commitment it is possible to separate the impact of the employment relationship and the impact of workplace characteristics, thereby elaborating the understanding of commitment.

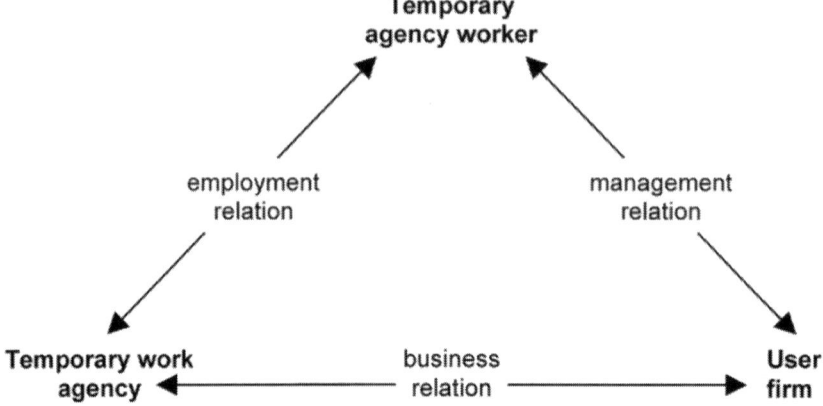

Figure 11.1   The triangular relationship between temporary agency worker, temporary work agency and user firm.

THE SWEDISH CONTEXT

The use of agency workers is a relatively new phenomenon in Sweden. Prior to the temporary work agency act in 1993 it was illegal to run private work agencies for profit-making purposes (Berg 2008: 106). In Sweden, as well as in most OECD countries, the number of agency workers increased rapidly during the last two decades. In the Netherlands and in the UK, where temporary work agencies have existed for several decades, a considerable increase took place in the 1990s with a stabilisation in the 2000s. Despite being the subject of rather extensive debate, temporary agency work is still a marginal phenomenon in the labour market. The proportion of agency workers accounts for around 1 percent of all workers in most EU countries (Storrie 2007). According to the employer organization of temporary work agencies, only a handful of countries have more than 2 percent agency workers (CIETT 2009: 22). In 2008 the number of employees in the Swedish temporary work agency industry was 58,850 according to statistics from the employer organization (Bemanningsföretagen 2009: 3), corresponding to 1.3 percent of all employees. Because of the economic downturn, sales turnover in the temporary agency work industry decreased almost 25 percent in 2009. Even though the industry accounts for a small fraction of employment, its effects on the labour market must not be underestimated; one third of all Swedish workplaces within the private sector with at least 100 employees use agency workers (Håkansson and Isidorsson 2007). The work organization in user firms has to be adjusted in response to the use of agency workers, meaning that the use of a small number of agency workers affects many more employees. Agency workers' commitment to the user firm might influence the commitment of the employees of the user firm as well.

Sweden has rather liberal regulations on agency work (Arrowsmith 2006). Temporary agency work is treated like any other industry and is not subject to any special legislation. This lack of specific legal regulation is in line with Swedish labour market practice, with the social partners given the responsibility for regulation via collective agreements. In the year 2000, the LO trade union confederation coordinated a unique collective agreement for blue-collar workers valid for fifteen affiliated trade unions (Bergström et. al. 2007: 55). The white-collar workers' union HTF was signatory to a collective agreement prior to the change in the legislation in 1993. The widespread use of agency workers and the regulation via collective agreements indicate that temporary work agencies could be seen as institutionalised in Sweden (Bergström et al. 2007).

According to Swedish legislation there are principally two different types of employment contracts: open-ended and of limited duration (SFS 1982: 80). Since temporary work agencies in Sweden are treated like any other business, the normal employment contract for an agency worker should be open-ended. It is quite common for temporary work agencies to employ staff on a probationary contract for the first six months. The practice of probationary work and the high turnover in the industry imply that there is a high proportion of limited duration contracts within the temporary work agency industry.

There is no legislation on equal pay in Sweden. The blue-collar workers' collective agreement stipulates that temporary agency workers must be paid according to the average at the workplace where they are posted (Avtal för bemanningsföretag 2007:§5 Mom 1). The white-collar workers' collective agreement stresses that salaries are based on individual qualifications (Förhandlingsprotokoll 2007 Bemanningsföretagen, HTF, Akademikerförbunden: Protokollsbilaga 1, HTF §1.1, 1.2, 1.3). The individually set salaries mean that two white-collar temporary agency workers doing the same work at the user firm can be paid differently. For both blue-collar and white-collar workers there are collective agreements stipulating a guarantee of approximately 80–90 percent pay even if the temporary agency worker does not have an assignment.

RESEARCH OVERVIEW AND THEORETICAL FRAMEWORK

In the following four sections we refer to previous research and the theoretical framework for our study. This part starts with two sections on the concept of commitment and its antecedents and is followed by a section on the position of temporary agency workers in the user firm. The research overview is finalized with a section on commitment and temporary agency workers.

The Concept of Organizational Commitment

Much research on commitment originates from psychology. In general, commitment is seen as a positive orientation to an organization, connected with the readiness to stay with the organization. In a 2001 article, Meyer and Herscovitch address the issue of what commitment is and how to define it. After an extensive research review encompassing some twenty studies, they identify a number of differences in the conception of commitment but they also find some important similarities. Most models of organizational commitment include a dimension reflecting an affective bond with the organization and a mindset characterised by a desire on the part of the employee to follow a course of action as to continue employment and exert effort to achieve organizational goals (Meyer and Herscovitch 2001: 307–308).

Allen and Meyer (1990) have developed the most used multidimensional model of organizational commitment. They distinguish three different dimensions: affective, normative and continuance commitment (see also Meyer and Allen 1991: 67–69). Affective commitment refers to the employee's emotional attachment to, identification with and involvement in the organization; the employee wants to stay. Normative commitment reflects moral obligations, a feeling of duty to remain in the organization. Continuance commitment refers to an individual's awareness of the high costs of leaving the organization, which means that he or she needs to stay. Different studies support their organizational commitment model (e.g., Dunham, Grube and Castaneda 1994). Since the normative component has shown similarities with the affective component regarding antecedents and consequences, many researchers use only the affective and the continuance components (Coleman, Irving and Cooper 1999: 996). This chapter focuses on temporary agency workers' emotional attachment to, identification with and involvement in organizations. We are interested in the voluntary attachment to the organization and the employee's willingness to get involved in the organization, that is, affective commitment. This view on organizational commitment is also put forward by Gallie et al. (1998).

Antecedents of Affective Organizational Commitment

Mowday, Porter and Steers (1982) found several antecedents of affective commitment: personal characteristics, structural characteristics, job-related characteristics and work experience. Allen and Meyer (1990: 4, 8–9) point to work experience as the strongest antecedent of affective commitment; employees who felt comfortable and competent in the job expressed greater affective commitment to the organization. The variables used to measure work experience were job challenge, role clarity, goal clarity, participation in decisions regarding their own work, feedback, management receptiveness, peer cohesion, equity and personal importance. Work experience thus includes factors connected both to job satisfaction and to the relationship with the organization. Meyer and Allen (1997: 42–49) examine the research on antecedents closely and introduce two further factors: individual fulfillment of self-worth and met expectations. Personal characteristics such as sex and education showed no correlation with affective commitment, while age seemed to be important—older people are more inclined to exhibit affective organizational commitment than are younger people (Meyer and Allen 1997: 43).

Commitment is a mutual relation and presupposes the organization's commitment to employees or at least an employee perception of such commitment (Eisenberger et al. 1986: 501). Baruch (1998) argues that commitment is declining because of the way organizations are dealing with economic crises. Frequent downsizing processes undermine employees' commitment to the organization. According to Baruch (1998), employment security is crucial for employees' commitment to the organization. However, Gallie et al. (1998: 243) report that there was no evidence that staff reductions reduced organizational commitment.

The Position of Temporary Agency Workers in the User Firm

There is a widespread conception of temporary work as a means to achieve flexibility. By using employees on temporary contracts and temporary agency workers, employers can easily adapt the number of workers to actual demand. This is illustrated in the model of the flexible firm by John Atkinson (1984). The same notion of temporary agency workers appears in several later studies (Houseman 2001; Kalleberg 2001; Kalleberg, Reynolds and Marsden 2003: 532; Kauhanen 2001; Mitlacher 2007). It is then assumed that agency workers are assigned to work tasks with short induction time, in practice often routine work tasks that can be carried out by unqualified and easily replaceable staff, while user firm employees perform the more qualified and firm-specific work tasks.

However, not all temporary agency workers belong to the periphery (Håkansson and Isidorsson 2011). When they are used for work tasks that require high qualifications and the assignment is expected to be long term, there is no obvious segmentation in core and periphery in the workplace. Rather, the temporary agency workers' situation is similar to that of core workers in the user firm. We can hypothesize that a core position would increase a temporary agency workers' commitment toward the user firm. It may also be assumed that their attachments to the agency and to the user firm differ depending on how they perceive their positions and opportunities by comparison with the user firm employees.

Temporary Agency Workers and Commitment

Temporary agency workers and their commitment have been dealt with in several studies. Unfortunately most researchers do not distinguish between different forms of non-standard employment contracts. Employees with non-standard contracts, sometimes called contingent or just non-permanent employees, may consist of very different categories: workers on short-term contracts, workers on fixed-term contracts, contractors and temporary agency workers. The studies on non-standard contracts show mixed results.

Some studies on employees on non-permanent contracts show that they have less affective commitment toward their employer than do employees with a permanent contract (e.g., Van Dyne and Ang 1998; Millward and Hopkins 1998: 1548; Forde and Slater 2006: 153–155). Gallie et al. (1998: 242–247) found that the differences in organizational commitment between employees on temporary contracts and those on open-ended contracts disappear when taking into account practices and policies which are usually applied to longer-term employees such as possibilities for competence development and participation in communication and decision-making. The results of their study boil down to the fact that dissatisfaction with perceived (job) security was linked to reduced organizational commitment. Comparing permanent employees and contractors, Pearce (1993: 1093) comes to a conclusion similar to that of Gallie et al. that there is no difference in organizational commitment between the two groups. In an explorative study, Coyle-Shapiro and Morrow (2006: 426–427) find that employees in outsourced work, that is, contractors, are committed both to their user firm and to their employer. One of the conclusions of the study is that researchers have to examine the nature of commitment in these non-standard employment relationships.

In many countries a merger of the different non-standard employment relations, including temporary agency work, has not been regarded as especially problematic. However, in most countries the temporary agency worker has a temporary contract at the agency, and the differences in commitment between agency workers and user firm employees might be explained by the different employment relations. Explaining these inconsistent and inconclusive findings, De Cuyper et al. (2008: 34–36) point to several shortcomings in previous research. One is that traditional antecedents of organizational commitment may not apply to temporary agency workers. They also identify the heterogeneity of the category 'temporary workers' as a problem, as working conditions can differ in relation to, for example, employment contracts and skill requirements. In a literature review, Connelly and Gallagher (2004: 962) notice that one explanation for the contradictory results may be the heterogeneity in the group of contingent workers. Broschak, Davies-Black and Block (2008: 30) emphasise agency workers' different possibilities of getting access to the internal labour market at the user firm. They found high commitment to the user firm in cases where the agency worker thought there was a chance of making a career at the user firm. This is in line with the results presented by Gallie et al. (1998).

Research focused solely on temporary agency workers and their commitment is scarce. This is also noted by Galais and Moser (2009: 595). Their focus is, however, the relationship between agency workers, commitment and well-being. Liden et al. (2003: 620) have written one of a small number of articles studying temporary agency workers' dual commitment to the agency and the user firm. Their main finding is that perceived organizational support from the agency is positively related to commitment to the agency and that perceived organizational support from the user firm is positively related to commitment to the user firm. Their study is somewhat limited as it is based on only 98 temporary agency workers placed at one user firm (Liden et al. 2003: 625). Connelly, Gallagher and Gilley (2007: 333) found that perceived organizational support from the agency was correlated with affective commitment to both the agency and to the user firm, a so-called spill-over effect. They also introduced the role of voluntariness into the analysis. It was shown that temporary agency workers who had actively chosen temporary work were more likely to form an emotional bond with their temporary agencies. Similar results concerning perceived organizational support were found by Van Breugel, Van Olffen and Olie (2005: 539) in their investigation of temporary agency workers' organizational commitment to the agency. Support from the agency could, for example, involve career support and close contacts between the agency manager and the agency worker. In contrast to the results in the study by Connelly, Gallagher and Gilley (2007), voluntary choice of an agency did not appear to create an affective bond with it.

To sum up, previous sections show that research on organizational commitment of traditional workers is quite extensive but scarce in relation to temporary agency workers. The ambiguous results in previous research indicate that there is a need for additional explanatory factors. Our analysis includes both explanatory variables from previous research and some new variables that are intended to capture how agency workers are used and integrated in the user firm.

DATA AND METHODOLOGY

Our intention was to have a sample representing Swedish temporary agency workers. Since there is no central register for these workers, we decided to approach temporary work agencies but there have been considerable difficulties in finding agencies willing to participate in our survey. There are several explanations for this. First, the temporary work agencies regarded the survey as badly timed because of the economic crisis in 2009, with most industries carrying out dismissals, including terminating many contracts with agency workers. This also affected temporary work agencies that were in a process of downsizing. Managers in the industry whom we approached were afraid that dismissals within their own companies would have a negative effect on organizational commitment, and therefore they chose not to participate. Second, during autumn 2009 the temporary work agency industry received some unfavourable attention on television and in other media, with reports of poor working conditions for its workers. This probably had a negative impact on the willingness to participate in our survey.

Altogether two regional branch offices and one national temporary work agency participated in the survey. The agency workers were assigned to a large number of user firms. We distributed the survey among four occupational groups: office and administration services; IT services; finance/accounting and manufacturing/logistics. Unfortunately, we received too few responses from agency workers in manufacturing/logistics to include them in the analysis. The study therefore only includes white-collar workers.

The questionnaire was distributed via the Internet during autumn 2009 and spring 2010. This was seen as the best method, as temporary agency workers are used to communicating with their employers via the Internet, for example when reporting working time. Our aim was to distribute the electronic survey directly to the temporary agency workers' e-mail addresses. This was possible in only one company where we also sent out two reminders. Neither of the other two agencies had a centralised e-mail list. In these cases an Internet link to a questionnaire was sent by e-mail to a branch office manager or regional manager. They distributed the link to their consultant managers (first line managers) who in turn forwarded the questionnaire link to his or her staff. We therefore did not have full control over distribution and in these two agencies it was only possible for us to send out one reminder. In total we have 533 respondents within office and administration, IT services and finance/accounting. The response rate was 41 per cent.

The questionnaire consisted of 35 questions covering, among other things, employment at the agency, the assignment at the user firm and personal characteristics such as age and educational level. The dependent variable in this study is affective organizational commitment, measured by four questions elaborated and used by Allen and Meyer (1990: 6). We used the same questions but asked for organizational commitment to the employer *and* to the user firm. A fifth question was added in relation to the user firm. Thus the following items were included:

1. I would be very happy to spend the rest of my career with my temporary work agency/user firm.
2. I enjoy discussing my temporary work agency/user firm with people outside it.
3. I think that I could easily become as attached to another organization as I am to this agency/user firm (reversed).
4. I really feel as if this agency's/user firm's problems are my own.

5. I would gladly accept an open-ended contract at my present user firm.

The questions on commitment are thus made up of four plus five statements and respondents were asked to take a stand on them. Five response alternatives were given on each statement: '1 strongly agree', '2 slightly agree', '3 neither agree nor disagree', '4 slightly disagree' and '5 strongly disagree'.

A principal component analysis using Varimax rotated factor analysis revealed three dimensions (Table 11.1). The two first components that

Table 11.1 Affective Organizational Commitment to the Temporary Work Agency (TWA) and to the User Firm. Principal Component Analysis

	Component 1 Committed to user firm	Component 2 Committed to TWA	Component 3 Easily committed/ volatile
I enjoy discussing my user firm with people outside it.	0.744	0.026	0.146
I would be very happy to spend the rest of my career with my user firm.	0.854	-0.017	0.065
I would gladly accept an open-ended contract at my present user firm.	0.847	-0.243	0.016
I really feel as if this user firm's problems are my own.	0.729	0.156	-0.086
I enjoy discussing my temporary work agency with people outside it.	0.017	0.836	0.146
I would be very happy to spend the rest of my career with my temporary work agency.	-0.090	0.828	-0.091
I really feel as if this agency's problems are my own.	0.050	0.841	0.040
I think that I could easily become as attached to another organization as I am to this user firm.	-0.081	0.045	0.803
I think that I could easily become as attached to another organization as I am to this agency.	0.130	0.023	0.786

n= 438[1]

Extraction method: Principal component analysis. Rotation method: Varimax with Kaiser Normalization. Rotation converged in 4 iterations.

emerged refer to user firm commitment and agency commitment, respectively. A third, 'mixed' component also appeared. It covers a set of responses indicating that the individuals are casual or volatile—they could easily be committed to any user firm or agency.

An index of commitment to the user firm was constructed by the four questions that loaded highly on component 1.[2] An index of commitment to the agency was constructed in a similar way to the questions that loaded highly on component 2.[3] Forming these indexes an average value of maximum 2 ('slightly agree') was coded as committed to the agency and the user firm, respectively. The third dimension did not fulfil the requirement to construct a scale.

Employment conditions include three items: type of employment contract, satisfaction with pay and satisfaction with employment security. Job experience was measured by a number of items used in previous research: A Varimax rotated factor analysis revealed three dimensions[4]: (1) satisfaction with variation and challenge; (2) satisfaction with influence; and (3) satisfaction with information and contact with the agency. The two first dimensions concern job satisfaction and appear, for example, in the research by Allen and Meyer (1990: 8) and Mowday, Porter and Steers (1982). The third dimension could be interpreted as perceived organizational support, also discussed by Liden et al. (2003) and Eisenberger et al. (1986). These dimensions were transformed into three indexes.

The core-periphery position of the agency worker was measured by a number of items on satisfaction with opportunities for training and the agency workers' possibility to participate in change projects[5] compared to user firm employees. The special situation as a mobile worker was measured by items on the number of previous assignments and the duration of the current assignment.

ANALYSES AND RESULTS

The respondents in this study differed from the average Swedish temporary agency worker, by having a higher educational level; 50 percent have a university level. The corresponding share in the industry is one third (Andersson and Wadensjö 2004: 37). From a work-content point of view one can label our sample the cream of temporary agency workers. The workers in our sample were also older than the average temporary worker and more likely to be union members. We expected this group of temporary agency workers to have the best working conditions and so the best prerequisites to be committed to both the agency and the user firm.

A brief picture of the respondents reveals that there was a dominance of women, 68 percent. Age ranged from 19 to 65, with a mean value of 38 years. Most of the respondents, 68 percent, had an open-ended contract with their temporary work agency, and the vast majority, 85 percent, were born in Sweden. Of the non-Swedes half were born within EU and half outside. In our sample we have three major occupational groups accounting for roughly one third each: office/clerical/call centre workers; IT/ technicians/engineers; and accounting/finance staff. Six percent of the temporary agency workers did not fit into any of these three groups and so we categorized them as 'other.'

The analysis of affective organizational commitment among temporary agency workers' dual employment relationship can involve four types: commitment to the user firm, to the temporary work agency, to both the user firm and the agency and to neither the agency nor the user firm (Table 11.2). The majority of the respondents, almost 60 percent, were committed to at least one organization, foremost to the user firm. Slightly more than 40 percent showed affective organizational commitment neither to the temporary work agency nor the user firm.

The analysis of organizational commitment among temporary agency workers will be carried out by means of logistic regressions. Two models are presented (Table 11.3). The independent variables in the first one, among other things, include sex, age, country of birth and education. At least age has previously turned out to be correlated with organizational commitment. Other independent variables are type of contract, satisfaction with pay and job security, tenure at the agency and occupational group. Finally, there are two variables on job satisfaction. These variables have been pointed out as the main antecedents for organizational commitment among employees in traditional employment relations, that is, employees with one employer and open-ended contracts. Our factor analysis above also confirmed the construction of two job satisfaction indexes. We now test their association with organizational commitment both to the employer (the agency) and to the user firm.

The second model adds variables intended to capture the specific character of agency work. Satisfaction with information and contact with the agency, satisfaction with training offered by the agency and development discussions with the agency are three aspects to be considered. Previous research has brought out perceived organizational support as an important antecedent for agency workers' commitment. Moreover we introduce some

Table 11.2 Organizational Commitment to the Temporary Work Agency and to the User Firm. Percent

		Commitment to user firm	
		yes	no
Commitment to temporary work agency	yes	9.6	10.1
	no	37.3	43.0

n=525

variables on how temporary agency workers are used and integrated in the user firms. The measures describe how respondents perceive their access to training in the user firm and their opportunities to participate in change projects. There are also two variables on the time of the present assignment and on the number of assignments the agency worker has been contracted for. It should be emphasised that these variables have not been examined in any quantitative study before. The results of our regression models appear in Table 11.3.

In Model 1 we find a large number of interesting results. Sex seems to have a significant effect; women were less likely to show organizational commitment to the agency. Age is strongly associated with organizational commitment, with older employees more likely to be organizationally committed. This is in line with previous research by Meyer and Allen (1997: 43). However, the age effect is reversed but not significant as regards commitment to the user firm. Educational level shows no clear impact on commitment to the agency, but respondents with a university education are less inclined to be committed to the user firm. Country of birth shows no obvious effects, neither in relation to the agency nor to the user firm.

In reference to the questions on type of contract, satisfaction with pay and satisfaction with employment security we find type of contract does not seem to matter. It is instead perceived employment security that affects commitment to the agency and to the user firm, positively in the first case and negatively in the second. Respondents were also more likely to be committed to the agency if they were satisfied with pay. We should note that these dimensions of satisfaction are factors that the agency can influence. Tenure at the agency turns out not to be an important variable, but we find some effects related to type of assignment. Respondents within the category accounting/financing tended more often to show commitment to the agency, whereas the category 'other' was more likely to be committed to the user firm. The items on job satisfaction at the current assignment do not affect commitment to the temporary work agency much, but they have considerable effects on commitment to the user firm. This commitment is obviously strongly linked to the situation where the work is performed.

With some exceptions, most of the significant results found in Model 1 are sufficiently robust to remain throughout Model 2, in which a number of other variables are introduced. One of the exceptions is the variable 'satisfaction with employment security'; in Model 2 those who were satisfied with their with employment security were no longer significantly more likely to be committed to the agency. However, they were still less likely to be committed to the user firm.

In Model 2 we take the specific character of temporary agency work into account. Temporary agency workers are engaged for a limited period of time in the user firm, even though an assignment can last for years. They could be assigned to simple and unattractive work tasks, to specific work tasks requiring high qualifications or to the same work tasks and the same

Table 11.3   Factors Impacting on Commitment to Temporary Work Agency (TWA) User Firm. Odds Ratios

Factors	Model 1 Commitment to:		Model 2 Commitment to:	
	TWA	user firm	TWA	user firm
Sex (ref: Male)	1	1	1	1
Female	0.447*	0.719	0.472+	0.801
Age (ref: 18-29)	1	1	1	1
30-45	2.088+	0.907	2.442+	0.958
46-64	3.747**	0.630	4.228**	0.688
Education (ref: Primary or secondary)	1	1	1	1
Post-secondary	1.686	0.749	2.058	0.763
University	0.929	0.503**	1.225	0.440**
Country of birth (ref: Sweden)	1	1	1	1
Outside Sweden	1.224	1.063	1.133	1.025
Type of contract (ref: Fixed-term)	1	1	1	1
Open-ended contract	1.288	1.124	1.366	1.558
Satisfied with employment security				
Yes	2.933***	0.498**	1.524	0.534*
No (ref.)	1	1	1	1
Satisfied with pay				
Yes	2.628**	1.044	2.797**	1.197
No (ref.)	1	1	1	1
Tenure at the agency (ref: Less than 1 year)	1	1	1	1
1-3 years	1.705	0.888	1.702	0.905
4 years and more	1.867	0.760	1.752	1.142
Occupation Office/clerical/call centre workers (ref.)	1	1	1	1
IT/ Technician/Engineer	1.049	1.449	1.281	1.794+
Accounting/finance	2.036+	0.989	1.779	1.482
Other	2.173	2.873*	1.998	2.234
Satisfied with variation and challenge at current assignment				
Yes	1.536	2.322***	0.904	2.459***
No (ref.)	1	1	1	1

(*continued*)

Table 11.3   (continued)

Factors	Model 1 Commitment to:		Model 2 Commitment to:	
	TWA	user firm	TWA	user firm
Satisfied with influence at work at the current assignment				
Yes	1.801+	2.302***	1.586	1.812*
No (ref.)	1	1	1	1
Satisfied with information and contact with agency				
Yes			6.945***	0.925
No (ref.)			1	1
Have had development discussion				
Yes (ref.)			1	1
No			0.466+	1.622
Satisfied with training offered by the agency				
Yes			1.221	0.266***
No (ref.)			1	1
Satisfied with training offered by the user firm				
Yes			0.801	2.268*
No (ref.)			1	1
Time at present assignment (ref: Max. 3 months)			1	1
4-12 months			0.479	1.155
more than one year			0.347+	1.725
Contracted to other user firms (ref: No)			1	1
Yes, 1-10 other user firms			1.164	0.543+
Yes, more than 10 other user firms			0.578	0.435
Opportunities to participate in change projects in the user firm				
Equal or better			1.861+	1.605*
Worse (ref.)			1	1
Constant	0.016***	1.096	0.015***	0.473
Nagelkerke R2	0.317	0.178	0.454	0.266
n	460	456	428	426

Note: + $p<0.1$, * $p<0.05$, ** $p<0.01$, *** $p<0.001$.

working conditions as the user firm employees. We assume that belonging to the core in the user firm is important in explaining commitment among temporary agency workers. Our indicators refer to employees' opportunities for training and development as well as opportunities to participate in change projects. We also expect that agency workers who stay in the same user firm for a long time are more likely to show commitment to the user firm than those who have changed user firms several times.

The added variables measuring the specific work situation of temporary agency workers have an effect on organizational commitment both to the agency and to the user firm, but in different ways. One of the most conspicuous results in this respect is the strong impact of the variable 'satisfied with information and contact with agency.' It is seven times more likely that agency workers satisfied with information and contact with the agency are committed to the agency than those who are not satisfied. The prevalence of development discussions at the agency has a significant effect in the same direction.

Satisfaction with training offered by the agency shows no significant effect on organizational commitment to the agency but a negative effect in relation to the user firm. Hence, agency workers satisfied with training offered by the agency were not significantly more often committed to the work agency, but they tended to be committed to the user firm to a significantly lower degree. An indicator of the agency worker's position in the user firm is the possibility to participate in change projects or development work. Having fewer possibilities than user firm employees could imply a peripheral position in the workplace. An interesting result is that employees reporting equal or better opportunities to participate in change projects than user firm employees were more likely to be committed to both the user firm and the agency; there is a clear spill-over effect; a core position at the user firm apparently also contributes to commitment to the agency.

A long assignment might reduce the probability of being committed to the agency and increase the probability of being committed to the user firm. However, only those who stayed more than one year showed significantly lower values for commitment to the agency, and no significant effect could be discovered for them on commitment to the user firm. Accordingly, it is not tenure at the user firm that explains commitment to it but rather the actual job situation at the workplace. At the same time, experience of assignments at many user firms seems to decrease the probability of being committed to the user firm, although the data are only partly statistically verified. Employees who actually face the unpredictability of agency work appear not to become attached to any workplace. We find a similar pattern regarding commitment to the agency, but this effect is not statistically significant.

The inclusion of variables measuring the specific work situation as an agency worker in Model 2 also implied that satisfaction with employment security lost its previous significance. This is in line with the studies by

Gallie et al. (1998) and Pearce (1993) who argue that the type of contract in itself is not important; commitment follows the practices and policies which are usually applied to longer-term employees. It seems that contact with and recognition by managers at the temporary work agency are more important in explaining commitment than are actual training courses.

DISCUSSION AND CONCLUSIONS

The aim of this chapter was to investigate if and how temporary agency workers are committed and if so whether they are committed to the temporary work agency or to the user firm and to explain why. Our analysis—based on the Allen and Meyer (1990: 6) questions on affective organizational commitment—shows that the majority, 57 percent, of the agency workers in our study were committed to at least one of the organizations. Most often they were committed to the user firm; 37 percent were committed only to the user firm and 10 percent were committed only to the agency, whereas 10 percent were committed to both. It must be mentioned that our sample was not completely representative and could best be described as covering the cream of agency workers.

Previous research has produced quite ambiguous explanations of temporary agency workers' affective organizational commitment. The role and importance of employment security is one point that has not been clear. Some researchers have found less commitment among fixed-term employees (Forde and Slater 2006; Van Dyne and Ang 1998; Millvard and Hopkins 1998), while others discovered no differences between employees on fixed-term and open-ended contracts (Gallie et al. 1998; Pearce 1993). Our study supports the latter result; perceived employment security does not seem to have any effect on affective commitment vis-à-vis the employer when taking perceived organizational support into account.

Agency workers are obviously committed to the two organizations for different reasons, although there are a few similarities. Job satisfaction turned out to be important when explaining commitment, which has also been emphasised by other researchers (Allen and Meyer 1990; Meyer and Allen 1997). However, the effects of job satisfaction on commitment are only connected to the workplace itself—the user firm. Agency workers who are satisfied with their influence on and the challenge provided by the actual work in the current assignment are more likely to show commitment to the user firm. The experience of job satisfaction is thus not connected to the employment relationship but to everyday work.

Commitment to the agency is strongly linked to perceived organizational support such as information and contacts with the manager at the agency and the prevalence of discussions about personal development. This has also been pointed out by Liden et al. (2003), Connelly, Gallagher and Gilley (2007) and Van Breugel, Van Olffen and Olie (2005). Their research indicates that support from the agency, for example career planning and close contact, increases commitment to the agency. Furthermore, including these variables in the analysis overrides the effect of perceived employment security, which ceases to have significant effects on commitment. Temporary agency workers' employment security is dependent on their employability, which is probably improved through discussions about personal development and contacts with the manager at the agency. Satisfaction with pay is also important in explaining commitment to the agency.

Access to training could be interpreted as organizational support (Liden et al. 2003; Connelly, Gallagher and Gilley 2007) but also as an indicator of integration. Even though we cannot assume that temporary agency workers belong to the core because of training, we could suppose that user firms that offer training for agency workers probably do not use them for peripheral work tasks (Håkansson and Isidorsson 2011). The variable satisfaction with training shows some interesting results. Agency workers who were satisfied with training offered by the user firm were more likely to show commitment to the user firm, but there were no corresponding results concerning training offered by the agency. One explanation could be that the agency worker has higher expectations of training from the employing organization. According to Meyer and Allen (1997), commitment decreases when expectations are not met.

Another indicator of integration and belonging to the core workers in the user firm is the possibility to participate in change projects and development work. Broschak, Davies-Black and Block (2008) found high commitment to the user firm in cases where the agency worker thought there were career opportunities at the workplace. Our findings modify these results to some extent. Even though participating in change projects and development work is closely connected to the actual workplace (the user firm), our study shows that this affects commitment to the user firm and to the agency in the same way. There is simply a commitment spill-over effect from the user firm to the agency. Also Connelly, Gallagher and Gilley (2007: 327, 333) notice a spill-over effect; however their study showed a spill-over effect for perceived organizational support, which was not confirmed in our study.

The effect of being mobile by working at different user firms has not been studied in previous research. Our analysis shows that mobility has a negative effect on commitment to the user firm. Frequent changes of workplace thus prevent affective commitment. Furthermore, the duration of assignment and tenure at the agency do not seem to matter. Hence, affective commitment does not emerge over time but is explained by the actual work situation.

To sum up, the analysis of the dual employment relationship reveals some interesting patterns. Job satisfaction is an important factor to take into account if one wants to understand affective organizational commitment. However, the importance of job satisfaction is linked to the workplace and it therefore influences the propensity of organizational commitment to the user firm but not to the employer. Organizational support, for example information, contact and discussions about personal development with the agency, is important when it comes to understanding and explaining temporary agency workers' organizational commitment to their employer. Furthermore, our analysis shows that factors capturing the specific work situation of temporary agency workers help explain organizational commitment. The mobile character of agency work seems to affect only commitment to the user firm—with several assignments the probability of showing affective commitment decreases. The way temporary agency workers are used in the user firm, and if they are integrated or not, seems to be important for affective commitment to both the agency and the user firm.

To conclude, agency workers' affective organizational commitment is foremost characterised by competing loyalties either to the agency or to the user firm—factors that explain commitment to one organization have a reverse or no effect on the commitment to the other organization. However, our analysis reveals one exception, a spill-over effect—if the agency worker is well integrated in the user firm, this leads not only to an increase in commitment to the user firm but also affects commitment to the agency.

NOTES

1. The item "I really feel as if this user firm's problems are my own" was missing in the questionnaire to the employees in one agency. Thus 101 people are missing in the principal component analysis. However, the same analysis including all respondents but without the missed question gives principally the same result. In order to keep as many responses as possible, the scale of commitment to the user firm consists of all four items that loaded high on user firm commitment, and the people who missed one item are coded manually on the basis of the average of three items instead of four.
2. Cronbach's alpha = 0.805.
3. Cronbach's alpha = 0.770.
4. The items satisfaction with task variety, job challenge and fit between tasks and skills loaded highly on the first dimension. The items satisfaction with influence how to perform the job, possibilities to plan the job, influence on working time schedule, job clarity, information from the user firm and contact with the supervisor at the user firm loaded highly on the second dimension. Finally, the items satisfaction regarding changes at the agency, the variation as an agency worker and the contact with the manager at the agency loaded highly on the third dimension.
5. 'Change project' is something separate from the daily production. It can be improvements of the production process or work process. The Lean Production concept Kaizen (continuous improvements) can be seen as a small-scale change project.

12 Work Travel
Stimulating or Stressful?

Bengt Furåker

Working conditions in economically advanced societies have been subject to numerous studies. Researchers have dealt with issues such as physical environments, working hours, workload, work intensity, occupational health and stress, pay systems, job contents, opportunities for training and career, job autonomy, task discretion and employees' influence over decision-making in the organization. After decades of research we have access to a huge body of knowledge regarding various aspects of people's working conditions. Yet, not much attention has been paid to the fact that travel is an important element in many jobs. The present chapter is an attempt to provide some remedy for this. It is aimed at contributing new knowledge about people's subjective relationship to travel because of work assignments. The main question raised is whether, or rather to what degree, job travelers consider travel stimulating and stressful, respectively. In either case, this kind of activity may have significant impact on job satisfaction. The empirical basis for the analysis is a Swedish survey among a random sample of employed individuals, carried out in 2005.

There are many different reasons why people travel in their jobs. Some are employed in the transportation sector as drivers of vehicles, ticket collectors, cabin attendants, etc. Work tasks then consist of driving, piloting or navigating or of activities performed while traveling. In other jobs, people go to different places more or less every day to carry out their work tasks; some electricians, sellers and health care workers can exemplify this. Furthermore, many employed leave their regular workplace occasionally to attend meetings, conferences, exhibitions and the like. Although work travel has increased in developed societies over a number of decades (e.g., Swarbrooke and Horner 2001), our knowledge about it is rather limited. It seems that we know more about commuting, which is a related but yet different phenomenon.

The purpose of this chapter is to examine how people conceive of job travel as an element of their working conditions. It starts out from two simple questions: Is this kind of travel mainly a stimulant for the employed or is it, to the contrary, above all something stressful—a burden—for them? Now we should not equate stimulating conditions with job satisfaction and stressful conditions with the opposite; the assumption is just that these factors are likely to influence the degree of satisfaction. It is then also essential to study how the experiences of work travel are affected by the circumstances under which it takes place. I will, for example, consider how often people travel in their jobs, whether and how often they stay overnight and to what extent they have control over when to travel.

WORK TRAVEL AND QUALITY OF WORK ISSUES

In modern societies, most people of working-age spend a large part of their time working, and the conditions under which the job is performed are highly important for them. These circumstances impinge on the individuals' commitment, effort and performance, their job satisfaction and their physical health and mental wellbeing. There are various negative consequences associated with poor physical environments, excessive workload and work intensity, degraded work tasks, job monotony, insufficient opportunities for training and absence of employee autonomy and influence. The research available shows considerable differences with respect to working conditions across countries, industries and social categories (e.g., Cully et al. 1999; Gallie 2007a; Gallie et al. 1998; Karasek and Theorell 1990; Parent-Thirion et al. 2007).

Despite an impressive bulk of knowledge regarding working conditions in modern societies, there are certain lacunas, and one aspect which has frequently been neglected is work travel. This activity forms an integral part of many jobs, but its role varies substantially across occupational categories. Many individuals travel in their jobs—to a greater or lesser extent—but often under very different circumstances which are likely to affect their work satisfaction or dissatisfaction. People who think that travel makes their job stimulating do not necessarily have to be very satisfied with their job—as there are many other aspects to take into consideration—but it can be a significant positive factor. Inversely, if work-related travel is experienced as stressful, it probably creates dissatisfaction, although there may be counteracting factors.

We have several reasons to believe that job travel can be an inspiring element in people's working conditions. Two aspects appear to be particularly significant. The first has to do with the potential positive effects on individuals of variation in their work situation. According to the fourth European survey of working conditions, conducted in 2005, more than four out of ten respondents characterize their jobs as monotonous (Parent-Thirion et al. 2007: 46–48). This is above all manifest among the young and among people with low educational level and manual jobs. Work travel can then provide an opportunity for breaking away from old routines. Travelers get a chance to gain other than the usual experiences, see different places, meet with new people and—especially when going abroad—come across new cultures. Journeys can be associated with staying in hotels and eating out in fancy restaurants, and they can sometimes resemble tourism by including sightseeing, visits to museums and concerts and the like (Høyer and Næss 2001; Lassen 2006). It has been shown that long-distance travelers often develop a cosmopolitan outlook, without thereby losing their local ties (Gustafson 2009).

All of the above are likely to contribute to preventing or reducing monotony. There is, however, an obvious reservation to be made: work travel can be or become a matter of routine as well. Some people travel every day, follow the same route, do the same things and meet more or less the same people. Consequently, on the whole, they have almost indistinguishable experiences day after day. The fact that they travel in their job does not mean much variation at all. Even people who go to different far-away places but do it frequently may have similar feelings; that is, they too become subject to monotony. Airports and big cities may have a great deal of attraction in the beginning, but after a while they can also become coupled with routine and boredom.

Another possible positive aspect of job travel is that it may offer some freedom and autonomy (Bergström 2006, 2008; Gustafson 2006; Presser and Hermsen 1996). In modern working life, employers make use of many different forms of control (Edwards 1979: 18–22; Furåker 2005: 79–85). These forms include personal supervision as well as control through 'bureaucratic' rules, through technical devices and of output. By being away from their regular workplace, employees are to some extent outside the control by managers and—not to be ignored—by workmates. This is likely to be most relevant for those who are normally under tight supervision in their jobs.

When job travelers carry out their work tasks in a vehicle and hence have their 'workplace' with them, they can frequently enjoy a considerable measure of freedom and autonomy. Truck drivers make up a good illustration of this (Ouellet 1994). Once on the road, they cannot so easily be controlled, although modern technology furnishes devices to be used for that purpose: black boxes, cell phones, portable computers, etc. It is nevertheless difficult to take away all freedom related to job travel. Work autonomy is important for job satisfaction and travel may be associated with a degree of autonomy that is otherwise less likely to appear.

There are thus certain reasons to believe that job travel is often perceived as stimulating, at least unless it is so common that it becomes dull and boring. However, we must also look at the other side of the coin. Besides the possibility that this kind of travel becomes a matter of routine, there may be other negative features associated with it. We can think of aspects such as leaving home early in the morning to go to distant places, coming back late, having long workdays, staying overnight (which is not always a pleasant thing to do) and being burdened by heavy workload and stress (Bergström 2006, 2008; Espino et al. 2002; Gustafson 2006; Ivancevic, Konopaske and DeFrank 2003; Striker et al. 1999). Sometimes work travel implies that employees must live up to employers' demands for flexibility (for a discussion of the concept of flexibility, see, e.g., Furåker 2005: ch. 8; Furåker, Håkansson and Karlsson 2007). For example, they may have to be continually prepared to visit various places at short notice. A full regular travel schedule can be arduous, but it is presumably more trying not to know much in advance where and when to go.

A key research question is here whether or to what extent various categories experience job travel mainly as a burden or as a stimulating element of their working conditions. In throwing light on these issues, several aspects must be taken into account. First, we need to consider traveling frequency; to be on the move every day or several days a week is very different from doing it just now and then. It is probably more stimulating to have some work travel than none at all, but once a certain limit is crossed this association may disappear. Moreover, from that—or some other—limit, people may become more likely to feel that travel makes their work stressful. Second, another relevant aspect is whether travelers stay overnight or not and—if they do so—how frequently this happens. Again, it is conceivable that we find certain thresholds. Some overnight stays per year may be exciting, but when a certain number is reached this effect may level off. It is more difficult to anticipate how overnight stays might be related to the experience of stress, and therefore I refrain from formulating any hypothesis in this respect.

A third issue to be dealt with is the impact of traveling abroad. Presumably, trips to foreign countries entail some stimulating features, but they may also bring about stress. We should be aware that work-related long-distance and overnight travel is most common among well-educated men in higher white-collar positions (Gustafson 2005; Presser and Hermsen 1996). Most work travelers do not go abroad at all. Fourth, an interesting theme is whether or to what extent people have control over when to travel. It can be supposed that a high degree of control has stress-reducing effects and as a result contributes to making travel stimulating. Fifth, I examine whether people go on trips alone or together with workmates and the implications of the one and the other. A reasonable hypothesis is that company renders travel both stimulating and less stressful. At the same time, however, it may include some element of social control. Finally, I consider the consequences of inconvenient hours associated with work travel. It seems indeed likely that people who have to leave their home early in the morning and/or come home late in the evening experience this as a burden.

Several other factors should also be taken into account, such as sex, marital status, having children at home, age, working time and socioeconomic category (class). As the social division of labour (in terms of paid and unpaid work, etc.) and work-family conflicts are clearly gendered, we might expect women to be more prone than men to consider work travel stressful. Moreover, I pay attention to people's marital status and what it means to have children at home, as the problem of combining travel with family obligations has been a crucial topic in previous research (Bergström 2006, 2008; Espino et al. 2002; Gustafson 2006; Striker et al. 1999; Westman, Etzion and Gattenio 2008). Another possibly relevant dimension is age, although it is difficult to anticipate the outcome. On the one hand, we may assume work travel to be more stimulating and less stressful for the young, but, on the other hand, many older workers who actually travel may do this because they enjoy it or have become accustomed to it. In other words, there is likely to be an element of self-selection involved. Working time is yet another factor to be considered, because long hours—in combination with work travel—can be anticipated to impact on whether people experience their situation as stressful or not. Finally, socioeconomic position presumably has a role to play, as the conditions under which workers travel are related to their position in the socioeconomic structure.

DATA, VARIABLES AND METHODS

The empirical basis for this chapter is a postal survey, carried out in 2005 among employed persons in Sweden. Data were collected by Statistics Sweden and, with a response rate of about 69 percent, 2,804 individuals were included in the dataset. The survey was set up in the following way. A large random sample of employed participants in the regular labour force surveys were asked whether they, in their job, go on at least one 100-kilometer trip (commuting not included) during a normal working month and if they would be willing to answer a questionnaire. On this account, travelers could provisionally be distinguished from non-travelers. Both categories were included in the survey, but the former were over-sampled, because they still constitute a rather small proportion of the employed and because we wished to incorporate a large number of respondents who travel frequently. To make up for this, data are weighted in the empirical analyses.

The questionnaire was designed to provide information, on the one hand, from all employed and, on the other, specifically from those who reported some work-related travel. Among other things, it was asked how often respondents travel in their job and one response option given was 'never'. Thus, we got another piece of information to separate travelers from non-travelers and this division is being used in the analyses below. A substantial part of the questionnaire was intended for all respondents and it includes general items on work and working conditions. The part aimed at travelers alone asked respondents to describe, in many different ways, their experience of job travel.

Dependent Variables

In view of the aim and direction of this chapter, the dependent variables refer to answers to a few questions. To begin with, there are two items dealing with both travelers' and non-travelers' descriptions of their jobs. One of them grasps to what extent respondents generally regard their job as stimulating and another to what extent they regard it as arduous. The remaining dependent variables concern work travelers. Most important, respondents were asked to agree or disagree with a number of statements, and two of these read as follows: (a) 'The travels make work stimulating'; and (b) 'The travels make work stressful.' There are also a few further items to which some attention will be paid. They deal with rather similar possible effects of job travel: whether it produces a feeling of freedom at work, gives people new perspectives on their lives, makes them tired and prevents them from being with their families as much as they wish.

We may regard the key dependent variables as too simple if anything, but there is a great advantage with simplicity; it is hard to misunderstand the statements involved. Although the items might well be combined, I have refrained from constructing scales, as I want to keep the analysis as close to the wordings as possible. The answers have been made dichotomous to allow binary logistic regression to be used. Respondents who have said it agrees 'totally' or 'rather well' that travel makes their job stimulating are collapsed into one category and those who have answered 'not very well' or 'not at all' are classified into another. The same is done with the other dependent variables subject to multivariate analysis.

Independent Variables

The main independent variables refer to work travel and, as outlined above, they deal with six different dimensions. A first variable is a simple measure of the frequency of such travel. Second, there is another quantitative item capturing the number of overnight stays during the last year. Third, respondents have been asked whether they have traveled abroad or not. In this case, I initially found it interesting to single out travel outside the Scandinavian countries. The reason for this was that the Scandinavian countries are adjacent to Sweden, which might be expected to influence outcomes at least for inhabitants in the border regions. After having run the data in several different combinations, however, I concluded that nothing could be gained from such an operation; it was sufficient to distinguish between those who had traveled abroad and those who had not.

A few other independent variables are derived from statements on which respondents were asked whether they agree 'totally', 'rather well', 'rather badly' or 'not at all.' Thus, fourth, we have a statement about whether people can decide when to travel. The idea is to get a measure of the individuals' control over travel activities. A fifth variable taps whether job travelers go alone or together with workmates. Finally, respondents have been asked whether work travels imply leaving home early and/or coming home late. All the six variables mentioned did not come across as significant in every analysis and my attention is from now on mainly focused on the most important.

Moreover, a number of other factors are also taken into consideration. Actually, six other variables have been tried in the analyses: sex, age, marital status, having children at home, working hours and socioeconomic status. As with the work travel variables, all of them did not emerge as essential in the regressions and the presentations just include the most interesting results.

RESULTS

In Table 12.1 the answers to a number of items are presented by frequency of travel. The first two of these questions deal with whether, on the one hand, respondents generally regard their job as stimulating and, on the other, whether they regard it as arduous. Merging those who have answered 'to a very large extent' or 'to a rather large extent', we find that about 65 percent of all respondents consider their job stimulating and half of them consider it arduous. It is of course possible for an individual to entertain these two opinions simultaneously. Both questions have been answered by travelers and non-travelers alike and we can thus compare the two categories. The lowest proportion considering their job stimulating (52.8%) is found for non-travelers. Even more interesting is perhaps that the second lowest proportion (58.9%) is noticed among those who travel the most (every day). Between the bottom and the top we discover rather high figures, especially for people who travel several times a year but less than every month.

As mentioned, about half of the respondents have judged their job as arduous, also in this case with some variation related to frequency of travel, although less so than on the previous measure. The lowest figure again crops up among non-travelers (47.4%), but the proportion for the respondents traveling most frequently is practically the same (47.5%). If job travel is arduous, it is not surprising that those who are non-mobile score low on this item, but it is noteworthy that those who travel every day basically have the same score. Every-day trips are perhaps so marked by routine that stress is kept at bay. However, this does not hold for people who travel several times a week; they are the ones with the highest figure.

It is not possible to say anything conclusive about causal mechanisms here. One interpretation is that jobs which are regarded as stimulating and/ or arduous by incumbents entail some or a great deal of travel. Another possibility is that work travel—at least up to a certain frequency—makes jobs stimulating and/or arduous, but thereafter patterns become more or less the same as for non-travelers. Both explanations might be reasonable.

The third row of figures shows the differences between each pair of figures above. As we have already seen, the proportions considering their job stimulating are higher than those considering it arduous and this goes for all the comparisons. For the total sample, the gap is more than 14 percentage points. With frequency of job travel, the largest positive difference comes

Table 12.1 Opinions on Work and Work Travel by Travel Frequency. Percent

			Frequency of work travel						
	Never	Occasionally	Several times a year*	Every month	Every week	Several times a week	Every day	All	n
Regard their job to a very or rather large extent as . . .									
stimulating	52.8	62.8	84.9	78.5	79.4	75.7	58.9	65.0	2,612
arduous	47.4	52.5	50.5	53.6	51.5	60.7	47.5	50.6	2,593
Difference	5.4	10.3	34.4	24.9	27.9	15.0	11.4	14.4	
It agrees totally or rather well that . . .									
the travels make work stimulating		79.3	82.5	77.7	73.5	69.0	61.3	74.8	1,550
the travels make work stressful		13.5	13.3	21.4	20.5	27.3	28.0	19.6	1,499
Difference		65.8	69.2	56.3	53.0	41.7	33.3	55.2	
It agrees totally or rather well that . . .									
the travels give me a feeling of freedom at work		57.2	64.4	69.5	74.4	73.8	75.4	67.6	1,498
I get new perspectives on my life through my traveling		52.0	58.4	61.0	57.0	52.8	32.6	52.3	1,409
I often feel tired after traveling		28.8	41.9	41.9	40.4	40.2	39.3	37.9	1,503
the travels prevent me from being with my family as much as I would like to		5.6	14.5	21.7	15.6	25.9	24.1	16.6	1,423

* The wording in the questionnaire is 'Not every month but several times a year.'

up among respondents who travel several times a year but less than every month, followed by the two categories answering 'every week' and 'every month.' At the opposite end of the scale, we have non-travelers who are not so inclined to judge their job as stimulating and arduous, respectively.

Turning to the question of how respondents assess the effects of traveling, we start out with the two items—dealing with whether the travels make work, on the one hand, stimulating and, on the other, stressful. Three out of four have endorsed the statement about a stimulating effect. At the same time, only one out of five has answered that the travels render their job stressful. As a consequence, the difference given in the row below reaches above 55 percentage points, that is, it is much higher than the corresponding difference for the previous question about how work in general is perceived. Again, it is possible to experience job travel as both stimulating and stressful and actually almost 12 percent have done so.

In terms of frequency, the highest proportion saying that the travels make job stimulating is found for the category 'not every month but some times a year.' The second highest figure appears for people who are mobile only occasionally. Apart from these two response alternatives, percentages decrease concurrently with increasing frequency of travel and we thus come across the lowest proportion among those who travel every day. Even in this category, however, more than six out of ten have agreed. With respect to the statement on stress, figures point in the opposite direction; rising frequency of travel seems to increase the likelihood that travel is conceived of as making work stressful, reaching 28 percent in the end.

By and large, the pattern of differences shows declining figures, because a larger proportion among the less mobile consider travel stimulating than among the more mobile, while it is the other way around on the 'stress' item. In other words, the largest differences come about among those individuals who travel rather seldom ('not every month but some times a year' and 'occasionally') and the smallest can be observed for those who travel most often. The percentage for the every-day category is basically half of the two in the beginning of the row.

Next, we shall look at the response patterns concerning some related indicators of how work travelers experience the effects of their travels. The indicators are selected in order to keep us as close as possible—given the data available—to the theoretical discussion earlier in this chapter. They are ranked according to proportions of respondents who have answered that a statement agrees totally or rather well with their own understanding.

To start with, we have an item asking respondents to take a stand on the statement that the travels give them a sense of freedom at work. Two thirds have answered that it agrees, totally or rather well, with their own experience. Moreover, the feeling of freedom appears to increase with frequency of job travel, but only up to a certain limit; the three top categories are quite close to one another with around 75 percent answering in the affirmative.

On the statement 'I get new perspectives on my life through my traveling', Table 12.1 shows that just above half of the respondents have answered that it agrees totally or rather much. The highest proportions appear among those who travel more than occasionally but not as often as every week or every day. Interestingly, the latter category has the clearly lowest proportion. A conceivable interpretation is thus that travel becomes a matter of routine for many who are frequently on the move; at least, there are quite a few who do not think it brings them any new perspectives on life.

The subsequent item in Table 12.1 refers to a statement in the questionnaire about whether respondents sense that travels make them tired. Less than four out of ten are in agreement with this. Except for those who travel only occasionally—they score the lowest—there are just minor differences across the categories. This outcome must be considered somewhat unanticipated.

Finally, I report the results on an item intended to grasp clashes with family matters. Respondents were asked whether the work travels prevent them from being with their family as much as they would wish to be. The proportions agreeing are rather small but are positively associated with the frequency variable. In other words, the more often people are traveling, the more this activity seems to interfere with family life.

To give a very brief summary so far, we have got unmistakable indications that job travel is above all a positive part of people's work situation. A more cautious conclusion would be that it mainly appears to be a positive factor among work travelers. The reason for some cautiousness is of course that we suspect a self-selection mechanism to be implicated. People who travel in their jobs—and in particular those who travel a lot—are probably often rather willing to do this. If they were not, we would not expect them to remain in their jobs—although, of course, it can be difficult to find other employment or other ways of supporting oneself. There are, however, also some negative aspects associated with work travel; to some extent, it is likely to make work stressful. In the next analytical step, I study the simultaneous impact of the previously discussed independent variables on the dependent variables.

Multivariate Analyses

As mentioned before, the multivariate analyses in this chapter will be carried out by means of binary logistic regressions. It should be observed that non-travelers are now excluded, as the questions at issue have been put to travelers only. I concentrate on the two most crucial variables, that is, whether respondents feel that the travels make their jobs stimulating and stressful, respectively. In addition, I shall mention some results concerning the dependent variables at the bottom of Table 12.1.

In Table 12.2 two different models are presented. Both models include five travel-related, independent variables: frequency of travel, frequency of

Table 12.2   Factors Impacting on Whether Work Travel Is Considered Making Work Stimulating. Logistic Regression. Odds Ratios

	Model 1	Model 2
Frequency of travel		
Occasionally (ref.)	1	1
Not every month but several times a year	0.96	1.02
Every month	0.98	1.03
Every week	0.70	0.83
Several times a week	0.58*	0.60*
Every day	0.46***	0.60*
Overnight stays		
None (ref.)	1	1
1–2	1.22	1.30
3–5	1.68**	1.74**
6–10	2.69***	2.83***
11–20	2.51**	2.70**
21–50	2.47**	2.97**
51–	2.96*	3.38**
Travel abroad		
Yes	1.30	1.45*
No (ref.)	1	1
Can decide when to travel		
Agrees totally	1.83*	2.20*
Agrees rather well	1.17	1.29
Agrees rather badly	1.07	1.14
Does not agree at all (ref.)	1	1
Travel together with workmates		
Agrees totally	2.64***	2.56**
Agrees rather well	1.72**	1.74**
Agrees rather badly	1.20	1.25
Does not agree at all (ref.)	1	1
Sex		
Male		0.65**
Female (ref.)		1
Age		
16–34		1.30
35–44		0.88
45–54 (ref.)		1
55–64		1.65*

(*continued*)

Table 12.2   (continued)

	Model 1	Model 2
Socioeconomic position		
Unskilled manual worker (ref.)		1
Skilled manual worker		0.55*
Lower white collar		0.89
Middle white collar		0.84
Higher white collar		0.72
Self-employed		0.43**
Constant	1.53*	1.85*
Nagelkerke R²	0.12	0.15
n	1,582	1,580

Levels of significance: *p<0.05; ** p<0.01; *** p<0.001.

overnight stays, whether trips involve travel abroad or are just domestic, to what degree respondents think they can decide when to travel and, finally, whether they travel together with workmates or not. The item measuring consequences of traveling in the form of early mornings and late homecomings is not included, as it did not turn out to be significant. Model 2 adds three general background variables: sex, age and socioeconomic position. The other three mentioned previously—marital status, having children at home and working hours—did not have much effect on the outcome and are therefore not included.

Looking first at the issue of whether job travel is conceived of as making work stimulating, we find that frequency of travel is partly a crucial factor. This conclusion can be drawn from both models. Respondents who travel every day or several times a week are less inclined than the reference category (those who travel only occasionally) to say that the travels have an encouraging effect. As regards the number of overnight days, it is instead the other way around. The likelihood of answering that travel renders one's job stimulating tends to increase with the number of such days. There is some indication that going abroad has a similar effect, but it is not statistically confirmed until in Model 2.

The next item, capturing influence over when to travel, turns out to have a rather important role to play. Respondents totally agreeing with the statement that they can decide when to travel more often consider job travel a stimulating factor. An even clearer outcome can be observed for the variable on travel companions. It is evidently more exciting to be out on journeys together with workmates than to go alone.

Controlling for background variables does not affect the outcome on the travel-related variables very much, but we can observe that travel abroad now appears as a statistically significant stimulating factor. Moreover, the background variables themselves show some interesting results. Men travel more frequently and longer distances than women (Gustafson 2005, 2006) and are perhaps therefore less inclined to regard job travel as having a stimulating impact on work. On the age variable, we discover the highest coefficient for the oldest category. This indicates that we are dealing with people who have remained in jobs in which travel is a significant element. There is also a high figure for the youngest category—for whom travel might still have the charm of novelty—but the effect cannot be confirmed statistically.

The outcome on socioeconomic position needs some comments. Two categories distinguish themselves with clearly lower scores than the reference category (unskilled manual workers). Both the skilled manual workers and the self-employed have a lower propensity to agree that travel is stimulating. To explain this outcome, we need to examine more closely the work tasks these two categories have as well as the kinds of travel they are usually involved in, but it is a task that goes beyond the scope of the present chapter.

Table 12.3 summarizes the results on the second main dependent variable referring to responses to the statement 'The travels make my job stressful.' Again, two models are presented. The independent variables common for both models are slightly different from those in the preceding table. One more is added, namely the measure on whether work travel implies early mornings and/or late homecoming. Two other variables—dealing with frequency of overnight stays and foreign trips—are excluded. There is no sign that many overnight stays contribute to rendering work stressful and whether respondents travel abroad or not does not turn out to be important at all. Regarding the general background variables—and in contrast to the previous table—Table 12.3 contains normal working hours but not socioeconomic position. Perhaps somewhat surprisingly, we find no significant results concerning the variables having children at home and marital status. The explanation may be that respondents were requested to state whether travels make their *job* stressful and not whether travels have such effects on their family life or their life in general.

The results on frequency of work travel indicate that respondents who travel several days a week are more apt to agree that they experience stress. We also find a high coefficient for the every-day category, but it is not statistically significant (although nearly so). The workers in this category should be particularly used to coping with travel-related stress, as they are on the move all working days. At any rate, it is reasonable to conclude that high frequency of travel is an important factor in people's working conditions; in Table 12.2, we find that it makes work less stimulating and in Table 12.3 there is some indication that it brings about stress.

To be able to decide when to travel is apparently a stress-reducing factor and the same is found for traveling with workmates. This fits with the results in Table 12.2, where these two factors stand for positive effects. In other words, they contribute to the feeling that jobs become both more

Table 12.3 Factors Impacting on Whether Work Travel Is Considered Making Work Stressful. Logistic Regression. Odds Ratios

	Model 1	Model 2
Frequency of travel		
Occasionally (ref.)	1	1
Not every month but several times a year	0.87	0.84
Every month	1.50	1.46
Every week	1.15	1.09
Several times a week	1.86*	1.96*
Every day	1.55	1.60
Can decide when to travel		
Agrees totally	0.44*	0.43*
Agrees rather well	0.58**	0.59**
Agrees rather badly	0.88	0.91
Does not agree at all (ref.)	1	1
Travel together with workmates		
Agrees totally	0.40**	0.36**
Agrees rather well	0.62*	0.55**
Agrees rather badly	0.79	0.71
Does not agree at all (ref.)	1	1
The travels often entail leaving home early and/or coming home late		
Agrees totally	4.20***	4.11***
Agrees rather well	1.76**	1.80**
Agrees rather badly	1.16	1.17
Does not agree at all (ref.)	1	1
Sex		
Male		0.73
Female (ref.)		1
Age		
16–34		0.91
35–44		1.30
45–54 (ref.)		1
55–64		0.63*
Normal working hours		
–29		0.86
30–39		0.67
40 (ref.)		1
41–49		1.09
50–		1.33
Constant	0.22***	0.32***
Nagelkerke R^2	0.12	0.15
n	1,506	1,503

Levels of significance: * $p<0.05$; ** $p<0.01$; *** $p<0.001$.

stimulating and less of a burden. The final travel-related variable on whether respondents have to leave home early and/or come home late is indeed important. Evidently, inconvenient hours as measured here strongly add to the experience that job travel makes work stressful.

There are also some comments to be made regarding the background variables in Table 12.3. To a lesser degree than females, males tend to think of work travel as causing stress, but the difference is not proved statistically, although not far from it. This can be compared with the outcome in Table 12.2, where males are less likely to answer 'stimulating.' In other words, it is suggested that women are more strongly affected positively and perhaps also negatively. With respect to age, it is the oldest category that scores the lowest and it has the highest score in the previous table. Both results can be interpreted in a similar way. If they did not consider traveling stimulating and were unable to avoid stress or keep it within reasonable limits, older travelers would be likely to quit their jobs to do something else. Thus, to repeat what has been said before, there is probably a selection mechanism in operation. On working hours, we find no significant differences, but the outcome is shown anyway because the variable ought to be a crucial factor and because some of the coefficients point in expected directions.

Multivariate analyses have also been run for the other variables in the lower part of Table 12.1. Although the results are not shown in tabular form, a few words should be said about them. The variables emanate from four statements dealing with, first, whether job travels give respondents a feeling of freedom at work; second, whether they furnish them with new perspectives on life; third, whether they make them tired; and finally, whether they prevent them from being with their families as much as they would like to.

Starting with the variable whether job travel gives respondents a feeling of freedom at work, we found that results are, to a considerable degree, in line with what we have already seen. However, some of them point in another direction. While people who travel frequently are less inclined to consider travel stimulating (Table 12.2), they are generally more apt to say that it makes them feel free at work. On the other hand, frequency of over-night stays seems to be positive for both the dimensions mentioned. It is obviously sufficient to be away for only a few nights to experience a sense of freedom. To be able to decide when to travel also has clear positive effects, whereas no significant differences can be detected regarding the variable on traveling with workmates. Feelings of freedom are not enhanced by having travel companions, which might suggest that company implies a certain degree of social control. Then again, the results do not point in the opposite direction either; they rather indicate that this aspect of traveling is not so important for making people feel free at work.

On the item concerning whether work travel generates new perspectives on life, it turns out that daily travel means a lower propensity to agree, but aside from that the frequency variable is not important in this regard. The pattern is close to the one recorded on the issue as to whether work becomes stimulating. In contrast, the results with respect to overnight stays go in the opposite direction, and, again, people do not have to be away more than a few nights to become more apt to answer that they get new perspectives on life through their travels. It does not matter much, however, whether people go abroad or not. Distinct influence over when to travel and traveling with colleagues are both positive factors for experiencing new perspectives.

The measure of whether people feel tired after travels is the third aspect. It does not seem to have much to do with frequency of travel. Other factors turn out to be more important. Staying often overnight is such a factor; those who have many nights away from home tend to feel tired to a larger degree than those who have none. Being able to decide when to travel reduces feelings of tiredness, whereas—far from astonishingly—early mornings and/or late evenings have a strong reverse impact.

As to being with one's family as much as desired, there are some significant results to report. High frequencies of travel and of overnight stays reduce this possibility and, in particular, we should note the negative effect of early mornings and/or late homecomings. Once more, being able to decide when to travel helps to make the situation better. In this case, having children at home and being married/cohabitant both play the role anticipated, that is, they make people more inclined to answer that travels prevent them from being with their family as much as they want to.

CONCLUSION

In contemporary economically advanced societies, job travel has become an increasingly important aspect of people's working conditions, but it is still a relatively neglected aspect in sociological research. This chapter has aimed at providing new knowledge about some of its possible consequences. The main research question has simply been whether job travel is looked upon as a stimulating or as a stressful phenomenon. On the one hand, it may be considered stimulating, a chance of getting away from dull daily routines, and bringing autonomy, freedom and other positive effects with it. On the other hand, it may be experienced as stressful, as a burden because of long working hours, early mornings, late homecomings, overnight stays and the like.

The principal dependent variables used here cover whether people think of job travel as stimulating and stressful, but some other dimensions are also taken into account. For example, respondents have been asked if they regard travel as creating a sense of freedom and as providing new perspectives on life. Among the independent variables, six work-related travel measures have been tested: frequency of travel, frequency of overnight stays; whether trips abroad are included; degree of control over when to go; if travel involves company; and whether it entails leaving home early and/or coming home late. A number of background variables are controlled for.

A general conclusion from the analysis is that work travel is clearly more often considered stimulating than stressful. However, the two most mobile categories are less likely than others to feel that it is stimulating. At the same time, it appears that these categories are more prone to feel that it creates stress, although in this case the coefficient for every-day travelers is not statistically verified. Spending many nights away from home tends to have a positive, inspiring impact and it does not seem to generate stress. Moreover, the experience of work travel as stimulating is enhanced by trips abroad, a high degree of control over travel schedules and traveling with workmates. The latter two factors also turn out to have stress-reducing effects. Finally, it must be noted that stress is strongly related to the inconveniences of early mornings and/or late homecoming that are sometimes implicated.

It may be seen as encouraging that work-related travel above all appears to be a positive, stimulating element in people's working conditions, in particular as it tends to increase. However, some comments need to be added. First, as mentioned several times, it is likely that the phenomenon under scrutiny is associated with a selection mechanism, which implies that many of those who travel a lot actually enjoy it or at least to find it tolerable. The fact that older workers more commonly think of job travel as stimulating and less often regard it as stressful is indicative of this. Had they disliked it very much, they would probably have tried to find something else, although this is not always easy. Second, we should underline that work travel—besides the damaging effects on the environment—may also be associated with negative consequences for the individuals involved. It may create stress, make people tired, make it impossible for them to be with their families as much as wanted, etc. These effects are to a large extent dependent on the differing circumstances under which travel takes place.

An overall conclusion in this chapter is that job-related travel is a significant aspect of many individuals' working conditions. It has mainly positive effects for the individuals, but to some extent we also find negative consequences. There is accordingly no doubt that job travel contributes to shaping work orientations and work attitudes. Not least because it will probably continue to expand, social researchers need to pay more attention to it.

Contributors

Tomas Berglund is associate professor at the Department of Sociology, University of Gothenburg. Most of his research lies in the field of working life and labour market sociology. In addition, he has an interest in the field of political sociology, in particular the significance of social class for ideological orientations. Berglund is currently coordinator of a research project on job, employment and income security among employees, which also involves Nordic cooperation.

Tuula Bergqvist is researcher and lecturer at the Department of Working Life Science, Karlstad University, where she also received her Ph. D. in 2004. Her research started in the empirical field of entrepreneurship and continued with studies on flexibility and changing conditions of work. During the last three years she has been taking part in a project on youth unemployment and social and political exclusion in Europe. Presently she is a co-researcher in a project dealing with gender issues within the Swedish rescue services.

Tómas Bjarnason has a B.A. in sociology and mass communication from the University of Iceland and a Ph.D. in sociology from the University of Gothenburg. He is currently research director and consultant at *Capacent* in Iceland and has specialized in employee and organizational surveys. Moreover, he is a part-time lecturer at the Department of Sociology, University of Iceland.

Birgitta Eriksson is professor at the Department of Working Life Science, Karlstad University, Sweden. Her main research fields are unemployment, people's attitudes to work and the organization of work and its impact on employees' working conditions. Eriksson is at present responsible for the Swedish part of a European project on youth unemployment and exclusion.

Bengt Furåker came as professor to the Department of Sociology, University of Gothenburg, in 1990. He had previously held positions at other Swedish universities and has later been a Visiting Fellow at Yale University in the US. His research is mainly focused on labour market and working life issues and the relationship between the labour market and the welfare state. In 2007–2010 Furåker was editor of *Acta Sociologica*, the journal of the Nordic Sociological Association. Among his more recent publications, three books can be mentioned: *Post-industrial Labour Markets. Profiles of North America and Scandinavia* (2003; ed. with Thomas P. Boje), *Sociological Perspectives on Labor Markets* (2005) and *Flexibility and Stability in Working Life* (2007; ed. with Kristina Håkansson and Jan Ch. Karlsson).

Frans Hikspoors is lecturer at Windesheim University for Applied Science in Zwolle, the Netherlands. Currently he is writing a Ph.D. thesis about work values. He is also engaged in teaching and supervising. Hikspoors has previously worked for consulting companies and educational institutions. Among other things, he has been editor of *de Gids voor Personeelsmanagement* (Dutch HR magazine). He has also published on political culture issues.

Kristina Håkansson is associate professor at the Department of Sociology, University of Gothenburg. Her main research interest is oriented toward work organization and strategies for flexibility. In particular, she focuses on examining the consequences of flexibility for individuals, work organizations and the labour market. Håkansson is currently involved in a research project on temporary agency workers' organizational commitment, besides being a teacher and supervisor. She has co-edited—with Bengt Furåker and Jan Ch. Karlsson—the book *Flexibility and Stability in Working Life* (2007).

Tommy Isidorsson is researcher at the Department of Work Science, University of Gothenburg. His thesis examined the development of working time in Sweden in a broad historical perspective. In addition to research on working time, he has carried out studies on flexibility issues, focusing on strategies for flexibility and their consequences for individuals, workplaces and society. Isidorsson is also responsible for the Master program in Work Science.

Dan Jonsson is professor emeritus of sociology, University of Gothenburg. His academic interests include general sociological theory, social psychology, theory and methods in social research, peace research, sociotechnical systems analysis and sociology of work. He has published extensively on these topics, besides being a teacher and supervisor at the Department of Sociology. For many years, Jonsson has collaborated with researchers at Chalmers University of Technology on workplace design and analysis.

Anette Karlsson received a Ph.D. in sociology at the University of Gothenburg in 2010 and she is presently lecturer at the sociology department. Her main teaching and research interests are within the fields of occupations and organizations, identity, intersectional analysis, and theories of work-related and other social change.

Jan Ch. Karlsson is professor of sociology at the Department of Working Life Science, Karlstad University. His publications are concerned with the concept of work, modern work organization, class and gender in everyday life and critical realism and methodology in the social sciences. He is co-author of *Explaining Society: An Introduction to Critical Realism in the Social Sciences* (2002), *Gender Segregation. Divisions of Work in Post-Industrial Welfare States* (2005) and *Flexibility and Stability in Working Life* (2007); he is also author of *Organizational Misbehaviour in the Workplace. Narratives of Dignity and Resistance* (2011).

Ylva Ulfsdotter Eriksson received her Ph.D. in 2006 and is now lecturer at the Department of Sociology, University of Gothenburg. Her overall research interest has to do with processes that create equality and inequality between people. She focuses on differences within and between occupations—differences which help to maintain inequalities in status, recognition and respect. Ulfsdotter Eriksson is also coordinator of the B.A. program in Human Resource Management and Labour Relations.

Bibliography

Abramson, P. and R. Inglehart (1999) 'Measuring Postmaterialism.' *American Political Science Review* 93(3): 665–677.

Adkins, C. L., J. D. Werbel and J.-L. Farh (2001) 'A Field Study of Job Insecurity during a Financial Crisis.' *Group & Organization Management* 26(4): 463–483.

Alcock, P., C. Beatty, S. Fothergill, R. Macmillan and S. Yeandle (2003) *Work to Welfare: How Men Become Detached from the Labour Market.* Cambridge: Cambridge University Press.

Allen, N. J. and J. P. Meyer (1990) 'The Measurement and Antecedents of Affective, Continuance and Normative Commitment to the Organization.' *Journal of Occupational Psychology* 63(1): 1–18.

Allen, N. J. and J. P. Meyer (1996) 'Affective, Continuance, and Normative Commitment to the Organization: An Examination of Construct Validity.' *Journal of Vocational Behavior* (49)3: 252–276.

Allen, T. D., D. M. Freeman, J. E. A. Russell, R. C. Reizenstein and J. O. Rentz (2001) 'Survivor Reactions to Organizational Downsizing: Does Time Ease the Pain?' *Journal of Occupational and Organizational Psychology* 74(2): 145–164.

Andersson, P. and E. Wadensjö (2004) *Hur fungerar bemanningsbranschen?* Rapport 2004: 15. Uppsala: Institute for Labour Market Policy Evaluation.

Anthony, P. D. (1977) *The Ideology of Work.* London: Tavistock.

Applebaum, H. (1992) *The Concept of Work. Ancient, Medieval, and Modern.* Albany: State University of New York Press.

Aristotle, (2006) *Nichomachean Ethics* X: VII. Oxford: Clarendon Press.

Armstrong, P., H. Armstrong and K. Scott-Dixon (2008) *Critical to Care: The Invisible Women in Health Services.* Toronto: University of Toronto Press.

Arrowsmith, J. (2006) *Temporary Agency Work in an Enlarged European Union.* Dublin: European Foundation for the Improvement of Living and Working Conditions.

Ashford, S. J., C. Lee and P. Bobko (1989) 'Content, Causes, and Consequences of Job Insecurity: A Theory-Based Measure and Substantive Test.' *Academy of Management Journal* 32(4): 803–829.

Ashforth, B. E. and F. Mael (1989) 'Social Identity Theory and the Organization.' *Academy of Management Review* 14(1): 20–39.

Asplund, J. (1991) *Essä om Gemeinschaft och Gesellschaft.* Göteborg: Korpen.

Atkinson, J. (1984) 'Manpower Strategies for Flexible Organization.' *Personnel Management* 16(8): 28–31.

Aurell, M. (2001) *Arbete och identitet. Om hur städare blir städare.* Linköping University: Department of Thematic Studies—Technology and Social Change.

Avtal för bemanningsföretag 2007–2010. Bemanningsföretagen och Svenska Byggnadsarbetareförbundet, Svenska Elektrikerförbundet, Fastighetsanställdas Förbund, Grafiska Fackförbundet, Handelsanställdas förbund, Hotell och Restaurang Facket, IF Metall, Svenska Kommunalarbetareförbundet, Svenska Livsmedelsarbetareförbundet, Svenska Musikerförbundet, Svenska Målareförbundet Svenska Pappersindustriarbetareförbundet, Skogs- och Träfacket, SEKO—facket för service och kommunikation, Svenska Transportarbetareförbundet. Signed in Stockholm 31, May 2007.

Baldamus, W. (1961) *Efficiency and Effort: An Analysis of Industrial Administration.* London: Tavistock.

Baldry, C., P. Bain, P. Taylor, J. Hyman, D. Scholarios, A. Mars, A. Watson, K. Gilbert, G. Gall and D. Bunzel (2007) *The Meaning of Work in the New Economy.* Houndmills, Basingstoke: Palgrave Macmillan.

Baldursson, F. M. and G. Zoëga (2011) 'Um óreiðumenn og annað fólk.' *Fréttabladið,* 2 April.

Baruch, Y. (1998) 'The Rise and Fall of Organizational Commitment.' *Human Systems Management* 17(2): 135–144.

Bauman, Z. (1998) *Work, Consumerism and the New Poor.* Buckingham: Open University Press.

Bauman, Z. (2007) *Consuming Life.* Cambridge: Polity Press.

Beck, U. (2000) *The Brave New World of Work.* Cambridge: Polity Press.

Becker, H. S. (1998) *Tricks of the Trade: How to Think about Your Research While You're Doing It.* Chicago: University of Chicago Press.

Bemanningsföretagen (2009) *Antal anställda och penetrationsgrad i bemanningsbranschen 2009. Bemanningsföretagens utveckling,* at http://www.bemanningsforetagen.se/web/9db1c872–0d96–4d44-bfec-ef7ec0cd816a_2.aspx.

Berg, A. (2008) *Bemanningsarbete, flexibilitet och likabehandling. En studie av svensk rätt och kollektivavtalsreglering med komparativa inslag.* Lund: Juristförlaget.

Berglund, T. (2001) *Attityder till arbete i Västeuropa och USA. Teoretiska perspektiv och analyser av data från sex länder.* University of Gothenburg: Department of Sociology.

Bergström, G. (2006) 'Ett arbetsliv i rörelse. Resandets positiva och negativa potential för arbetstillfredsställelsen bland resande säljare.' *Arbetsmarknad & Arbetsliv* 12(3): 147–160.

Bergström, G. (2008) 'Ett könsperspektiv på resor i arbetet.' *Arbetsmarknad & Arbetsliv* 14(2): 29–50.

Bergström, O., K. Håkansson, T. Isidorsson and L. Walter (2007) *Den nya arbetsmarknaden. Bemanningsbranschens etablering i Sverige.* Lund: Academica Adacta.

Bernard, T. J. (1980) *The Consensus-Conflict Debate: Form and Content in Social Theories.* New York: Columbia University Press.

Bianchi, S. M., L. M. Casper and R. Berkowitz King (eds.) (2005) *Work, Family, Health and Well-Being.* Mahwah, NJ: Lawrence Erlbaum.

Bielby, W. T. and D. D. Bielby (1989) 'Family Ties: Balancing Commitment to Work and Family in Dual Earner Households.' *American Sociological Review* 54 (5): 776–789.

Bjarnason, T. (2009) *Social Recognition and Employees' Organizational Support. The Impact of Social Recognition on Organizational Commitment, Intent to Stay, Service Effort, and Service Improvements in an Icelandic Service Setting.* University of Gothenburg: Department of Sociology.

Björk, M. (2008) 'Fighting Cynicism: Some Reflections on Self-Motivation in Police Work.' *Police Quarterly* 11(1): 88–101.

Björnberg, U., G. Eydal and S. Ólafsson (2006) 'Education, Employment and Family Formation: Differing Patterns', 199–219 in J. Bradshaw and A. Hatland (eds.) *Social Policy, Employment and Family Change in Comparative Perspective*. Cheltenham: Edward Elgar.

Blau, P. M. (1967) *Exchange and Power in Social Life*. New York: Wiley.

Blauner, R. (1960) 'Work Satisfaction and Industrial Trends in Modern Society', 339–360, in W. Galenson and S. M. Lipset (eds.) *Labor and Trade Unionism: An Interdisciplinary Reader*. New York: John Wiley & Sons.

Blauner, R. (1964) *Alienation and Freedom. The Factory Worker and His Industry*. Chicago & London: University of Chicago Press.

Bleijenbergh I. and C. Roggeband (2007) *Equality Machineries Matter, The Impact of Women's Political Pressure on European Social-Care Policies*. Oxford: Oxford University Press.

Blomqvist, M. (1994) *Könshierarkier i gungning. Kvinnor i kunskapsföretag*. Acta Universitatis Upsaliensis. Stockholm: Almqvist & Wiksell.

Blomqvist, M. (2001) 'Arbetsorganisatorisk förändring ur ett genusperspektiv', 73–83, in L. Gonäs, G. Lindgren and C. Bildt (eds.) *Könssegregering i arbetslivet*. Stockholm: National Institute for Working Life.

Blossfeld, H.-P. and H. Hofmeister (eds.) (2006) *Globalization, Uncertainty and Women's Careers. An International Comparison*. Cheltenham: Edward Elgar.

Blossfeld, H.-P., M. Mills and F. Bernardi (eds.) (2006) *Globalization, Uncertainty and Men's Careers: An International Comparison*. Cheltenham: Edward Elgar.

Blumer, H. (1986) *Symbolic Interactionism: Perspective and Method*. Berkeley: University of California Press.

Bollé, P. (2009) 'Labour Statistics: The Boundaries and Diversity of Work.' *International Labour Review* 148: 183–193.

Bolton, S. (2005) *Emotion Management in the Workplace*. New York: Palgrave Macmillan.

Bourdieu, P. (1989) *Distinction. A Social Critique of the Judgment of Taste*. New York & London: Routledge.

Bourdieu, P. (2000) *Pascalian Meditations*. Cambridge: Polity Press.

Bradley, H. (1996) *Fractured Identities*. Cambridge: Polity Press.

Braverman, H. (1974) *Labour and Monopoly Capital. The Degradation of Work in the Twentieth Century*. New York: Monthly Review Press.

Brockner, J., J. Greenberg, A. Brockner, J. Bortz, J. Davy and C. Carter (1988) 'Threat of Future Layoffs, Self-Esteem, and Survivors Reactions: Evidence from the Laboratory and the Field'. *Strategic Management Journal* 14 (special issue): 153–166.

Brockner, J., G. Spreitzer, A. Mishra, W. Hochwarter, L. Pepper and J. Weinberg (2004) 'Perceived Control as an Antidote to the Negative Effects of Layoffs on Survivors' Organizational Commitment and Job Performance.' *Administrative Science Quarterly* 49(1): 76–100.

Brooke Jr., P. P., D. W. Russell and J. L. Price (1988) 'Discriminant Validation of Measurements of Job Satisfaction, Job Involvement, and Organizational Commitment.' *Journal of Applied Psychology* 73(2): 139–145.

Broschak, J. P., A. Davies-Blake and E. S. Block (2008) 'Nonstandard, Not Substandard. The Relationship among Work Arrangements, Work Attitudes, and Job Performance.' *Work and Occupations* 35(1): 3–43.

Brown, A., M. Dif, L. Helemäe, S. Kirpal, S. Koniordos, G. Laske, N. Patiniotis and O. Strietska-Ilina (2007) 'Decomposing and Recomposing Occupational identities—A Survey of Theoretical Concepts', 13–44, in A. Brown, S. Kirpal and F. Rauner (eds.) *Identities at Work*. Dordrecht: Springer.

Buchanan, J. (1971) 'The Backbending Supply Curve of Labor: An Example of Doctrinal Retrogression?' *History of Political Economy* 3(2): 383–390.

Burchell, B. (1993) 'A New Way of Analyzing Labour Market Flows Using Work History Data.' *Work, Employment & Society* 7(2): 237–258.

Burrell, G. and G. Morgan (1979) *Sociological Paradigms and Organizational Analysis.* London: Heinemann.

Capacent (2009a), at http://www.capacent.is/Frettir-og-frodleikur/Thjodarpulsinn/Thjodarpulsinn/2009/03/03/Traust-til-stofnana-og-embaetta/.

Capacent (2009b), at http://www.capacent.is/Frettir-og-frodleikur/Frettir/Frett/2009/11/04/Traust-til-althjodastofnana-/.

Capacent (2009c), at http://www.capacent.is/Frettir-og-frodleikur/Thjodarpulsinn/Thjodarpulsinn/2009/12/04/Ahrif-fjarhags-a-lidan-/.

Casey, C. (1995) *Work, Self and Society. After Industrialism.* New York: Routledge.

Castles, F. G. (ed.) (1993) *Families of Nations: Patterns of Public Policy in Western Democracies.* Aldershot: Dartmouth.

Castles, F. G. (2004) *The Future of the Welfare State: Crisis Myths and Crisis Realities.* Oxford: Oxford University Press.

Cheng, G. H.-L. and D. K.-S. Chan (2008) 'Who Suffers More from Job Insecurity? A Meta-Analytic Review.' *Applied Psychology* 57(2): 272–303.

CIETT (2009) *The Agency Work Industry around the World. Main Statistics.* Brussels: International Confederation of Private Employment Agencies.

Clark, A. E. (1997) 'Job Satisfaction and Gender: Why Are Women So Happy at Work?' *Labour Economics* 4(4): 341–372.

Coleman, D. F., G. P. Irving and C. L. Cooper (1999) 'Another Look at the Locus of Control—Organizational Commitment Relationship: It Depends on the Form of Commitment.' *Journal of Organizational Behavior* 20(6): 995–1001.

Connelly, C. and D. G. Gallagher (2004) 'Emerging Trends in Contingent Work Research.' *Journal of Management* 30(6): 959–983.

Connelly, C., D. G. Gallagher and K. M. Gilley (2007) 'Organizational and Client Commitment among Contracted Employees: A Replication and Extension with Temporary Workers.' *Journal of Vocational Behavior* 70: 326–335.

Conradson, B. (1988) *Kontorsfolket.* Stockholm: Nordiska Museet.

Cowherd, D. M. and D. I. Levine (1992) 'Product Quality and Pay Equity between Lower-level Employees and Top Management: An Investigation of Distributive Justice Theory.' *Administrative Science Quarterly* 37(2): 302–319.

Coyle-Shapiro, J. A. M. and P. C. Morrow (2006) 'Organizational and Client Commitment among Contracted Employees.' *Journal of Vocational Behavior* 68: 416–431.

Crompton, R. (2006) *Employment and the Family. The Reconfiguration of Work and Family Life in Contemporary Societies.* Cambridge: Cambridge University Press.

Crompton, R. (2008) *Class and Stratification. An Introduction to Current Debates.* 3rd ed. Cambridge: Polity Press.

Crompton, R. and G. Jones (1984) *A White Collar Proletariat? Deskilling and Gender in Clerical Work.* Basingstoke: Macmillan.

Crompton, R. and F. Harris (1998) 'Explaining Women's Employment Patterns: "Orientations to Work" Revisited.' *British Journal of Sociology* 49(1): 118–149.

Crompton, R. and C. Lyonette (2006) 'Work-life 'Balance' in Europe.' *Acta Sociologica* 49(4): 379–393.

Cross, G. (1993) *Time and Money. The Making of Consumer Culture.* London: Routledge.

Cully, M., S. Woodland, A. O'Reilly and G. Dix (1999) *Britain at Work. As Depicted by the 1998 Workplace Employee Relations Survey.* London: Routledge.

Dahrendorf, R. (1969) *Homo Sociologicus. Om människan och rollerna*. Uppsala: Argos Förlag.

Danielsson, J. and G. Zoëga (2009) *The Collapse of a Country*. 2nd ed. Downloaded May 2, 2010, at www.Riskresearch.org.

Davies, C. (1995) *Gender and the Professional Predicament in Nursing*. Buckingham: Open University Press.

Davies, K. (1942) 'A Conceptual Analysis of Stratification.' *American Sociological Review* 7(3): 309–321.

Davies, M. (1982) *Woman's Place Is at the Typewriter. Office Work and Office Workers, 1870–1930*. Philadelphia: Temple University Press.

Davy, J. A., A. J. Kinicki, J. Angelo and C. L. Scheck (1997) 'A Test of Job Security's Direct and Mediated Effects on Withdrawal Cognitions.' *Journal of Organizational Behavior* 18(4): 323–349.

De Cuyper, N., J. de Jong, H. De Witte, K. Isaksson, T. Rigotti and R. Schalk (2008) 'Literature Review of Theory and Research on the Psychological Impact of Temporary Employment: Towards a Conceptual Model.' *International Journal of Management Review* 10(1): 25–51.

De Vroom, B. (2004) 'The Shift from Early to Late-Exit: Changing Institutional Conditions and Individual Preferences: The Case of The Netherlands', 120–153, in T. Maltby, B. De Vroom, M. L. Mirabile and E. Øverbye (eds.) *Ageing and the Transition to Retirement: A Comparative Analysis of European Welfare States*. Aldershot: Ashgate.

De Witte, H. (1999) 'Job Insecurity and Psychological Well-being: Review of the Literature and Exploration of Some Unresolved Issues.' *European Journal of Work and Organizational Psychology* 8(2): 151–177.

Dobbin, F. and T. Boychuk (1999) 'National Employment Systems and Job Autonomy: Why Job Autonomy Is High in the Nordic Countries and Low in the United States, Canada and Australia.' *Organizations Studies* 20(2): 257–291.

Dose, J. J. (1997) 'Work Values: An Integrative Framework and Illustrative application to Organizational Socialization.' *Journal of Occupational and Organizational Psychology* 70(3): 219–224.

du Gay, P. (1994) 'Making Up Managers: Bureaucracy, Enterprise and the Liberal Art of Separation.' *British Journal of Sociology* 45(4): 655–674.

du Gay, P. (1996) *Consumption and Identity at Work*. London: Sage.

Dubin, R. (1956) 'Industrial Workers' Worlds: A Study of the "Central Life Interests" of Industrial Workers.' *Social Problems* 3(3): 131–142.

Dunham, J. (ed.) (2001) *Stress in the Workplace: Past, Present, Future*. London: Whurr Publishers.

Dunham, R. B., J. A. Grube and M. B. Castaneda (1994) 'Organizational Commitment: The Utility of an Integrative Definition.' *Journal of Applied Psychology* 79(3): 370–380.

Durkheim, E. (1964) *The Division of Labor in Society*. New York: Free Press.

Eagly, A. H. and S. Chaiken (1993) *The Psychology of Attitudes*. Fort Worth: Harcourt Brace Jovanovich.

Economic Indicators (2009) Central Bank of Iceland. Accessed January 2011, at http://www.sedlabanki.is/lisalib/getfile.aspx?itemid=6767.

Edwards, R. (1979) *Contested Terrain. The Transformation of the Workplace in the Twentieth Century*. New York: Basic Books.

Ehrenreich, B. (2002) *Nickel and Dimed. On (Not) Getting By in America*. New York: Henry Holt and Company.

Eisenberger, R., R. Huntington, S. Hutchison and D. Sowa (1986) 'Perceived Organizational Support.' *Journal of Applied Psychology* 71(3): 500–507.

Ellingsæter, A. L. (1995) *Gender, Work and Social Change. Beyond Dualistic Thinking*. Oslo: Institute for Social Research.

England, G. W. and J. Misumi (1986) 'Work Centrality in Japan and the United States.' *Journal of Cross-Cultural Psychology* 17(4): 399–416.

Engström, T. (1983) *Materialflödessystem och serieproduktion*. University of Gothenburg/Chalmers University of Technology: Department of Transport and Logistics.

Engström, T., D. Jonsson and L. Medbo (1996) 'Production Model Discourse and Experiences from the Swedish Automotive Industry.' *International Journal of Operations and Production Management* 16(2): 141–158.

Erickson, R. A. and M. E. Roloff (2007) 'Reducing Attrition after Downsizing.' *International Journal of Organizational Analysis* 15(1): 35–55.

Erikson, R. and J. H. Goldthorpe (1993) *The Constant Flux: A Study of Class Mobility in Industrial Societies*. Oxford: Clarendon Press.

Eriksson, B. (1998) *Arbetet i människors liv*. University of Gothenburg: Department of Sociology.

Esping-Andersen, G. (1990) *The Three Worlds of Welfare Capitalism*. Princeton: Princeton University Press.

Esping-Andersen, G. (1999) *Social Foundations of Postindustrial Economies*. Oxford: Oxford University Press.

Espino, C. M., S. M. Sundstrom, H. L. Frick, M. Jacobs and M. Peters (2002) 'International Business Travel: Impact on Families and Travellers.' *Occupational and Environmental Medicine* 59(5): 309–322.

Esser, I. (2005) *Why Work? Comparative Studies on Welfare Regimes and Individuals' Work Orientations*. Stockholm University: Swedish Institute for Social Research.

Esser, I. (2009) 'Has Welfare Made Us Lazy? Employment Commitment in Different Welfare States', 79–105, in A. Park, J. Curtice, K. Thomson, M. Philips and E. Clery (eds.) *British Social Attitudes. The 25ᵗʰ Report*. London: Sage.

Essy, D. (1993) 'Unemployment and Mental Health: A Critical Review.' *Social Science and Medicine* 37(1): 41–52.

Eurostat (2011) Labour Market Statistics. Accessed January 2011, at http://epp.eurostat.ec.europa.eu/portal/page/portal/employment_unemployment_lfs/data/main_tables.

EVS (1990, 1999, 2008) European Values Study.

Fältholm, Y. (1998) *Work, Cooperation and Professionalization. A Multiple Case Study*. Luleå University of Technology: Department of Human Work Sciences.

Felski, R. (2000) *Doing Time. Feminist Theory and Postmodern Culture*. New York: New York University Press.

Ferrie, J. E. (2001) 'Is Job Insecurity Harmful to Health?' *Journal of the Royal Society of Medicine* 94(2): 71–76.

Ferrie, J. E., M. J. Shipley, M. G. Marmot, S. Stansfeld and G. D. Smith (1998) 'An Uncertain Future: The Health Effects of Threats to Employment Security in White-Collar Men and Women.' *American Journal of Public Health* 88(7): 1030–1036.

Festinger, L. (1954) 'A Theory of Social Comparison Processes.' *Human Relations* 7(2): 117–140.

Festinger, L. (1957) *A Theory of Cognitive Dissonance*. Evanston & White Plains, NY: Row, Peterson and Company.

Fevre, R. (2007) 'Employment Insecurity and Social Theory: The Power of Nightmares.' *Work, Employment & Society* 21(3): 517–535.

Fisher, B. and J. Tronto (1990) 'Toward a Feminist Theory of Caring', 48–61, in E. K. Abel and M. K. Nelson (eds.) *Circles of Care*. New York: SUNY Press.

Fjármálastöðugleiki (2010) Seðlabanki Íslands, fyrra hefti. Accessed January 2011, at http://www.sedlabanki.is/lisalib/getfile.aspx?itemid=7910.

Flisbäck, M. (2008) 'Att framhäva val och hävda möjligheter. Det rationella som strategi för erkännande i lågstatusyrken.' *Arbetsmarknad & Arbetsliv* 14(4): 27–42.

Flisbäck, M. (2010) 'Från generell bild till individuellt ansikte. Att hantera oförståelse i fyra lågstatusyrken.' *Sociologisk forskning* 10(1): 29–50.

Forde, C and G. Slater (2006) 'The Nature and Experience of Agency Working in Britain. What Are the Challenges for Human Resource Management?' *Personnel Review* 35(2): 141–157.

Förhandlingsprotokoll 2007–2010. Bemanningsföretagen, HTF, Akademikerförbunden. Signed 23 May 2007.

Fredholm, E. (1989) *Sin lön värd*. University of Gothenburg: Department of Sociology.

Freud, S. (1930) *Civilization and Its Discontents*. London: Hogarth.

Friedlander, D. and G. T. Burtless (1995) *Five Years After: The Long-term Effects of Welfare-to-Work Programs*. New York: Russell Sage Foundation.

Frone, M. R., M. Russell and M. L. Cooper (1997) 'Relation of Work-family Conflict to Health Outcomes: A Four-year Longitudinal Study of Employed Parents.' *Journal of Occupational and Organizational Psychology* 70(4): 325–335.

Fryer, D. M. (1986) 'Employment Deprivation and Personal Agency during Unemployment: A Critical Discussion of Jahoda's Explanation of the Psychological Effects of Unemployment.' *Social Behaviour* 1(1): 3–23.

Fukami, C. V. and E. W. Larson (1984) 'Commitment to Company and Union: Parallel Models.' *Journal of Applied Psychology* 69(3): 367–371.

Furåker, B. (2003) 'Post-industrial Profiles. North American, Scandinavian and Other Western Labour Markets', 241–261, in T. P. Boje and B. Furåker (eds.) *Post-industrial Labour Markets. Profiles of North America and Scandinavia*. London: Routledge.

Furåker, B. (2005) *Sociological Perspectives on Labor Markets*. Houndmills, Basingstoke: Palgrave Macmillan.

Furåker, B., K. Håkansson and J. Ch. Karlsson (eds.) (2007) *Flexibility and Stability in Working Life*. Houndmills, Basingstoke: Palgrave Macmillan.

Furåker, B. and A. Hedenus (2009) 'Gambling Windfall Decisions: Lottery Winners and Employment Behavior.' *UNLV Gaming Research & Review Journal* 13(2): 1–15.

Galais, N. and K. Moser (2009) 'Organizational Commitment and the Well-being of Temporary Agency Workers: A Longitudinal Study.' *Human Relations* 62(4): 589–620.

Gallie, D. (ed.) (2007a) *Employment Regimes and the Quality of Work*. Oxford: Oxford University Press.

Gallie, D. (2007b) 'Production Regimes, Employment Regimes, and the Quality of Work', 1–33, in Gallie (2007a).

Gallie, D. and M. White (1993) *Employee Commitment and the Skills Revolution*. London: PSI Publishing.

Gallie, D. and C. Vogler (1994) 'Unemployment and Attitudes to Work', 115–153, in D. Gallie, C. Marsh and C. Vogler (eds.) *Social Change and the Experience of Unemployment*. Oxford: Oxford University Press.

Gallie, D., M. White, Y. Cheng and M. Tomlinson (1998) *Restructuring the Employment Relationship*. Oxford: Oxford University Press.

Gallie, D. and S. Alm (2000) 'Unemployment, Gender and Attitudes to Work', 109–133, in D. Gallie and S. Paugam (eds.) *Welfare Regimes and the Experience of Unemployment in Europe*. Oxford: Oxford University Press.

Gallie, D. and S. Paugam (eds.) (2000) *Welfare Regimes and the Experience of Unemployment in Europe*. Oxford: Oxford University Press.

Gaskell, J. (1992) *Gender Matters from School to Work*. Buckingham: Open University Press.

Gellerman, S. W. (1963) *Motivation and Productivity*. New York: American Management Association.

Gellerman, S. W. (1998) *How People Work: Psychological Approaches to Management Problems*. Westport, CT: Quorum Books.

Gesser, B. (1977) 'Campanella och AMS—manuellt och mentalt arbete i yrkesvägledningen.' *Sociologisk Forskning* 2–3: 1–14.

Goldthorpe, J. H. (2000) *On Sociology: Numbers, Narratives, and the Integration of Research and Theory*. Oxford: Oxford University Press.

Goldthorpe, J. H., D. Lockwood, F. Bechhofer and J. Platt (1968) *The Affluent Worker: Industrial Attitudes and Behaviour*. Cambridge: Cambridge University Press.

Goodman, P. S. and A. Friedman (1971) 'An Examination of Adams' Theory of Inequity.' *Administrative Science Quarterly* 16(3): 271–288.

Gorz, A. (1999) *Reclaiming Work. Beyond the Wage-Based Society*. Cambridge: Polity Press.

Grant, D. (1999) 'HRM, Rhetoric and the Psychological Contract: A Case of "Easier Said than Done".' *International Journal of Human Resource Management* 10(2): 327–350.

Greenhalgh, L. and Z. Rosenblatt (1984) 'Job Insecurity: Toward Conceptual Clarity.' *Academy of Management Review* 9(3): 438–448.

Gunnarsson, E. (1994) *Att våga väga jämnt!* Luleå University of Technology: Division of Industrial Work Environment.

Gustafson, P. (2005) *Resor i arbetet: En kartläggning av svenskarnas tjänsteresor 1995–2001*. University of Gothenburg: Department of Sociology.

Gustafson, P. (2006) 'Work-related Travel, Gender and Family Obligations.' *Work, Employment & Society* 2(3): 513–530.

Gustafson, P. (2009) 'More Cosmopolitan, No Less Local. The Orientations of International Travellers.' *European Societies* 11(1): 25–47.

Hackman, R and G. Oldham (1980) *Work Redesign*. Reading, MA: Addison Wesley.

Håkansson, K. and T. Isidorsson (2007) 'Flexibility, Stability and Agency Work: A Comparison of the Use of Agency Work in Sweden and the UK', 123–147, in Furåker, Håkansson and Karlsson.

Håkansson, K. and T. Isidorsson (2011) 'Work Organizational Outcomes of the Use of Temporary Agency Workers.' Manuscript. University of Gothenburg: Department of Sociology.

Hakim, C. (1996) *Key Issues in Women's Work. Female Heterogeneity and the Polarisation of Women's Employment*. London: Athlone Press.

Hakim, C. (2000) *Work-Lifestyle Choices in the 21st Century. Preference Theory*. Oxford: Oxford University Press.

Hakim, C. (2002) 'Lifestyle Preferences as Determinants of Women Have Differentiated Labour Market Careers.' *Work and Occupations* 29(4): 428–459.

Hakim, C. (2003) *Models of the Family in Modern Societies. Ideals and Realities*. Aldershot: Ashgate.

Hall, P. A. and D. Soskice (2001a) 'An Introduction to Varieties of Capitalism, 1–68, in Hall and Soskice (2001b).

Hall, P. A. and D. Soskice (eds.) (2001b) *Varieties of Capitalism: The Institutional Foundations of Comparative Advantage*. New York: Oxford University Press.

Hall, P. A. and D. W. Gingerich (2009) 'Varieties of Capitalism and Institutional Complementarities in the Political Economy: An Empirical Analysis.' *British Journal of Political Science* 39(3): 449–483.

Hall, R. H. (1969) *Occupations and the Social Structure*. Englewood Cliffs: Prentice-Hall.

Halvorsen, K. (1997) 'The Work Ethic under Challenge?' 119–149, in J. Holmer and J. Ch. Karlsson (eds.) *Work—Quo Vadis? Re-thinking the Question of Work*. Aldershot: Ashgate.

Hamermesh, D. S. (1979) 'Entitlement Effects, Unemployment Insurance and Unemployment Spells.' *Economic Inquiry* 17(3): 317–332.

Hamermesh, D. S. (1980) 'Unemployment Insurance and Labor Supply.' *International Economic Review* 21(3): 517–527.

Hammer, T. and H. Russell (2004) 'Gender Differences in Employment Commitment among Unemployed Youth', 81–104, in D. Gallie (ed.) *Resisting Marginalization. Unemployment Experience and Social Policy in the European Union*. Oxford: Oxford University Press.

Harding, S. D. and F. J. Hikspoors (1995) 'New Work Values: In Theory and in Practice.' *International Social Science Journal* 145(3): 441–456.

Harpaz, I. (2002) 'Expressing a Wish to Continue or Stop Working as Related to the Meaning of Work.' *European Journal of Work and Organizational Psychology* 11(2): 177–198.

Harpaz, I., B. Honig and P. Coetsier (2002) 'A Cross-cultural Longitudinal Analysis of the Meaning of Work and the Socialization Process of Career Starters.' *Journal of World Business* 37(4): 230–244.

Harpaz, I. and R. Snir (2003) 'Workaholism: Its Definition and Nature.' *Human Relations* 56(3): 291–319.

Hasselbladh, H. (2002) 'Kvalitetsrörelsen—konsekvenser för individ, organisation och samhälle', 236–252, in E. Bejerot and H. Hasselbladh (eds.) *Kvalitet utan gränser?* Lund: Academia Adacta.

Hedenus, A. (2011) *At the End of the Rainbow. Post-winning Life among Swedish Lottery Winners*. University of Gothenburg: Department of Sociology.

Helgason, M. S. (2010) 'Bubblicious! The Icelandic Economic Miracle as Epidemic of Bubblethinking.' *The Reykjavík Grapevine* July–August.

Herriot, P., W. E. G. Manning and J. M. Kidd (1997) 'The Content of the Psychological Contract.' *British Journal of Management* 8(2): 151–162.

Hertting, A. and T. Theorell (2002) 'Physiological Changes Associated with Downsizing of Personnel and Reorganisation in the Health Care Sector.' *Psychotherapy and Psychosomatics* 71(2): 117–122.

Hertting, A., K. Nilsson, T. Theorell and U. Sätterlund Larsson (2003) 'Personnel Reductions and Structural Changes in Health Care: Work-life Experiences of Medical Secretaries.' *Journal of Psychosomatic Research* 54 (2): 161–170.

Herzberg, F. (1966) *Work and the Nature of Man*. Cleveland: World Publishing.

Herzberg, F., B. Mausner and B. B. Snyderman (1959) *The Motivation to Work*. New York: John Wiley.

Hirschfeld, R. R. and H.S. Feild (2000) 'Work Centrality and Work Alienation: Distinct Aspects of a General Commitment to Work.' *Journal of Organizational Behavior* 21(7): 789–800.

Hochschild, A. R. (2003) *The Managed Heart. Commercialization of Human Feeling*. Berkeley: University of California Press.

Homans, G. C. (1961) *Social Behaviour. Its Elementary Forms*. London: Routledge & Kegan Paul.

Houseman, S. N. (2001) 'Why Employers Use Flexible Staffing Arrangements: Evidence from an Establishment Survey.' *Industrial and Labor Relations Review* 55(1): 149–170.

Høyer, K. G. and P. Næss (2001) 'Conference Tourism: A Problem for the Environment, as Well as for Research?' *Journal of Sustainable Tourism* 9(6): 451–470.

Hughes, E. C. (2008) *The Sociological Eye. Selected Papers*. New Brunswick: Transaction Books.

Hult, C. (2004) *The Way We Conform to Paid Labour. Commitment to Employment and Organization from a Comparative Perspective.* Umeå University: Department of Sociology.

Hult, C. (2008) 'Gender, Culture and Non-Financial Employment Commitment in Great Britain and Sweden.' *European Societies* 10(1): 73–96.

Hult, C. and S. Svallfors (2002) 'Production Regimes and Work Orientations: A Comparison of Six Western Countries.' *European Sociological Review* 18(3): 315–331.

Inglehart, R. (1990) *Culture Shift in Advanced Industrial Society.* Princeton: Princeton University Press.

Inglehart, R. (1997) *Modernization and Postmodernization. Cultural, Economic, and Political Change in 43 Societies.* Princeton: Princeton University Press.

Inglehart, R. (2008) 'Changing Values among Western Publics from 1970 to 2006.' *West European Politics* 31(1/2): 130–146.

Inglehart, R. and W. Baker (2000) 'Modernization, Cultural Change, and the Persistence of Traditional Values.' *American Sociological Review* 65(1): 19–51.

Inglehart, R. and C. Welzel (2005) *Modernization, Cultural Change, and Democracy. The Human Development Sequence.* Cambridge: Cambridge University Press.

Isacson, M. and E. Silvén (2002) 'Yrken och yrkeskonstruktion i det moderna och senmoderna samhället', 267–281, in K. Abrahamsson, L. Abrahamsson, T. Björkman, P-E. Ellström and J. Johansson *Utbildning, kompetens och arbete.* Lund: Studentlitteratur.

ISSP (2005) Work Orientation. International Social Survey Programme.

Ivancevic, J. M., R. Konopaske and R. S. DeFrank (2003) 'Business Travel Stress: A Model, Propositions and Managerial Implications.' *Work and Stress* 17(2): 138–157.

Jahoda, M. (1982) *Employment and Unemployment. A Social-Psychological Analysis.* Cambridge: Cambridge University Press.

Jenkins, R. (1996) *Social Identity.* London: Routledge.

Jenkins, R. (2000) 'Categorization: Identity, Social Process and Epistemology.' *Current Sociology* 48(3): 7–25.

Johansson, G., K. Isaksson and A. Sjöberg (1996) 'Drivkrafter för arbete—attityder och värderingar i arbetskraften', in SOU 1996:34 *Aktiv arbetsmarknadspolitik. Expertbilaga.* Stockholm: Fritzes.

Johansson, M. (1991) 'Lönearbetet som mål eller medel', 175–195, in B. Furåker (ed.) *Arbetets villkor.* Lund: Studentlitteratur.

Jonsson, D. (1980) *Ideas, Individuals, Interaction. A Formal Theory.* Lund: Dialog.

Joseph, N. and A. Nicholas (1972) 'The Uniform: A Sociological Perspective.' *American Journal of Sociology* 77(4): 719–730.

Judge, T. A. and R. J. Larsen (2001) 'Dispositional Source of Job Satisfaction: A Review and Theoretical Extension.' *Organizational Behavior and Human Decision Processes* 86(1): 67–98.

Kalleberg, A. L. (1977) 'Work Values and Job Rewards: A Theory of Job Satisfaction.' *American Sociological Review* 42(1): 124–143.

Kalleberg, A. L. (1983) 'Aging, Values, and Rewards: Explaining Age Differences in Job Satisfaction.' *American Sociological Review* 48(1): 78–90.

Kalleberg, A. L. (2000) 'Nonstandard Employment Relations: Part-time, Temporary and Contract Work.' *Annual Review of Sociology* 26: 341–365.

Kalleberg, A. L. (2001) 'Organizing Flexibility: The Flexible Firm in a New Century.' *British Journal of Industrial Relations* 39(4): 479–504.

Kalleberg, A. L., J. Reynolds and P. V. Marsden (2003) 'Externalizing Employment: Flexible Staffing Arrangements in US Organizations.' *Social Science Research* 32(4): 525–552.

Kan, M. Y. (2007) 'Work Orientation and Wives' Employment Careers: An Evaluation of Hakim's Preference Theory.' *Work and Occupations* 34(4): 430–462.

Kanter, R. M. (1993) *Men and Women of the Corporation.* New York: Basic Books.

Kaplan, F. I. (1968) *Bolshevik Ideology and the Ethics of Soviet Labor. 1917–1920: The Formative Years.* New York: Philosophical Library.

Karasek, R. A. (1979) 'Job Demands, Job Decision Latitude, and Mental Strain: Implications for Job Redesign.' *Administrative Science Quarterly* 24(2): 285–308.

Karasek, R. and T. Theorell (1990) *Healthy Work. Stress, Productivity and the Reconstruction of Working Life.* New York: Basic Books.

Karlsson, A. (2009) 'Occupational Identity in Administrative Service Work: The Aspect of Carefulness.' *Gender, Work and Organization,* at doi:10.1111/j.1468–0432.2009.00472.x.

Karlsson, A. (2010) *I moderniseringens skugga? Om förändring och identitet i två administrativa serviceyrken.* University of Gothenburg: Department of Sociology.

Karlsson, J. C. (2004) 'The Ontology of Work: Social Relations and Doing in the Sphere of Necessity', 84–104, in S. Fleetwood and S. Ackroyd (eds.) *Critical Realist Applications in Organisation and Management Studies.* London: Routledge.

Katz, D. and R. L. Kahn (1978) *The Social Psychology of Organizations.* New York: John Wiley and Sons.

Kauhanen, M. (2001) *Temporary Agency Work in Finland.* Helsinki: Labour Institute for Economic Research.

Kennelly, I. (2006) 'Secretarial Work, Nurturing, and the Ethic of Service.' *Feminist Formations* 18(2): 170–192.

Kets de Vries, M. F. R. and K. Balazs (1997) 'The Downside of Downsizing.' *Human Relations* 50(1): 11–50.

Kivimäki, M., J. Vahtera, J. Pentti, L. Thomson, A. Griffiths and T. Cox (2001) 'Downsizing, Changes In Work, And Self-Rated Health Of Employees: A 7-Year, 3-Wave Panel Study.' *Anxiety, Stress and Coping* 14(1): 59–73.

Kleinbeck, U., H.-H. Quast, H. Thierry and H. Häcker (eds.) (1990) *Work Motivation.* Hillsdale, NJ: Lawrence Erlbaum.

Korpi, W. (1978) *Arbetarklassen i välfärdskapitalismen.* Stockholm: Prisma.

Korpi, W. (2000) 'Faces of Inequality: Gender, Class, and Patterns of Inequalities in Different Types of Welfare States.' *Social Politics* 7(2): 127–191.

Korpi, W. and J. Palme (1998) 'The Paradox of Redistribution and the Strategy of Equality: Welfare State Institutions, Inequality and Poverty in the Western Countries.' *American Sociological Review* 63(5): 661–687.

Korvajärvi, P. (1998) *Gendering Dynamics in White-Collar Work Organizations.* Tampere: Taju.

Kouvonen, A., M. Kivimäki, M. Elovainio, M. Virtanen, A. Linna and J. Vahtera (2005) 'Job Strain and Leisure-time Physical Activity in Female and Male Public Sector Employees.' *Preventive Medicine* 41(2): 532–539.

Kraimer, M. (1997) 'Organizational Goals and Values: A Socialization Model.' *Human Resource Management Review* 7(4): 425–447.

Krause, E. A. (1971) *The Sociology of Occupations.* Boston: Little, Brown and Company.

Lacroix, J. (1952) 'La notion du travail.' *La vie intellectuelle* 32(1): 4–31.

Lamont, M. (2000) *The Dignity of Working Men. Morality and the Boundaries of Race, Class and Immigration.* New York: Russell Sage Foundation.

Lassen, C. (2006) 'Aeromobility and Work.' *Environment and Planning A* 38(2): 301–312.

Leahy, M. and J. Doughney (2006) 'Women, Work and Preference Formation: A Critique of Catherine Hakim's Preference Theory.' *Journal of Business Systems, Governance and Ethics* 1(1): 37–48.

Liden, R. C., S. J. Wayne, M. L. Kraimer and R. T. Sparrowe (2003) 'The dual Commitments of Contingent Workers: An Examination of Contingents' Commitment to the Agency and the Organization.' *Journal of Organizational Behavior* 24(5): 609–625.

Lincoln, J. R. and A. L. Kalleberg (1990) *Culture, Control, and Commitment. A Study of Work Organization and Work Attitudes in the United States and Japan.* Cambridge: Cambridge University Press.

Lindbeck, A. (1995) 'Welfare State Disincentives with Endogenous Habits and Norms.' *Scandinavian Journal of Economics* 97(4): 477–494.

Lindbeck, A. (2003) *An Essay on Welfare State Dynamics.* Stockholm University: Institute for International Economic Studies. Published in CESifo Working Paper Series. No. 976.

Lindgren, G. (1999) *Klass, kön och kirurgi. Relationer bland vårdpersonal i organisationsförändringarnas spår.* Malmö: Liber.

Lødemel, I. and H. Trickey (eds.) (2001) *'An Offer You Can't Refuse'. Workfare in International Perspective.* Bristol: Policy Press.

Löfström, C. (2003) *Hur Posten blev företag.* University of Gothenburg: School of Business and Law.

Lovett, S., T. Coyle, G. Banerjee and S. Hardebeck (2008) 'Measuring Managerial Effectiveness in Handling Pay-cuts.' *Journal of Applied Management and Entrepreneurship* 13(4): 23–46.

Luke, T. W. (1985) *Ideology and Soviet Industrialization.* Westport, CT: Greenwood Press.

Lundgren, B. (1990) *Allmänhetens tjänare. Kvinnlighet och yrkeskultur i det svenska postverket.* Stockholm: Carlssons Bokförlag.

Lysgaard, S. (1967) *Arbeiderkollektivet. En studie i de underordnedes sosiologi.* Oslo: Universitetsforlaget.

MacKinnon, M. H. (1980) 'Work Instrumentalism Reconsidered: A Replication of Goldthorpe's Luton Project.' *British Journal of Sociology* 31(1): 1–27.

Malinowski, B. (1922) *Argonauts of the Western Pacific.* New York: Dutton.

March, J. G. and J. P. Olsen (1989) *Rediscovering Institutions. The Organizational Basis of Politics.* New York: Free Press.

Marsden, P.V., A.L. Kalleberg and C.R. Cook (1993) 'Gender Differences in Organisational Commitment: Influences of Work Positions and Family Roles.' *Work and Occupations* 20(3): 368–390.

Marx, K. (1933) *Wage-Labour and Capital.* New York: International Publishers.

Marx, K. (1996) *Capital. A Critique of Political Economy* (vol. 1), in K. Marx and F. Engels *Collected Works* 35. London: Lawrence & Wishart.

Maslach, C. (1982) *Burnout: The Cost of Caring.* Englewood Cliffs, NJ: Prentice-Hall.

Maslow, A. H. (1970) *Motivation and Personality.* New York: McGraw-Hill.

Mauss, M. (1923–1924) *Essai sur le don. Forme et raison de l'échange dans les sociétés archaïques,* at http://dx.doi.org/doi:10.1522/cla.mam.ess3.

McGregor, D. (1985) *The Human Side of Enterprise.* New York: Harper & Row.

Merton, R. K. (1964) *Social Theory and Social Structure.* Revised and enlarged ed. Toronto: Collier-Macmillan.

Meyer, J. P. and N. J. Allen (1991) 'A Three-component Conceptualization of Organizational Commitment.' *Human Resource Management Review* 1: 61–89.

Meyer, J. P. and N. J. Allen (1997) *Commitment in the Workplace: Theory, Research, and Application.* Thousand Oaks, CA: Sage.

Meyer, J. P. and L. Herscovitch (2001) 'Commitment in the Workplace: Toward a General Model.' *Human Resource Management Review* 11(3): 299–336.

Meyer, J. P., D. J. Stanley, L. Herscovitch and L. Topolnytsky (2002) 'Affective, Continuance, and Normative Commitment to the Organization: A Meta-analysis of Antecedents, Correlates, and Consequences.' *Journal of Vocational Behavior* 61(1): 20–52.

Millward, L.J. and L.J. Hopkins (1998) 'Psychological Contracts, Organizational and Job Commitment.' *Journal of Applied Social Psychology* 28(16): 1530–1556.

Mitlacher, L. (2007) 'The Role of Temporary Agency Work in Different Industrial Relations Systems—A Comparison between Germany and the USA.' *British Journal of Industrial Relations* 45(3): 581–606.

Moore, S., L. Grunberg and E. Greenberg (2006) 'Surviving Repeated Waves of Organizational Downsizing: The Recency, Duration, and Order Effects Associated with Different Forms of Layoff Contact.' *Anxiety, Stress and Coping* 19(3): 309–329.

Moorhouse, H. F. (1987) 'The "Work" Ethic and "Leisure" Activity: The Hot Rod in Post-War America', 237–257, in P. Joyce (ed.) *The Historical Meanings of Work*. Cambridge: Cambridge University Press.

Morgan, W. R, D. F. Alwin and L. J. Griffin (1979) 'Social Origins, Parental Values, and the Transmission of Inequality.' *American Journal of Sociology* 85(1): 156–166.

Mottaz, C. J. (1985) 'The Relative Importance of Intrinsic and Extrinsic Rewards as Determinants of Work Satisfaction.' *Sociological Quarterly* 26(3): 365–385.

MOW International Research Team (1987) *The Meaning of Work*. London: Academic Press.

Mowday, R. T. (1998) 'Reflections on the Study and Relevance of Organizational Commitment.' *Human Resource Management Review* 8(4): 387–401.

Mowday, R. T., L. M. Porter and R. M. Steers (1982) *Employee-Organization Linkages: The Psychology of Commitment, Absenteeism and Turnover*. New York: Academic Press.

Mulinari, P. (2007) *Maktens fantasier och servicearbetets praktik. Arbetsvillkor inom hotell- och restaurangbranschen i Malmö*. Linköping University: Linköping Studies in Arts and Science.

Musson, G. and J. Duberley (2007) 'Change, Change or Be Exchanged: The Discourse of Participation and the Manufacture of Identity.' *Journal of Management Studies* 44(1): 143–164.

Newman, K. S. (2000) *No Shame in My Game. The Working Poor in the Inner City*. New York: Vintage Books.

Niles, F. S. (1999) Towards a Cross-Cultural Understanding of Work-Related Beliefs.' *Human Relations* 52(7): 855–867.

Nisbet, R. A. (1993) *The Sociological Tradition*. New Brunswick, NJ: Transaction Publishers.

Nissen, J. and L. Olsson (1996) 'Förutsättningarna för postverksamhet i ett modernt samhälle. Postens egen syn', 111–139, in J. Nissen (ed.) *Posten och informationssamhället. En förstudie*. Stockholm: Kommunikationsforskningsberedningen.

Noon, M. and P. Blyton (2007) *The Realities of Work. Experiencing Work and Employment in Contemporary Society*. New York: Palgrave Macmillan.

Nordenmark, M. (1999) *Unemployment, Employment Commitment and Well-being. The Psychosocial Meaning of (Un)employment among Women and Men*. Umeå University: Department of Sociology.

Oakes P. J., S. A. Haslam and J. C. Turner (1994) *Stereotyping and Social Reality*. Oxford: Blackwell.

O'Connell Davidson, J. (1994) 'The Sources and Limits of Resistance in a Privatized Utility', 69–101, in J. Jermier, D. Knights and W. Nord (eds.) *Resistance and Power in Organizations*. London: Routledge.

OECD (various years) *OECD Employment Outlook*. Paris.

Offe, C. (1985) *Disorganized Capitalism. Contemporary Transformations of Work and Politics*. Cambridge: Polity Press.

Ólafsdóttir, K. (2008) *Er íslenskur vinnumarkaður sveigjanlegur?* Reykjavík: Háskólinn í Reykjavík.

Ólafsson, S. (1999) *Íslenska leiðin—Almannatryggingar og velferð í fjölþjóðlegum samanburði*. Reykjavík: Tryggingarstofnun Ríkisins.

Østhus, S. (2007) 'For Better or Worse? Workplace Changes and the Health and Well-being of Norwegian Workers.' *Work, Employment & Society* 21(4): 731–750.

Ouellet, L. J. (1994) *Pedal to the Metal: The Work Lives of Truckers*. Philadelphia: Temple University Press.

Pakulski, J. and M. Waters (1996) *The Death of Class*. London: Sage Publications.

Parboteeah, K. P. and J. B. Cullen (2003) 'Social Institutions and Work Centrality: Explorations beyond National Culture.' *Organization Science* 14(2): 137–148.

Parent-Thirion, A., E. F. Macías, J. Hurley and G. Vermeylen (2007) *Fourth European Working Conditions Survey*. Dublin: European Foundation for the Improvement of Working and Living Conditions.

Parker, S. R., R. K. Brown, J. Child and M. A. Smith (1972) *The Sociology of Industry*. London: Allen & Unwin.

Parsons, T. (1951) *The Social System*. Glencoe, Ill.: Free Press.

Parsons, T. and N. J. Smelser (1956) *Economy and Society. A Study in the Integration of Economic and Social Theory*. London: Routledge & Kegan Paul.

Paules, G. F. (1991) *Dishing It Out. Power and Resistance among Waitresses in a New Jersey Restaurant*. Philadelphia: Temple University Press

Paullay, I. M., G. Alliger and E. Stone-Romero (1994) 'Construct Validation of Two Instruments Designed to Measure Job Involvement and Work Centrality.' *Journal of Applied Psychology* 79(2): 224–228.

Pearce, J. L. (1993) 'Toward an Organizational Behavior of Contract Laborers: Their Psychological Contract and Effect on Co-workers.' *Academy of Management Journal* 36: 1082–1096.

Peterson, H. (2005) *Gender, Power and Post-Bureaucracy*. Uppsala: Uppsala University.

Peterson, M. and S. Ruiz-Quintanilla (2003) 'Cultural Socialization as a Source of Intrinsic Work Motivation.' *Group and Organizational Management* 28(2): 188–216.

Phelps Brown, H. (1990) 'The Counter-revolution of Our Time.' *Industrial Relations* 29(1): 1–14.

Porter, L. W., R. M. Steers, R. T. Mowday and P. V. Boulian (1974) 'Organizational Commitment, Job Satisfaction, and Turnover among Psychiatric Technicians.' *Journal of Applied Psychology* 59(5): 603–609.

Porter, M. E. and C. Ketels (2007) *Iceland: Small Fish in a Global Pond*. Harvard Business School Case 708–472. Harvard: Harvard Business School Press.

Presser, H. B. and J. M. Hermsen (1996) 'Gender Differences in the Determinants of Work-Related Overnight Travel among Employed Americans.' *Work and Occupations* 23(1): 87–115.

Pringle, R. (1988) *Secretaries Talk*. London: Verso.

Probst, T. M. (2003) 'Development and Validation of the Job Security Index and the Job Security Satisfaction Scale: A Classical Test Theory and IRT Approach.' *Journal of Occupational and Organizational Psychology* 76(4): 451–467.

Ransome, P. (2005) *Work, Consumption and Culture. Affluence and Social Change in the Twenty-first Century*. London: Sage.

Regini, M., J. Kitay and M. Baethge (eds.) (2000) *From Tellers to Sellers*. Cambridge, MA: MIT Press.

Reichers, A. E. (1985) 'A Review and Reconceptualization of Organizational Commitment.' *Academy of Management Review* 10(3): 465–576.

Reiss, A. (1961) *Occupations and Social Status*. New York: Free Press of Glencoe.

Rifkin, J. (1995) *End of Work: The Decline of the Global Labor Force and the Dawn of the Post-market Era*. New York: G. P. Putnam's Sons.

Robinson, S. L. and D. M. Rousseau (1994) 'Violating the Psychological Contract: Not the Exception but the Norm.' *Journal of Organizational Behavior* 15(3): 245–259.

Rose, M. (1985) *Re-Working the Work Ethic*. London: Batsford.

Rose, M. (1994) 'Skill and Samuel Smiles: Changing the British Work Ethic', 281–335, in R. Penn, M. Rose and J. Rubery (eds.) *Skill and Occupational Change*. Oxford: Oxford University Press.

Rosenberg, M. J. and C. I. Hovland (1960) 'Cognitive, Affective and Behavioral Components of Attitudes', 1–14, in M. J. Rosenberg, C. I. Hovland, W. J. McGuire, R. P. Abelson and J. W. Brehm *Attitude Organization and Change: An Analysis of Consistency among Attitude Components*. New Haven, CT: Yale University Press.

Rothman, R. A. (2002) *Inequality and Stratification. Race, Class, and Gender*. Upper Saddle River, N.J.: Prentice Hall.

Rousseau, D. M. (1995) *Psychological Contracts in Organizations. Understanding Written and Unwritten Agreements*. Thousand Oaks, CA: Sage.

Rousseau, D. M. (1996) 'Changing the Deal While Keeping the People.' *Academy of Management Executive* 10(1): 50–59.

Rousseau, D. M. (2001) 'Schema, Promise and Mutuality: The Building Blocks of the Psychological Contract.' *Journal of Occupational and Organizational Psychology* 74(4): 511–541.

Rowe, R. and W. E. Snizek (1995) 'Gender Differences in Work Values: Perpetuating the Myth.' *Work and Occupations* 22(2): 215–229.

Ruiz-Quintanilla, S. A. and B. Wilpert (1988) 'The Meaning of Work—Scientific Status of a Concept', 3–14, in V. de Keyser, T. Qvale, B. Wilpert, S.A. Ruiz-Quintanilla and B. Wilpert (eds.) *The Meaning of Work and Technological Option*. Chichester: Wiley.

Ruiz-Quintanilla, S. A. and B. Wilpert (1991) 'Are Work Meanings Changing?' *European Work and Organizational Psychologist* 91(2/3): 91–109.

Sahlins, M. (2004) *Stone Age Economics*. London: Routledge.

Salzer, M. (1995) *Postens själ*. Stockholm: Posten AB.

Scholz, E., J. Harkness, and T. Faaß (2008) *ISSP Study Monitoring 2005 Report to the ISSP General Assembly on Monitoring Work Undertaken for the ISSP*. GESIS-Methodenberichte Nr. 4/2008.

Sennett, R. (1998) *The Corrosion of Character. The Personal Consequences of Work in the New Capitalism*. New York: W. W. Norton.

Sennett, R. (2003) *Respect. The Formation of Character in an Age of Inequality*. London: Allen.

SFS 1982: 80.

Sharabi M. and I. Harpaz (2007) 'Changes in Work Centrality and Other Life Areas in Israel.' *Journal of Human Values* 13(2): 95–106.

Sharabi, M. and I. Harpaz (2010) 'Improving Employees' Work Centrality Improves Organizational Performance: Work Events and Work Centrality Relationships.' *Human Resource Development International* 13(4): 379–392.

Siegelbaum, L. H. (1988) *Stakhanovism and the Politics of Productivity in the USSR, 1935–1941*. Cambridge: Cambridge University Press.

Skeggs, B. (1998) *Formations of Class and Gender. Becoming Respectable*. London: Sage.

Sloman, J. (2010) *Economics*. 6th ed. Harlow: Pearson Education.

Smith, C. (2006) 'The Double Indeterminacy of Labour Power: Labour Effort and Labour Mobility.' *Work, Employment & Society* 20(2): 389–402.

Smola, K. W. and C. D. Sutton (2002) 'Generational Differences: Revisiting the Generational Work Values for the New Millennium.' *Journal of Organizational Behavior* 23(4): 363–382.

Snir, R. and I. Harpaz (2009a) 'Cross-Cultural Differences concerning Heavy Work Investment.' *Cross-Cultural Research* 43(4): 309–319.

Snir, R. and I. Harpaz (2009b) 'Workaholism from a Cross-cultural Perspective.' *Cross-Cultural Research* 43(4): 303–308.

Sörensen, B. A. (1982) 'Ansvarsrasjonalitet: Om mål-middeltenkning blant kvinner', 392–424, in H. Holter (ed.) *Kvinner i felleskap*. Oslo: Universitetsforlaget.

Soskice, D. (1999) 'Divergent Production Regimes: Coordinated and Uncoordinated Market Economies in the 1980s and 1990s', 101–134, in H. Kitschelt, P. Lange, G. Marks, J. D. Stephens (eds.) *Continuity and Change in Contemporary Capitalism*. Cambridge: Cambridge University Press.

Statistics Iceland (2010) Accessed October 2010, at www.hagstofa.is.

Statistics Sweden (2010) Table retrieved from online database 2010–09–03.

Stokes, D. E. (1963) 'Spatial Models of Party Competition.' *American Political Science Review* 57(2): 368–377.

Storrie, D. (2007) 'Temporary Agency Work in the European Union—Economic Rationale and Equal Treatment', 103–122, in Furåker, Håkansson and Karlsson.

Striker, J., R. S. Luippold, L. Nagy, B. Liese, C. Bigelow and K. A. Mundt (1999) 'Risk Factors for Psychological Stress among International Business Travellers.' *Occupational and Environmental Medicine* 56(4): 245–252.

Strümpfer, D. J. W. and G. P. de Bruin (2009) 'Antonovsky's Sense of Coherence and Job Satisfaction: Meta-analyses of South African Data.' *SA Journal of Industrial Psychology* 35(1): 172–174.

Stuckler, D., S. Basu, M. Suhracke, A. Coutts and M. McKee (2009) 'The Public Health Effect of Economic Crisis and Alternative Policy Responses in Europe: An Empirical Analysis.' *Lancet* 374(9686): 315–323.

Suls, J. and L. Wheeler (2000) *Handbook of Social Comparison. Theory and Research*. New York: Kluwer Academia/Plenum Publishers.

Svallfors, S., K. Halvorsen and J. G. Andersen (2001) 'Work Orientations in Scandinavia: Employment Commitment and Organizational Commitment in Denmark, Norway and Sweden.' *Acta Sociologica* 44(2): 139–156.

Svensson, L. G. (2003) 'Yrkes- och professionssociologi', 27–43, in M. Blomsterberg and T. Soidre (eds.) *Reflektioner. Perspektiv i forskning om arbetsliv och arbetsmarknad*. University of Gothenburg: Department of Sociology.

Svensson, L. G. and Y. Ulfsdotter Eriksson (2009) *Yrkesstatus. En sociologisk studie av hur yrken uppfattas och värderas*. University of Gothenburg: Department of Sociology.

Sverke, M., J. Hellgren and K. Näswall (2002) 'No Security: A Meta-Analysis and Review of Job Insecurity and Its Consequences.' *Journal of Occupational Health Psychology* 7(3): 242–264.

Swarbrooke, J. and S. Horner (2001) *Business Travel and Tourism*. Oxford: Butterworth-Heinemann.

Tajfel, H. and J. C. Turner (1979) 'An Integrative Theory of Intergroup Conflict', 33–47, in W. G. Austin and S. Worchel (eds.) *The Social Psychology of Intergroup Relations*. Monterey, CA: Brooks-Cole.

Tausig, M. and R. Fenwick (1999) 'Recession and Well-Being.' *Journal of Health and Social Behavior* 40(1): 1–16.

Tolbert, P. and P. Mohen (1998) 'Men's and Women's Definitions of "Good" Jobs: Similarities and Differences by Age and across Time.' *Work and Occupations* 25(2): 168–194.

Tönnies, F. (1887) *Gemeinschaft und Gesellschaft: Grundbegriffe der reinen Soziologie*. Berlin: R. Curtius.

Tourish, D., N. Paulsen, E. Hobman and P. Bordia (2004) 'The Downsides of Downsizing: Communication Processes and Information Needs in the Aftermath of a Workforce Reduction Strategy.' *Management Communication Quarterly* 17(4): 485–516.

Treiman, D. (1977) *Occupational Prestige in Comparative Perspective*. New York: Wiley.

Twenge, J. M., S.M. Campbell, B. J. Hoffman, and C.E. Lance (2010) 'Generational Differences in Work Values: Leisure and Extrinsic Values Increasing, Social and Intrinsic values Decreasing.' *Journal of Management* 36(5): 1117–1142.

Ulfsdotter Eriksson, Y. (2006) *Yrke, status och genus*. University of Gothenburg: Department of Sociology.

Van Breugel, G., W. Van Olffen and R. Olie (2005) 'Temporary Liaisons: The Commitment of "Temps" towards Their Agencies.' *Journal of Management Studies* 42(3): 539–566.

Van Dyne, L. and S. Ang (1998) 'Organizational Citizenship Behavior of Contingent Workers in Singapore.' *Academy of Management Journal* 41(6): 692–704.

Veblen, T. (1953) *The Theory of the Leisure Class. An Economic Study of Institutions*. New York: Mentor Books.

Vecernik, J. (2003) 'Skating on Thin Ice, a Comparison of Work Values and Job Satisfaction in EU and CEE Countries.' *International Journal of Comparative Sociology* 44(5): 444–471.

Vlasblom J. and J. Schippers (2006) 'Changing Dynamics in Female Employment around Childbirth.' *Work, Employment & Society* 20(2): 329–347.

von Otter, C. (1978) 'Några kritiska reflektioner kring frågan om behovstillfredsställelse och arbetsorganisation.' *Sociologisk Forskning* (16)1: 3–11.

Vroom, V. (1964) *Work and Motivation*. New York: Wiley.

Waerness, K. (1984) 'The Rationality of Caring.' *Economic and Industrial Democracy* 5(2): 185–211.

Wallace, J. E. (1993) ''Professional and Organizational Commitment: Compatible or Incompatible? *Journal of Vocational Behavior* 42 (3): 333–349.

Wang, G. T. (1996) *A Comparative Study of Extrinsic and Intrinsic Work Values of Employees in the United States and Japan*. New York: Edwin Mellen Press.

Warhurst, C., D. R. Eikhof and A. Haunschild (2008) *Work Less, Live More? Critical Analysis of the Work-life Boundary*. Basingstoke: Palgrave Macmillan.

Warr, P. (1982) 'A National Study of Non-financial Employment Commitment.' *Journal of Occupational Psychology* 55: 297–312.

Warr, P. (2008) 'Work Values: Some Demographic and Cultural Correlates.' *Journal of Occupational and Organizational Psychology* 81(4): 751–775.

Weber, M. (1930) *The Protestant Ethic and the Spirit of Capitalism*. London: Allen & Unwin.

Weber, M. (1978) *Economy and Society. An Outline of Interpretive Sociology* (ed. G. Roth and C. Wittich). Two vols. Berkeley: University of California Press.

Welzel, C. and R. Inglehart (2010) 'Agency, Values, and Well-Being: A Human Development Model.' *Social Indicators Research* 97(1): 43–63.

Westman, M., D. Etzion and E. Gattenio (2008) 'International Business Travels and the Work-family Interface: A Longitudinal Study.' *Journal of Occupational and Organizational Psychology* 81(3): 459–480.

Wiendieck, G. (1980) 'Arbeitszufriedenheit: Ein Kunstprodukt der Sozialforsc-hung?', 191–216, in W. Bungard (Hrsg.) *Die 'gute' Versuchsperson denkt nicht. Artefakte in der Sozialpsychologie.* Munich: Urban & Schwarzenberg.

Witz, A. and M. Savage (eds.) (1992) *Gender and Bureaucracy.* Oxford: Blackwell.

Wright, E. O. (1997) *Class Counts. Comparative Studies in Class Analysis.* Cam-bridge: Cambridge University Press.

WVS (1996) World Values Survey.

Yousef, D. A. (2001) 'Islamic Work Ethic: A Moderator between Organizational Commitment and Job Satisfaction in a Cross-cultural Context.' *Personnel Review* 30(2): 152–169.

Index